MathFlare

Name: ________________________

Class: ___________

Teacher: ________________________

Introduction

As parents and educators, we recognize the pivotal role mathematics plays in shaping a child's academic journey and future success. Yet, the path to mathematical proficiency can often seem daunting, fraught with challenges and complexities. That's where the transformative power of MathFlare Workbooks shine through, illuminating the way forward with clarity, precision, and purpose.

Introducing MathFlare Workbooks – a beacon of guidance, a testament to excellence, and a catalyst for achievement. Crafted with meticulous care and expertise, MathFlare Workbooks stand as paragons of educational excellence, designed to nurture young minds, ignite a passion for learning, and develop a deep-rooted understanding of mathematical concepts.

Picture this: your child eagerly delves into the pages of Mathflare Workbook, greeted by a step-by-step guide illuminated with vivid examples that demystify complex mathematical concepts. With each turn of the page, they embark on a journey of discovery, encountering thoughtfully curated practice questions that reinforce learning and hone problem-solving skills. And when they unveil the answers to those very questions, a sense of accomplishment blossoms within them – a tangible reward for their hard work and dedication.

But MathFlare Workbooks are more than just tools for learning; they are pathways to comprehension, fostering a deep-seated understanding of mathematical concepts through a sequential, logical flow. From fundamental principles to advanced problem-solving strategies, every chapter builds upon the last, ensuring a robust foundation upon which future knowledge can be constructed.

As parents, we yearn for nothing more than to see our children thrive, to witness the spark of inspiration ignited within them as they conquer academic challenges with confidence and poise. MathFlare Workbooks serve as partners in this noble endeavor, offering not just practice questions, but the keys to unlocking a world of opportunity.

And for teachers, MathFlare Workbooks stand as invaluable allies in the quest to cultivate mathematical proficiency in the classroom. With answers readily available, instructors can focus on guiding and nurturing their students, confident in the knowledge that MathFlare Workbooks provide a solid framework upon which to build.

In the pages of MathFlare Workbooks, we find not just the promise of academic excellence, but the seeds of a brighter tomorrow. So let us embrace the power of mathematics, let us champion the journey of learning, and let us pave the way for a generation of young minds poised to shape the world. With MathFlare Workbooks as our guide, the possibilities are infinite, and the future, bright.

Table of Contents

MathFlare
Grade 2
MATH WORKBOOK
Step by Step Guide and Essential Practice with Answers
Addition Subtraction
Multiplication
Place Value and Expanded Notations
Geometry
MathFlare Publishing

MathFlare
Grade 2-3
MATH WORKBOOK
Step by Step Guide and Essential Practice with Answers
Addition Subtraction
Multiplication and Division
Place Value and Expanded Notations
Geometry
MathFlare Publishing

MathFlare
Grade 3
MATH WORKBOOK
Step by Step Guide and Essential Practice with Answers
Multiplication and Division
Decimals
Place Value and Expanded Notations
Fractions and Geometry
MathFlare Publishing

MathFlare
Grade 1
MATH WORKBOOK
Step by Step Guide and Essential Practice with Answers
Counting and Numbers
Addition and Subtraction
Place Value and Expanded Notations
Understanding Time
MathFlare Publishing

MathFlare
Grade 1-2
MATH WORKBOOK
Step by Step Guide and Essential Practice with Answers
Counting and Numbers
Addition and Subtraction
Place Value and Expanded Notations
Understanding Time
MathFlare Publishing

MathFlare
Grade 3-4
MATH WORKBOOK
Step by Step Guide and Essential Practice with Answers
Addition Subtraction
Multiplication Division
Place Value and Expanded Notations
Fractions and Geometry
MathFlare Publishing

MathFlare
Grade 4
MATH WORKBOOK
Step by Step Guide and Essential Practice with Answers
Addition Subtraction
Multiplication Division
Place Value and Expanded Notations
Fractions and Geometry
MathFlare Publishing

MathFlare
Grade 4-5
MATH WORKBOOK
Step by Step Guide and Essential Practice with Answers
Multiplication Division
Place Value and Expanded Notations
Fractions and Geometry
Unit Conversion
MathFlare Publishing

MathFlare
Grade 5
MATH WORKBOOK
Step by Step Guide and Essential Practice with Answers
Multiplication Division
Place Value and Expanded Notations
Fractions and Geometry
Unit Conversion
MathFlare Publishing

MathFlare
Grade 5-6
MATH WORKBOOK
Step by Step Guide and Essential Practice with Answers
Multiplication Division
Place Value and Expanded Notations
Fractions and Geometry
Units and Statistics
MathFlare Publishing

MathFlare
Grade 6
MATH WORKBOOK
Step by Step Guide and Essential Practice with Answers
Integers and Statistics
Arithmetic and Pre-Algebra
Fractions and Geometry
Ratio and Percentage
MathFlare Publishing

MathFlare
Grade 6-7
MATH WORKBOOK
Step by Step Guide and Essential Practice with Answers
Arithmetic and Pre-Algebra
Ratio, Percent Proportion
Geometry
Statistics
MathFlare Publishing

MathFlare
Grade 7
MATH WORKBOOK
Step by Step Guide and Essential Practice with Answers
Pre-Algebra
Ratio, Percent Proportion
Geometry
Statistics
MathFlare Publishing

MathFlare
Grade 7-8
MATH WORKBOOK
Step by Step Guide and Essential Practice with Answers
Pre-Algebra
Ratio, Percent Proportion
Geometry and Cartesian Plane
Statistics
MathFlare Publishing

MathFlare
Grade 8-9
MATH WORKBOOK
Step by Step Guide and Essential Practice with Answers
Pre-Algebra
Ratio, Proportion and Percentage
Linear Equations
Geometry and Cartesian Plane
MathFlare Publishing

MathFlare
Grade 8
MATH WORKBOOK
Step by Step Guide and Essential Practice with Answers
Pre-Algebra
Percentage
Linear Equations
Geometry
MathFlare Publishing

Chapter. 01

Pre-Algebra

Order of Operations (PEMDAS)

The order of operations, often remembered by the acronym PEMDAS, stands for:

- **Parentheses**: Perform operations inside parentheses first.
- **Exponents**: Evaluate exponents (powers and roots) next.
- **Multiplication and Division**: Perform multiplication and division from left to right.
- **Addition and Subtraction**: Perform addition and subtraction from left to right.

The order of operations helps to clarify which operations should be performed first in a mathematical expression to ensure consistent and accurate results.

- **Parentheses**: Evaluate expressions within parentheses first. If there are nested parentheses, start with the innermost ones and work your way out.

  1. Example: $2 \times (3 + 4) = 2 \times 7 = 14$

- **Exponents**: Evaluate expressions with exponents (powers and roots) next.

  1. Example: $2^3 + 4 = 8 + 4 = 12$

- **Multiplication and Division**: Perform multiplication and division from left to right.

  1. Example: $2 \times 3 + 4 = 6 + 4 = 10$

  2. Example: $6 \div 2 \times 3 = 3 \times 3 = 9$

- **Addition and Subtraction**: Perform addition and subtraction from left to right.

  1. Example: $2 + 3 \times 4 = 2 + 12 = 14$

  2. Example: $10 - 4 \div 2 = 10 - 2 = 8$

Solving Equations (One Step)

Solving one-step equations involves performing a single operation to isolate the variable and find its value.

Let's solve an equation step by step: $16 + x = 31$

1. **Identify the Goal**:

   The goal is to isolate the variable x on one side of the equation.

2. **Simplify the Equation**: Combine like terms on both sides of the equation, if necessary.

   The equation is already simplified.

3. **Undo Addition or Subtraction**: If there's addition or subtraction involving the variable, undo it by performing the opposite operation on both sides of the equation.

   Since x is being added to 16, we'll undo this operation by subtracting 16 from both sides of the equation:

   $$16 + x - 16 = 31 - 16$$

4. **Isolate the Variable**: Ensure that the variable is alone on one side of the equation.

   $$X = 15$$

5. **Check Your Solution**: Substitute the value of x back into the original equation to verify that it satisfies the equation.

   $$16 + 15 = 31$$

   $$31 = 31$$

   The equation is balanced, so the solution.

<u>Equations (Two Sides)</u>

A two-sided equation is an equation where both sides have expressions with variables and constants. The goal when solving a two-sided equation is to find the value of the variable that makes both sides equal.

For example: Let's solve an equation:

$$9 + 8x + 8 = 64 + x + 2$$

- **Combine Like Terms:** Simplify each side of the equation by combining like terms (terms with the same variable or constants).

$$9 + 8x + 8 = 64 + x + 2$$
$$17 + 8x = 66 + x$$

- **Isolate the Variable:** Use inverse operations to isolate the variable on one side of the equation.

subtract x from both sides:

$$17 + 8x - x = 66 + x - x$$

$$17 + 7x = 66$$

subtracting 17 from both sides:

$$17 - 17 + 7x = 66 - 17$$

$$7x = 49$$

divide both sides by 7:

$$\frac{7x}{7} = \frac{49}{7} = x = 7$$

- **Check Solution:** Once you find the solution, substitute it back into the original equation to ensure it makes the equation true.

Substitute $x = 7$ back into the original equation:

$$9 + 8(7) + 8 = 64 + 7 + 2$$

$$9 + 56 + 8 = 64 + 7 + 2$$

$$73 = 73$$

Evaluate Expressions

Evaluating expressions involves substituting given values for variables in an expression and then performing the indicated operations to find the result.

For example: Let's evaluate $4x - 10$, when $x = 3$:

Step 1: Substitute the given value for the variable:

Replace every occurrence of x in the expression $4x - 10$ with the given value, which is 3:

$$= 4(3) - 10$$

Step 2: Perform the operations:

Perform the indicated operations according to the order of operations (PEMDAS - Parentheses, Exponents, Multiplication and Division, Addition and Subtraction):

$$= 4 \times 3 - 10$$

Step 3: Simplify:

Calculate the result:

$$12 - 10 = 2$$

Find Numbers (Verbal Algebra)

Verbal algebra involves translating word problems or verbal statements into algebraic expressions or equations.

For example: The product of the two numbers is 91. One number is six less than the other. What are the numbers?

We're given a verbal description of a problem, and we need to represent it using algebraic symbols and equations.

Let's break down the given problem into algebraic expressions:

- Given that the product of the two numbers is 91, we can write the equation: $xy = 91$
- Also, given that one number is six less than the other, we can write another equation: $x = y - 6$

Now, we can use algebraic techniques to solve the system of equations to find the values of x and y, which represent the two numbers.

$$x(x - 6) = 91$$

1. Solve the equation:

    - Expand the equation:

    $$x^2 - 6x = 91$$

    - Rearrange the equation into standard quadratic form:

    $$x^2 - 6x - 91 = 0$$

    - Factor the quadratic equation:

    $$(x - 13)(x + 7) = 0$$

2. Find the solutions for x.

    - From the factored form, we have two possible values for x.

    $$x = 13 \text{ or } x = -7$$

3. **Check the validity of the solutions:**

- Since one number is six less than the other, we discard the negative solution.

- Therefore, the solution is $x = 13$.

4. **Find the other number:**

- Substitute $x = 13$ into the expression for the other number:

Other number $= x - 6 = 13 - 6 = 7$

So, the two numbers are 13 and 7.

Solving Inequalities

Inequalities are mathematical expressions that compare the relative sizes of two values. They are used to express relationships where one quantity is:

- "<" (less than),
- ">" (greater than),
- "<=" (less than or equal to),
- ">=" (greater than or equal to),
- and "≠" (not equal to) another quantity.

For example:

$$y + -10 \leq -8$$

To isolate y, we need to get rid of the constant term -10. Since -10 is being subtracted from y, we can undo this operation by adding 10 to both sides of the inequality:

$$y - 10 + 10 \leq -8 + 10$$

$$y \leq 2$$

To check the solution:

$$2 - 10 \leq -8$$

$$-8 = -8$$

The inequality is true when $y = 2$

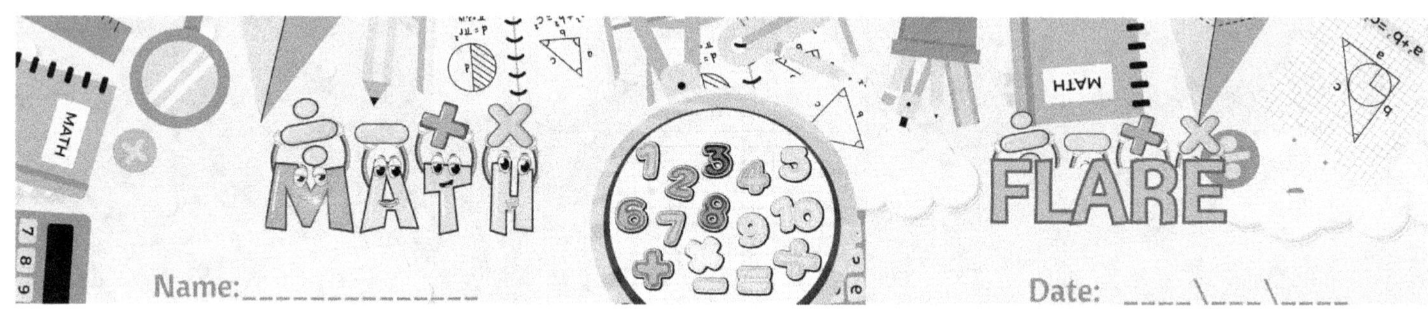

Order of Operations (PEMDAS)
Evaluate Expressions.

1) $(7 + 4)(5 + 3) =$

2) $(4^2) \times (3^2) + 2 =$
$$= 16 \times 9 + 2$$
$$= 144 + 2$$
$$= 146$$

3) $(9 + 10) \times (8 + 9) =$

4) $(5^2) \times (10^2) + 2 =$

5) $2 + 9^2 + 8 + 4^2 =$

6) $[7 - (8 - 8)] \times 9 =$

7) $(7^2) \times (2^2) + 8 =$

8) $2 + 4^2 + 8 + 4^2 =$

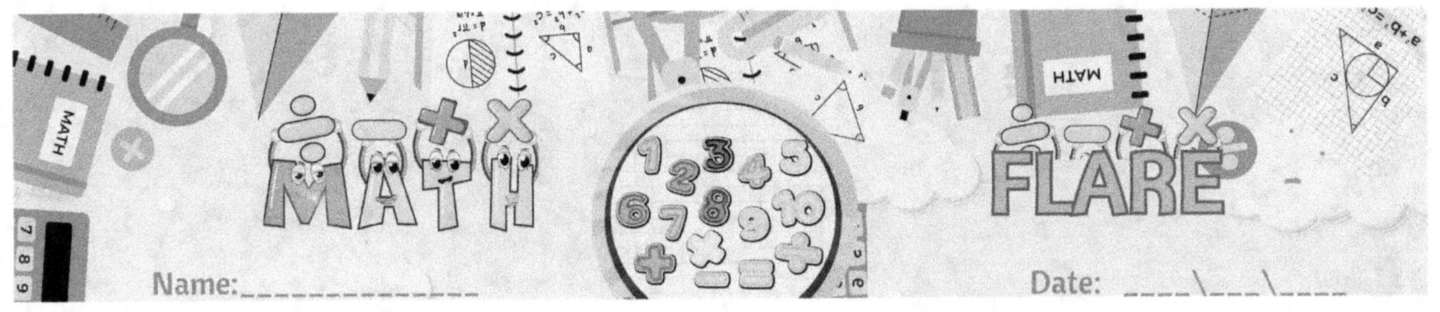

9) $3 \times (7 + 5) =$

10) $(2 + 4)^2 =$

11) $[8 - (1 + 5)] \div 6 =$

12) $(8 + 5)(9 + 1) =$

13) $(10 \times 10) - (5 + 4) =$

14) $(5^2) \times (6^2) + 3 =$

15) $(8 + 6) \div 8 =$

16) $(8 + 5) \div 5 =$

17) $(8 + 7) \div 4 =$

18) $6 + 2 + 10 =$

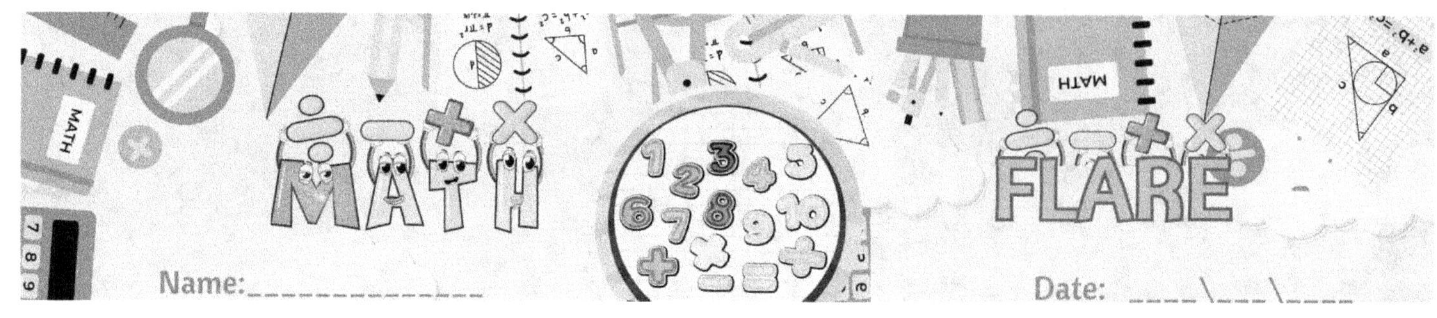

19) $4 + 5 + 8 + 2 =$

20) $4 \times 4 + 7 =$

21) $5 + 2 + 4 =$

22) $(3 \times 6) - (2 + 9) =$

23) $8 \times 10 \times 7 =$

24) $7 + 4 + 8 =$

25) $(9 + 6)^2 =$

26) $7 + 7 - 10 + 8 =$

27) $(7^2) \times (10^2) + 10 =$

28) $4 \times 2 \times 1 =$

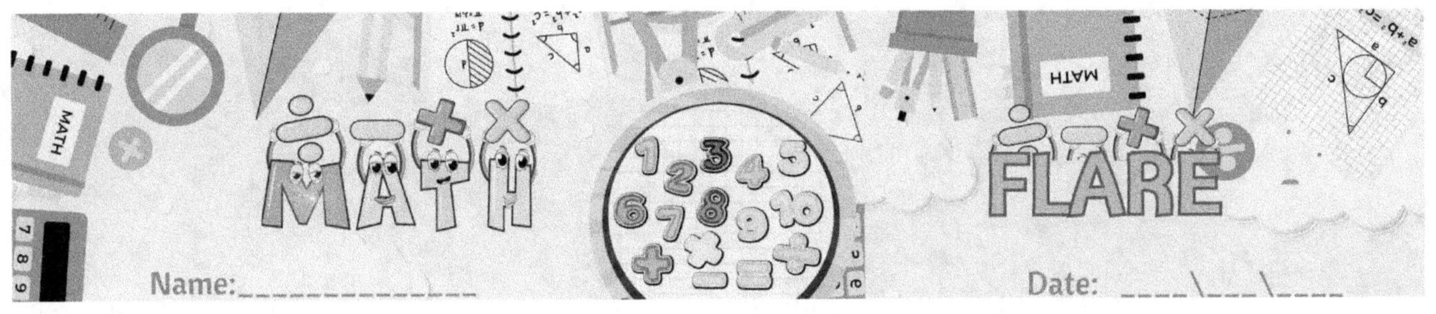

29) $7 + 6 - 5 + 6 =$

30) $(3 + 9)(2 + 1) =$

31) $(9^2) \times (2^2) + 1 =$

32) $4 \times 4 \times 2 =$

33) $6 + 6 - 7 + 9 =$

34) $1 + 7 + 2 + 4 =$

35) $2 + 9^2 =$

36) $9 + (1 + (3 - 6))^2 =$

37) $(7^2) \times (7^2) + 5 =$

38) $(8 + 3)^2 + (2 + 10)^2 =$

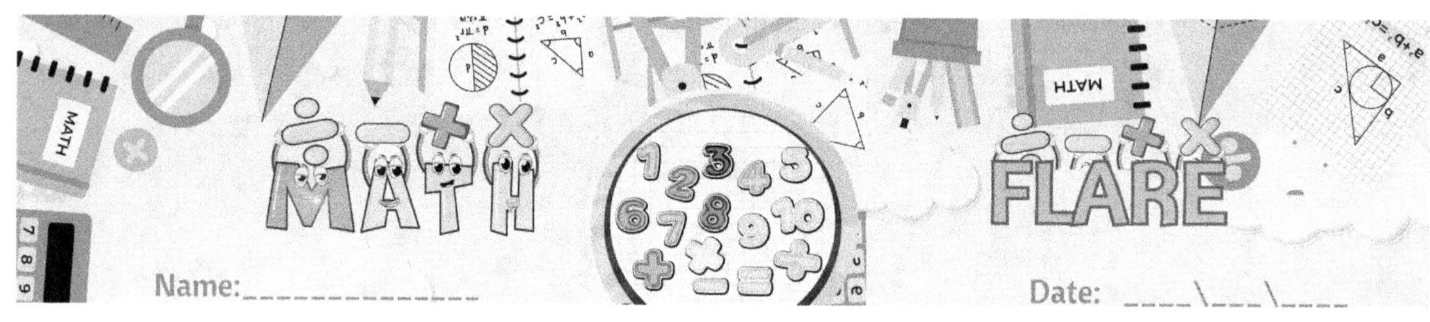

39) $(7 + 5)^2 + (2 + 8)^2 =$

40) $(8^2) \times (6^2) + 4 =$

41) $10 + 7 + 5 =$

42) $3 + 4 + 9 + 3 =$

43) $[2 - (3 + 2)] \div 4 =$

44) $5 \times 9 + 3 =$

45) $(5 + 7) \times (8 + 3) =$

46) $7 + (6 + (5 - 2))^2 =$

47) $7 + 3 + 2 =$

48) $(3 \times 2) - (10 + 2) =$

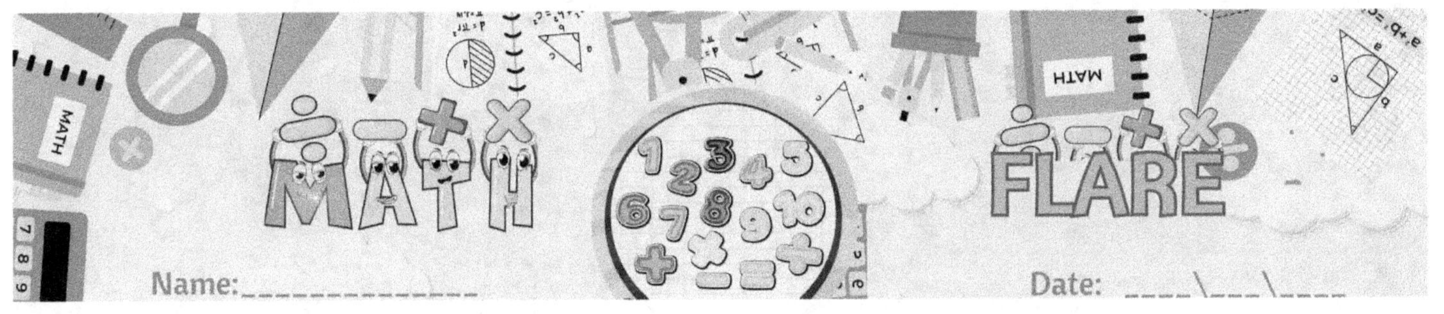

49) $(5 + 2) \times (3 + 2) =$

50) $8 + (5 - (5 - 4)) =$

51) $7 \times 8 =$

52) $5 + 4 + 5 =$

53) $(5^2) \times (3^2) + 5 =$

54) $(9^2) \times (4^2) + 7 =$

55) $2 + 9 - 5 + 6 =$

56) $2 \times 1 =$

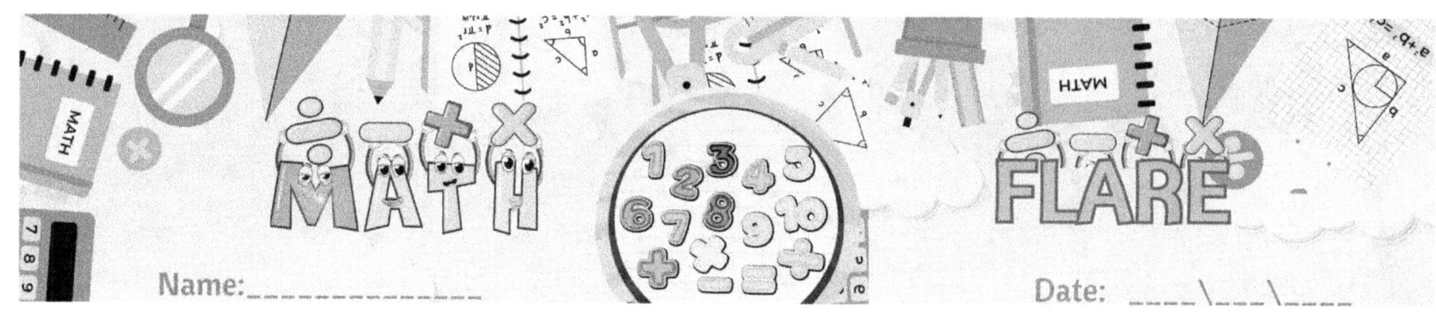

Solving Equations: (One Step)

1) $20 - y = 3$

   = $\ 20 - y - 20 = 3 - 20$

   = $\ -y = -17$

   = $\ (-1) \cdot (-y) = (-1) \cdot (-17)$

   = $\ y = 17$

2) $19 = 13 + y$

3) $7 = x + 2$

4) $5 + x = 7$

5) $34 = y + 19$

6) $209 \div y = 19$

7) $15 = 12 + x$

8) $65 = 11x + 10$

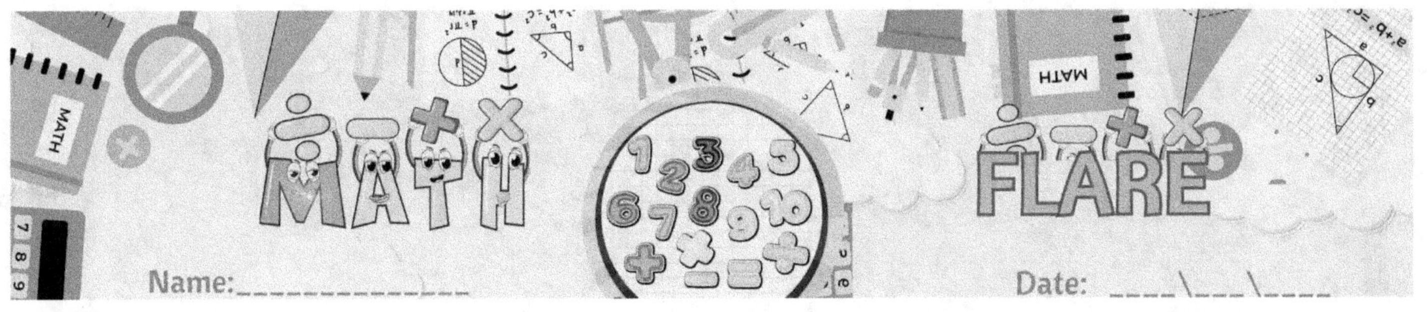

9) $13y - 2 = 128$

10) $x \times 13 = 65$

11) $26 = 18y + 8$

12) $14 = y + 2$

13) $11 = y \div 2$

14) $20 \times y = 40$

15) $20 + 18y = 236$

16) $10 + x = 12$

17) $182 = 12x + 14$

18) $18 = 6x - 12$

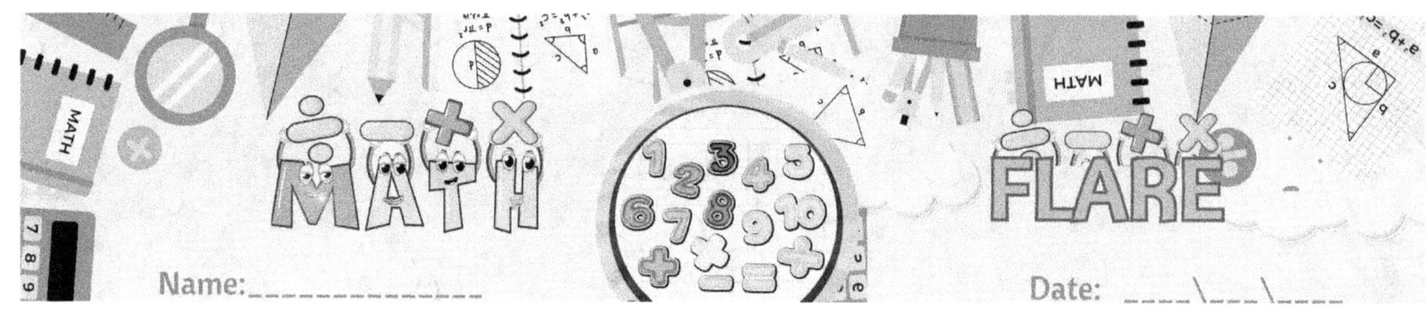

19) $14y + 19 = 285$

20) $292 = 19y - 12$

21) $220 = y \times 11$

22) $56 = 10x + 16$

23) $18y + 1 = 145$

24) $20y + 8 = 408$

25) $0 = 16 - y$

26) $173 = 2 + 9y$

27) $14 \times y = 56$

28) $15 + x = 17$

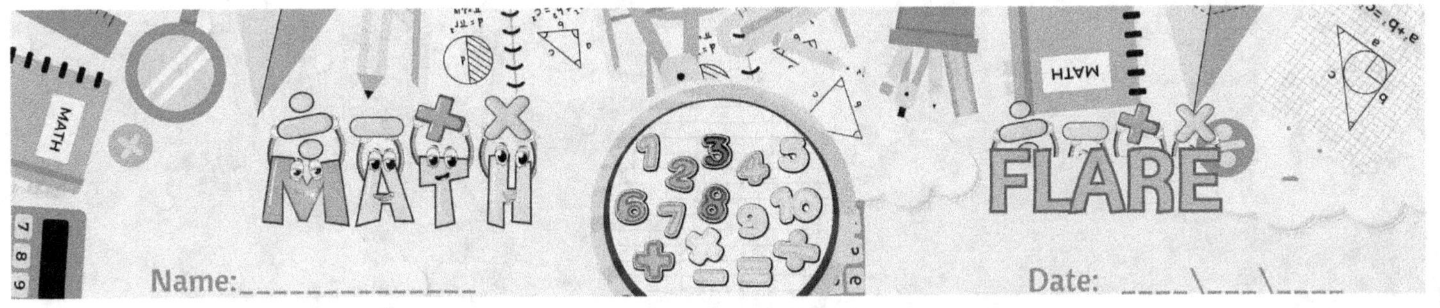

29) $15 - y = 7$

30) $31 = 11 + 10x$

31) $204 = x \times 12$

32) $235 = 20y + 15$

33) $17 + 15y = 242$

34) $x - 18 = 1$

35) $27 - 18x = 9$

36) $4x + 1 = 29$

37) $y + 1 = 11$

38) $18 - x = 12$

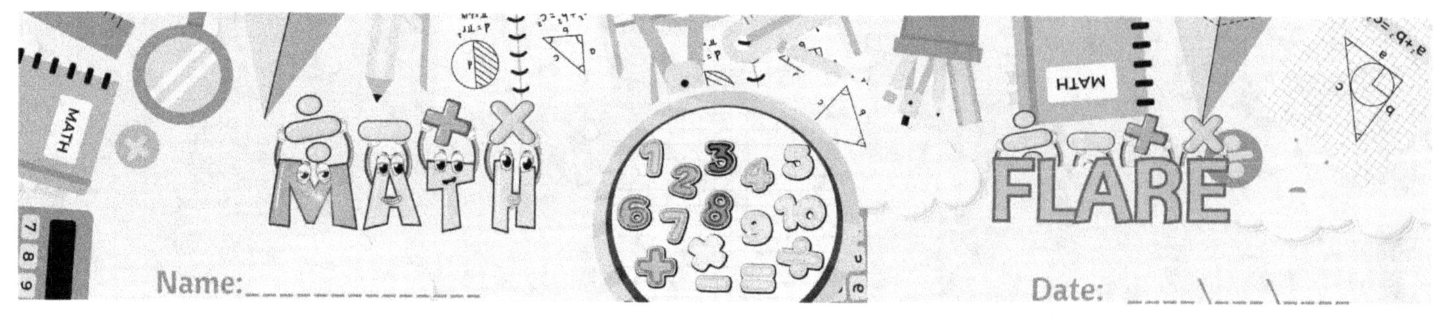

39) $y + 13 = 33$

40) $y + 12 = 31$

41) $121 = 9 + 16y$

42) $8 + 8x = 48$

43) $4 = y - 8$

44) $5 + 6y = 11$

45) $4 = 5 - x$

46) $169 - 13x = 0$

47) $25 = 5 + x$

48) $15y - 11 = 199$

49) $6y + 4 = 70$

50) $36 - 2x = 0$

51) $4 = y + 1$

52) $5y - 20 = 80$

53) $y \times 9 = 108$

54) $8 = x \div 16$

55) $276 - 16x = 4$

56) $11 \times x = 132$

57) $60 = 8x - 12$

58) $12 + y = 14$

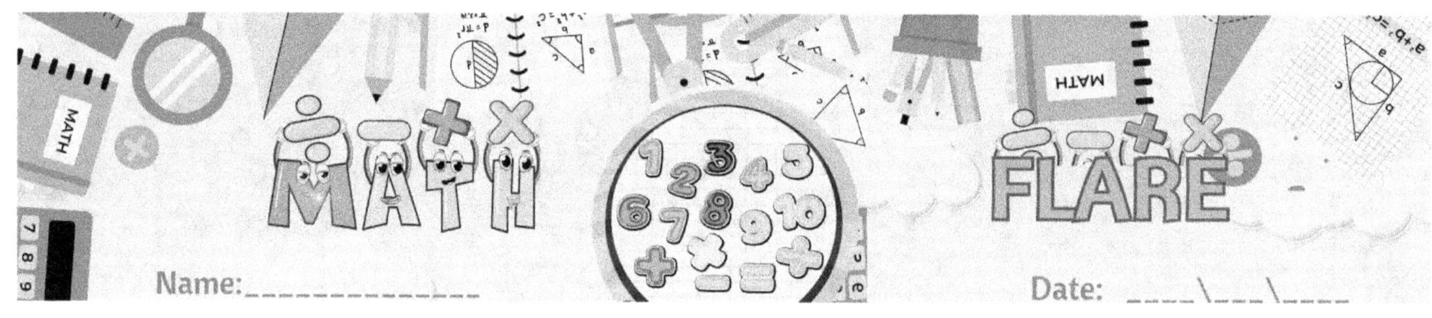

59) $x + 19 = 21$

60) $7 = 15 - 1x$

61) $7 = y \div 19$

62) $18 - y = 15$

63) $12 = x + 4$

64) $162 \div x = 18$

65) $28 \div x = 7$

66) $x - 6 = 4$

67) $y \div 10 = 20$

68) $12 - x = 8$

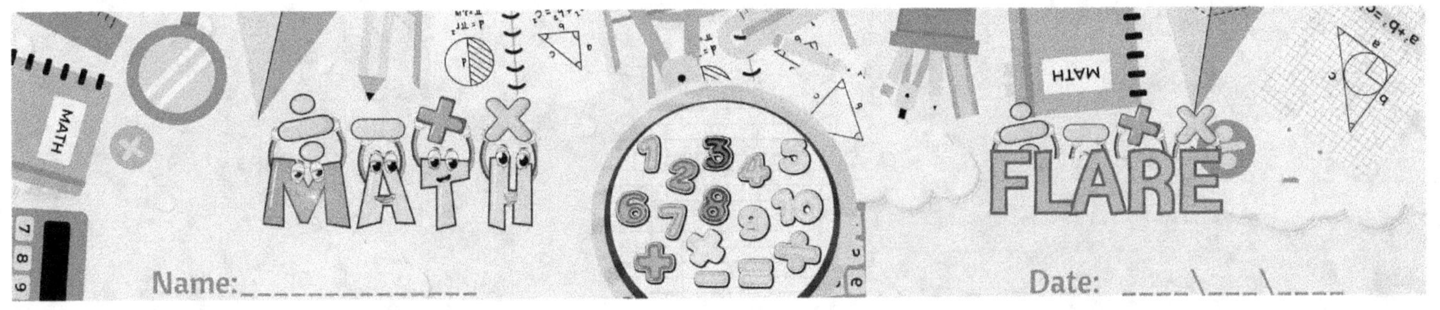

69) $4 = x - 12$

70) $x - 15 = 2$

71) $98 = 14 \times y$

72) $19 - x = 11$

73) $168 - 10x = 8$

74) $1 = x - 6$

75) $20 = 4 + y$

76) $25 = 10 + y$

77) $110 = x \times 11$

78) $95 \div y = 5$

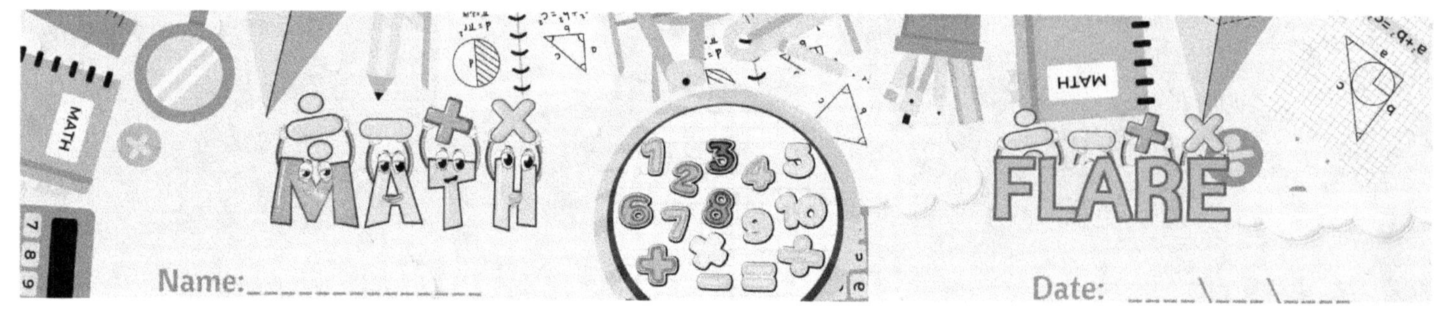

79) $15x + 17 = 272$

80) $20 + 8y = 76$

81) $10 = 10 \div x$

82) $1 = x \div 19$

83) $238 = 14 \times y$

84) $360 \div y = 18$

85) $137 - 15y = 2$

86) $24 \div x = 3$

87) $13 - y = 3$

88) $6 = 20 - y$

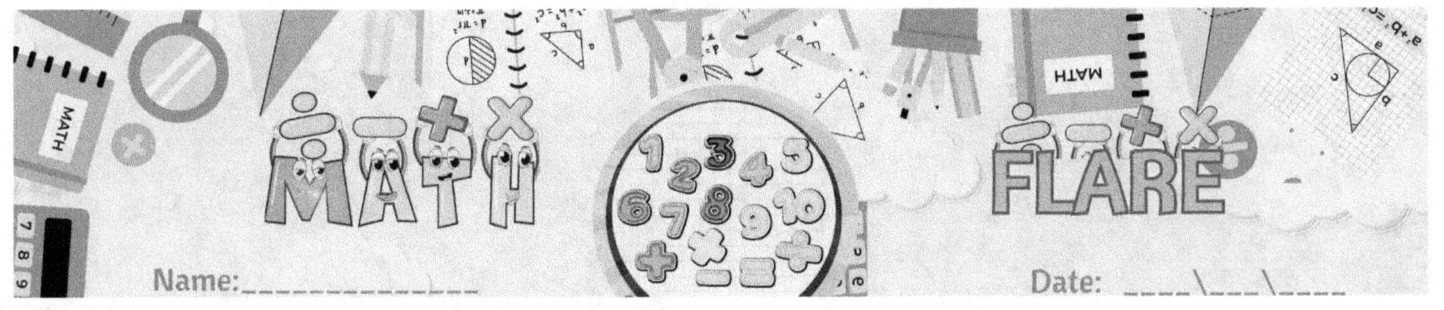

Equations (Two Steps)
Solve for the variable.

1) $9 + 8x + 8 = 64 + x + 2$

   = 8x+9+8=64+x+2   = 8x=x+49
   = 8x+17=64+x+2   = 7x=49
   = 8x+17=x+64+2   = x = 7
   = 8x+17=x+66

2) $1 + 8x = 7x + 8$

3) $9 + 6y + 6 = 21 - y + 8$

4) $28 + 2z = 5z + 7$

5) $7 + 5y = 15 + 3y$

6) 25 + z + -4 = 1 + 4z + 2

7) 54 – 2z = 4z + 6

8) 8x + 9 = 5 + 9x

9) 10 + 7x = 5 + 8x

10) 3x + 9 = 10 + 2x

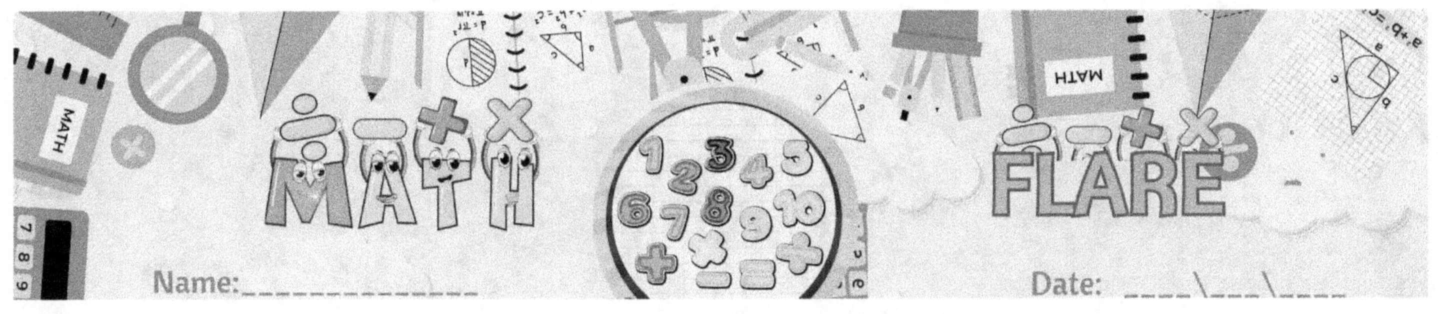

11) $9 + 7y = 1 + 9y$

12) $3 + 2x + 9 = 25 - x + 11$

13) $1 + 2y + 7 = 19 + y + -2$

14) $2 + 9x = 54 - 4x$

15) $9y + 8 = 17 + 8y$

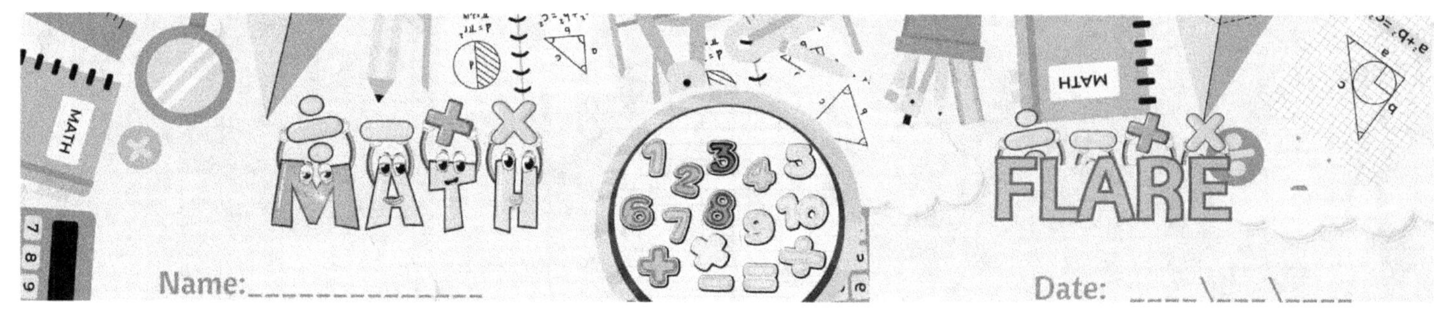

16) $158 - 8y = 5 + 9y$

17) $16 + 2z = 2 + 9z$

18) $11 - 2z = 7z + 2$

19) $5 + 6z + 5 = 45 + z$

20) $18 + y + 2 = 9 + 2y + 4$

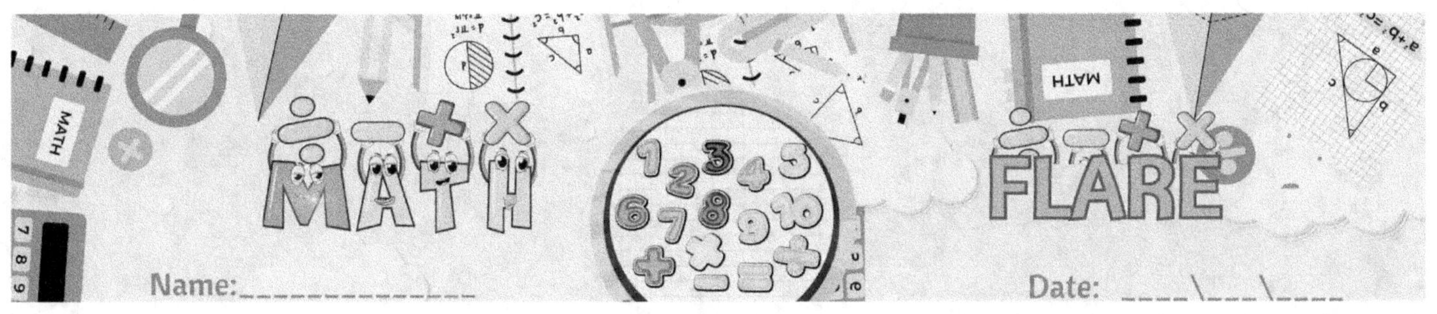

21) $28 + x = 6 + 4x + 7$

22) $7x + 3 = 51 - 5x$

23) $1 + 6x + 9 = 63 + x + -8$

24) $3x + 8 = 4x + 6$

25) $20 + x + 2 = 8 + 2x + 8$

26) $9 + 2y + 9 = 25 + y$

27) $82 - 7z = 2 + 9z$

28) $1 + 9x = 105 - 4x$

29) $4 + 9z = 10 + 7z$

30) $38 - 8x = 4 + 9x$

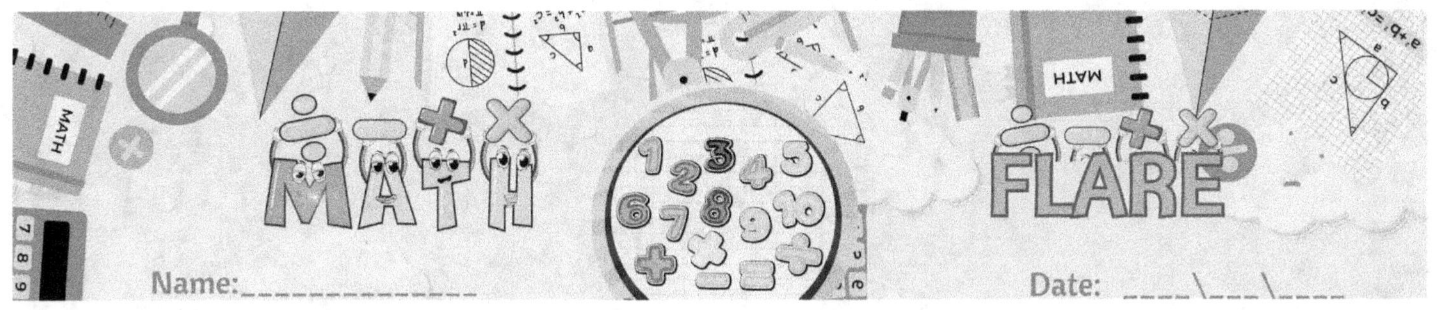

31) 15 – x + 11 = 9 + 6x + 3

32) 9z + 3 = 66 + 2z

33) 2 + 8z = 128 – 6z

34) 3x + 1 = 3 + 2x

35) 8 + 2z + 1 = 14 + z

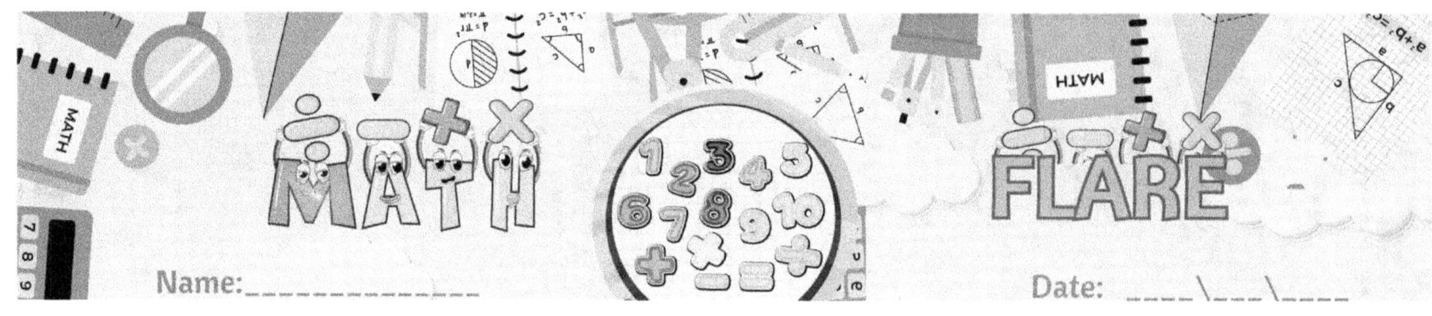

36)   58 − y = 7 + 4y + 6

37)   1 + 8y + 4 = 40 + y

38)   7y + 10 = 8 + 8y

39)   7 + 7x + 3 = 52 − x + 14

40)   56 − y = 6 + 7y + 2

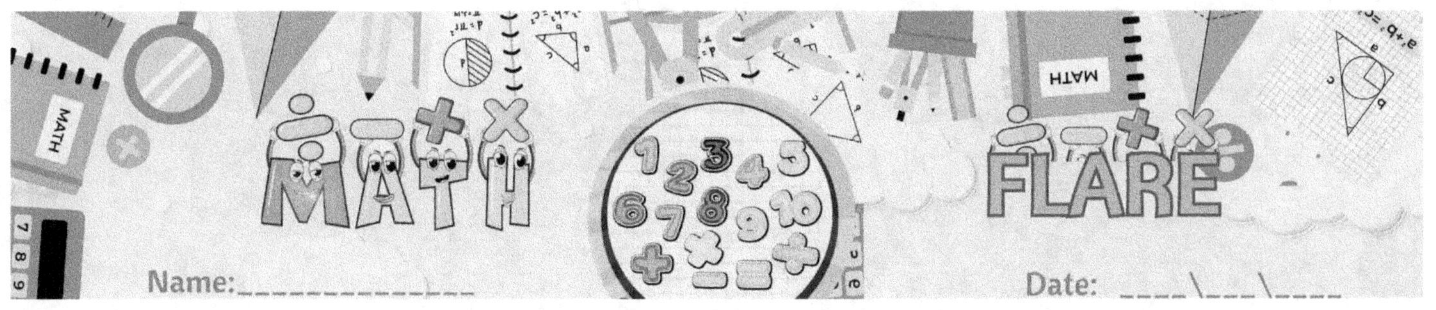

41) $5 + 5x + 8 = 29 + x$

42) $15 - z + 8 = 5 + 5z + 6$

43) $21 - x + 11 = 9 + 2x + 5$

44) $7 + 6z + 7 = 21 - z$

45) $8 + 4y = 43 - 3y$

46) 24 + z = 4 + 3z + 4

47) 33 – y + 12 = 9 + 8y + 9

48) 2 + 6z + 2 = 38 + z + -4

49) 7 + 2y + 5 = 27 – y

50) 28 + y + -3 = 1 + 6y + 4

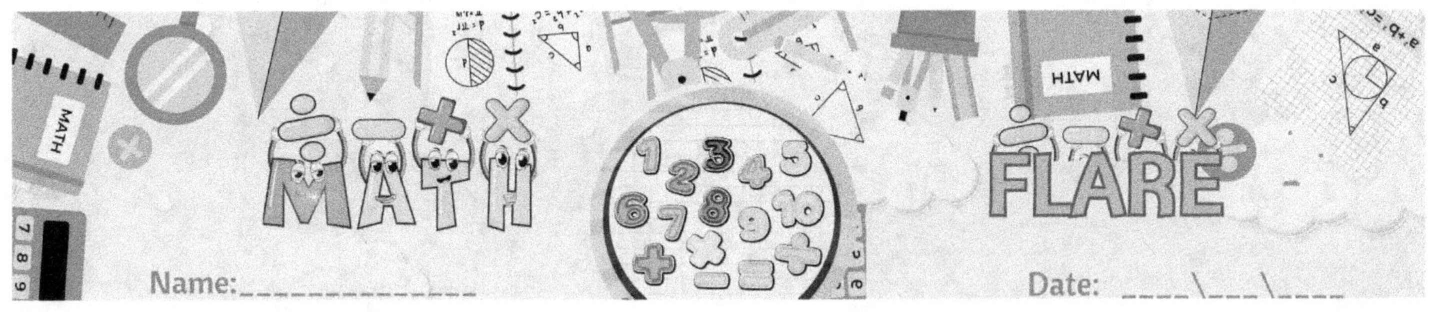

51) 84 – 7y = 8y + 9

52) 1 + 2z + 5 = 17 – z + 7

53) 2 + 6x + 7 = 61 + x + -7

54) 3 + 2y + 9 = 24 – y

55) 16 + z = 2 + 2z + 6

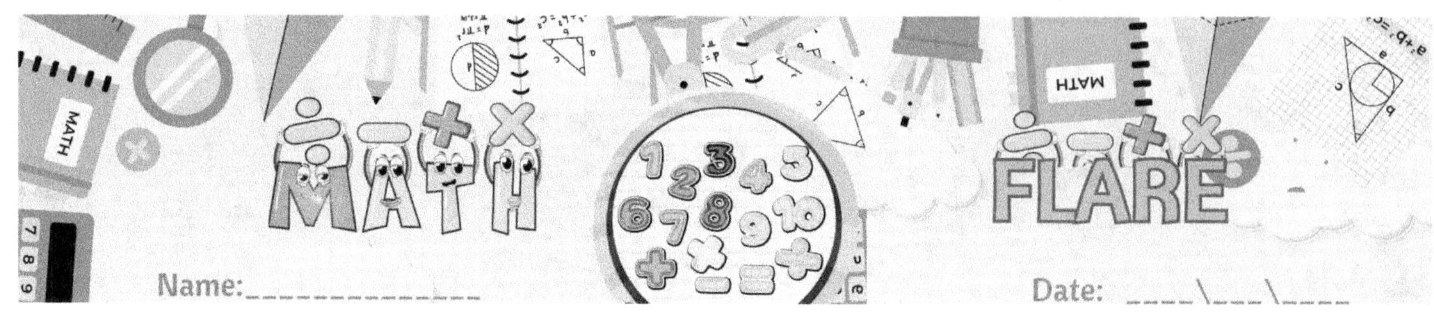

56) $3 + 7x = 4 + 6x$

57) $70 - 3x = 4 + 8x$

58) $5 + 4x + 1 = 13 + x + 2$

59) $47 - 5y = 8y + 8$

60) $23 - z = 9 + 5z + 8$

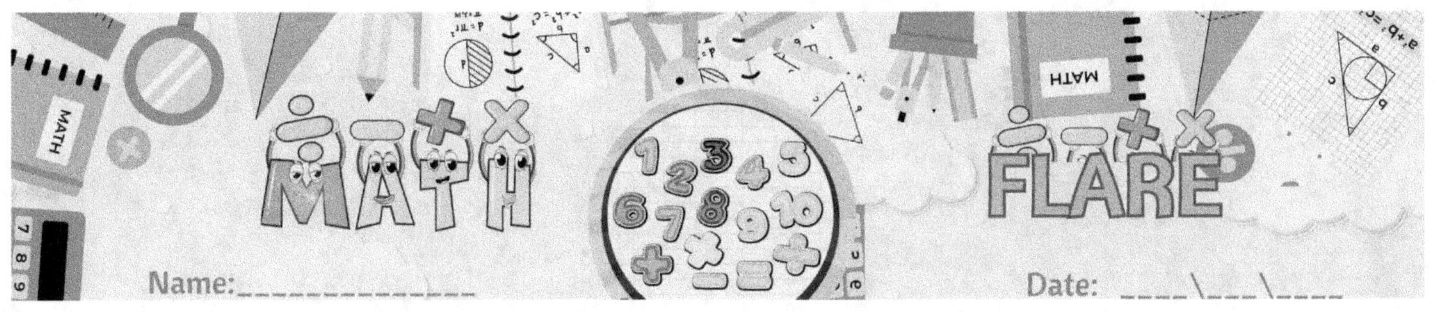

61) $8 + 5x + 2 = 52 - x$

62) $2 + 2y + 6 = 29 - y$

63) $7 + 6y = 4y + 11$

64) $1 + 4z + 7 = 31 + z + -5$

65) $3 + 5x + 4 = 9 - x + 4$

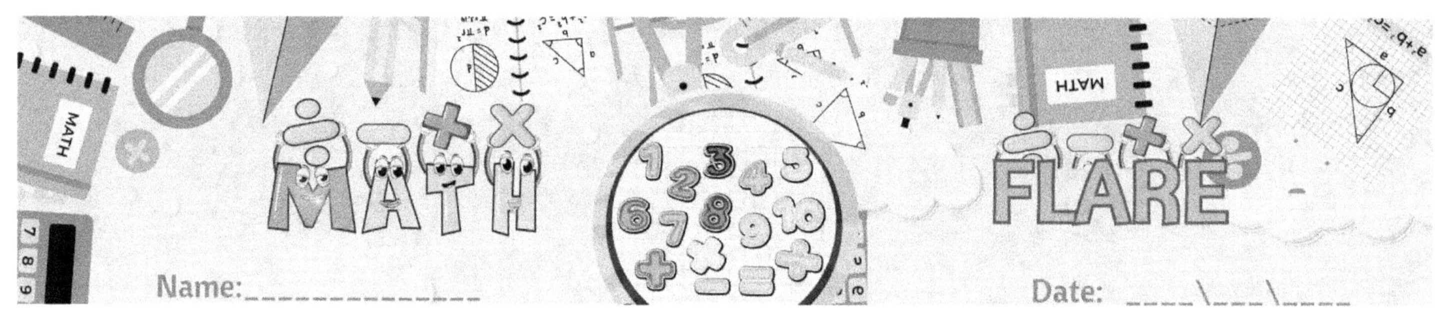

66) $7y + 6 = 50 - 4y$

67) $10 + 8y = 9y + 7$

68) $7 + 9x = 55 + 3x$

69) $11 + x + -1 = 5 + 2x + 2$

70) $8x + 6 = 18 - 4x$

71) $5 + x + 1 = 2 + 4x + 1$

72) $59 - x + 11 = 3 + 7x + 3$

73) $3 + 4z = 38 - 3z$

74) $33 + x = 8 + 4x + 1$

75) $29 + x = 3 + 7x + 8$

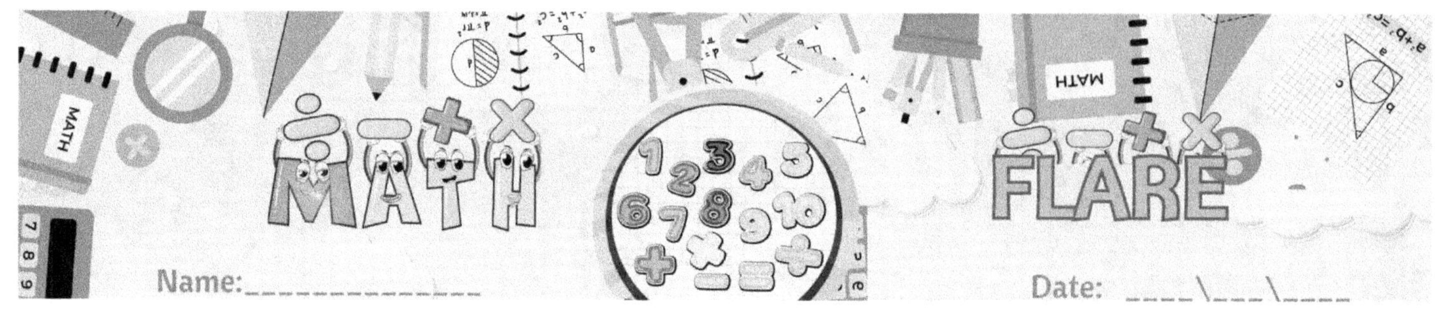

76) $8 + x + 4 = 2 + 2x + 7$

77) $5 + 9x = 7x + 7$

78) $3 + 5x + 8 = 33 - x + 14$

79) $2 + 4y + 6 = 17 + y$

80) $4 + 9y = 22 + 7y$

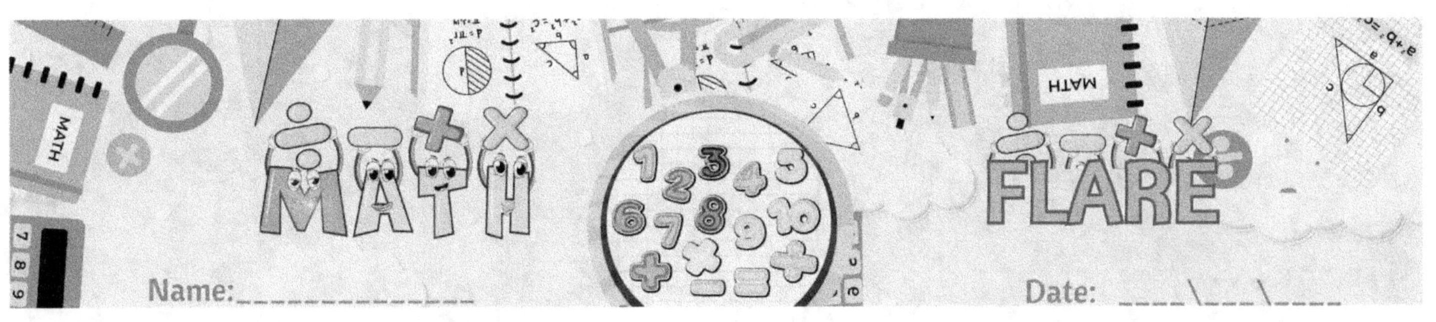

Evaluate Expressions

Evaluate the expression when: $x = 2$

1) $10x - 3 + x =$

$= 10(2) - 3 + 2$

$= 10(2) - 1$

$= 20 - 1 = 19$

2) $x + 3x - 5 =$

3) $5 \div x + 3 =$

4) $2x + 6 =$

5) $x + x =$

6) $(4 + 4x) + (8x - 3) - (5 + 2x) =$

7) $3x + 1 + (3x - 6) =$

8) $10 + (8x + 8) =$

Evaluate Expressions

Evaluate the expression when: $x = 1$

1) $1 - x =$

2) $3x - 1 + x =$

3) $\dfrac{7}{x} =$

4) $3 + (5x + 9) - 8 + (x) =$

5) $10 + x =$

6) $8x - 5 + 2x =$

7) $6x + 3 =$

8) $\dfrac{x}{1} + 3 =$

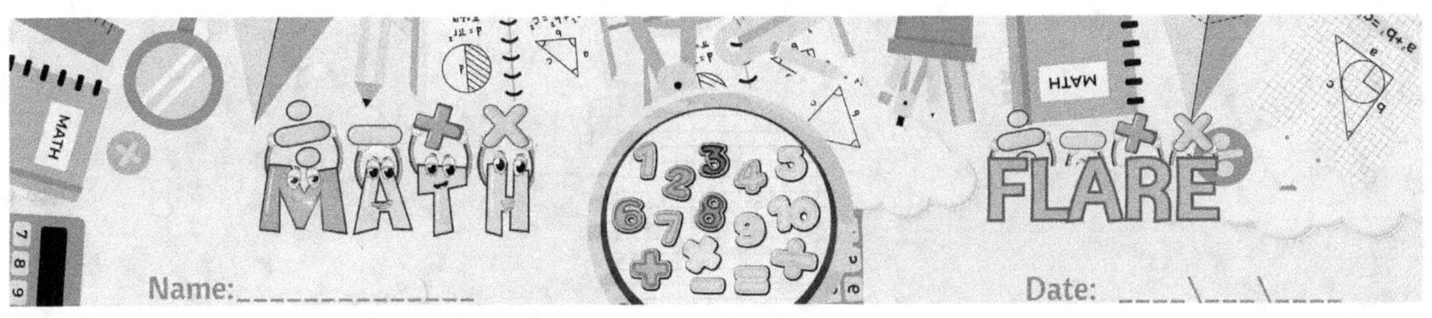

Evaluate Expressions

Evaluate the expression when: $x = 3$

1) $x + 2 =$

2) $x \div 5 =$

3) $4x + 10 - x =$

4) $5^3 + x^1 =$

5) $4x - x =$

6) $3 \div x + 4 =$

7) $\dfrac{x}{1} =$

8) $6x + x =$

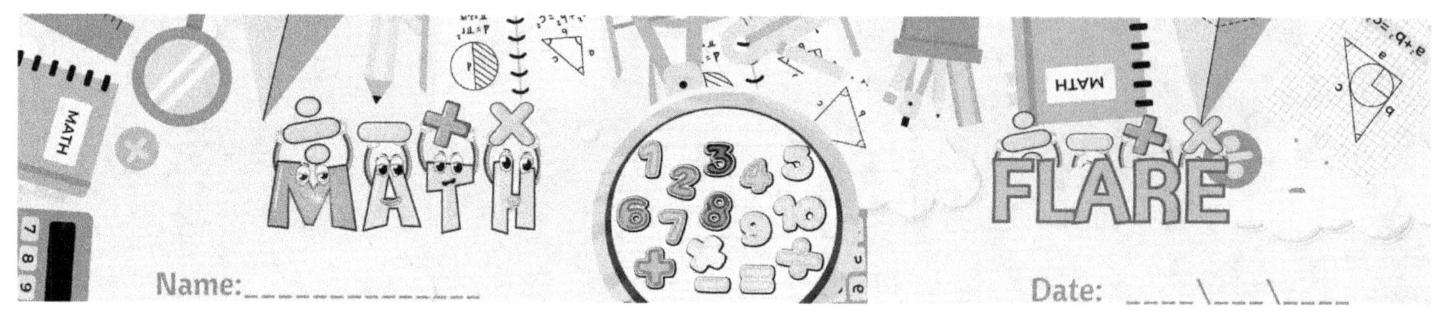

Evaluate Expressions

Evaluate the expression when: x = 7

1) $\dfrac{x}{1} + 3 =$

2) $(x^3 + 9) - 6(7 + x) =$

3) $9x^2 + 5x^2 =$

4) $4x - x =$

5) $\dfrac{3 + 28}{x + 2} =$

6) $x - 1 =$

7) $3x - x =$

8) $\dfrac{5 + 7}{x + 8} =$

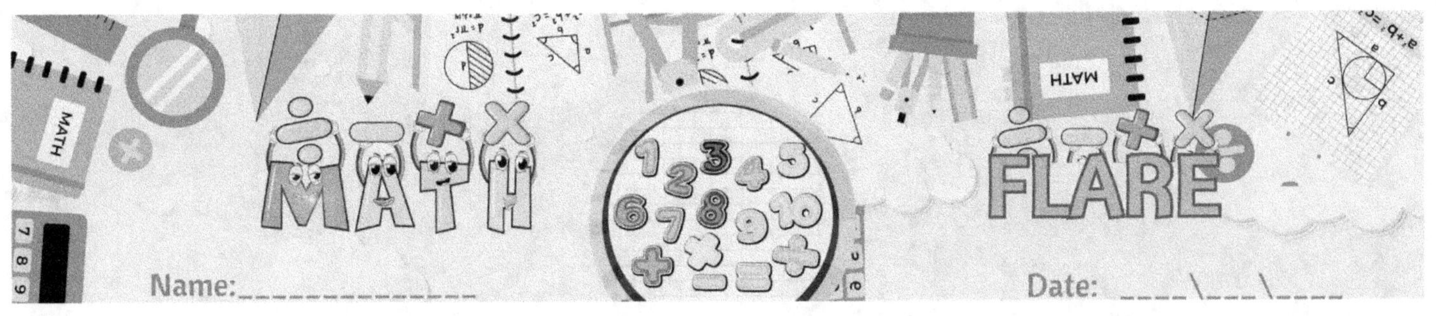

Evaluate Expressions

Evaluate the expression when: x = 7

1) $(2x)(8x) =$

2) $x + 4 - 8x =$

3) $x + 5 =$

4) $6 + (2x + 1) - 6 + (x) =$

5) $3x - 6 =$

6) $\dfrac{8 + 28}{x + 5} =$

7) $6 - x =$

8) $7 \div x + 3 =$

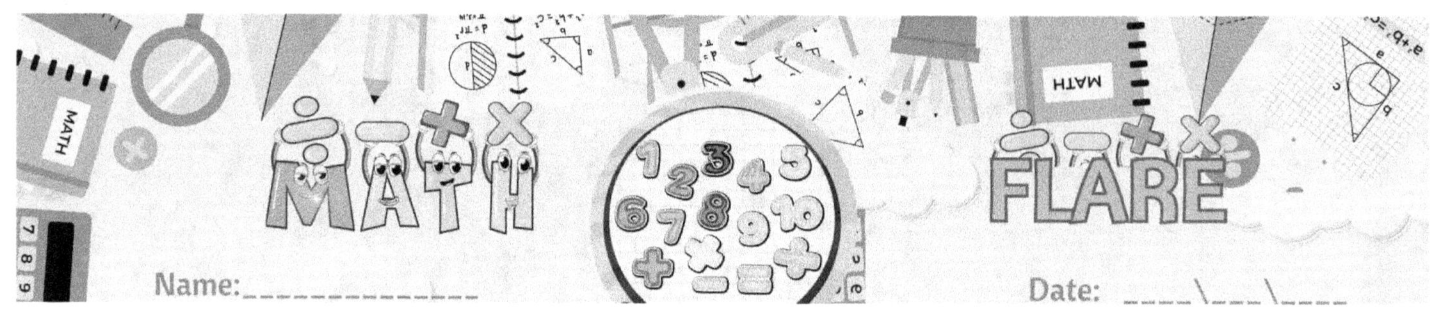

Evaluate Expressions

Evaluate the expression when: x = 6

1) $(x + 2) \div 6 =$

2) $\dfrac{x}{2} =$

3) $x - 1 =$

4) $8(1 + x) =$

5) $\dfrac{x}{1} + 10 =$

6) $(4x)^2 =$

7) $9 + \dfrac{9 + x}{2x} - 2 =$

8) $\dfrac{6 + x}{x + 2} =$

Evaluate Expressions

Evaluate the expression when: $x = 5$

1) $9 \div x =$

2) $x + 6 =$

3) $x \div 4 =$

4) $\dfrac{10 + x}{x + 10} =$

5) $7 \div x + 2 =$

6) $5 + (3x + 7) - 1 + (6x) =$

7) $(x + 7) \div 5 =$

8) $x + 7 =$

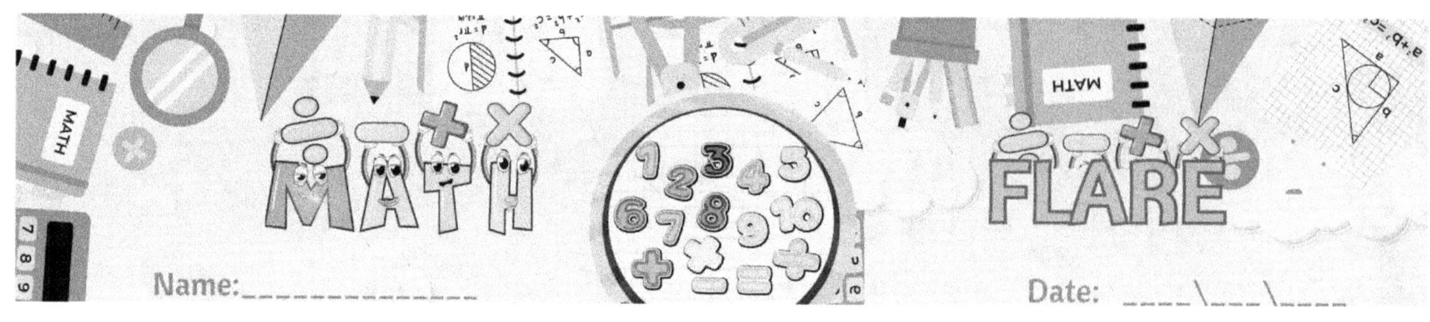

Evaluate Expressions

Evaluate the expression when: x = 1

1) $1 - x =$

2) $(6x + 8) + (9x + 1) =$

3) $9 + x =$

4) $8 + x =$

5) $8 + \dfrac{2 + x}{x} - 3 =$

6) $10x^1 + 7x^2 =$

7) $x(8 + x) =$

8) $1^2 + x^3 =$

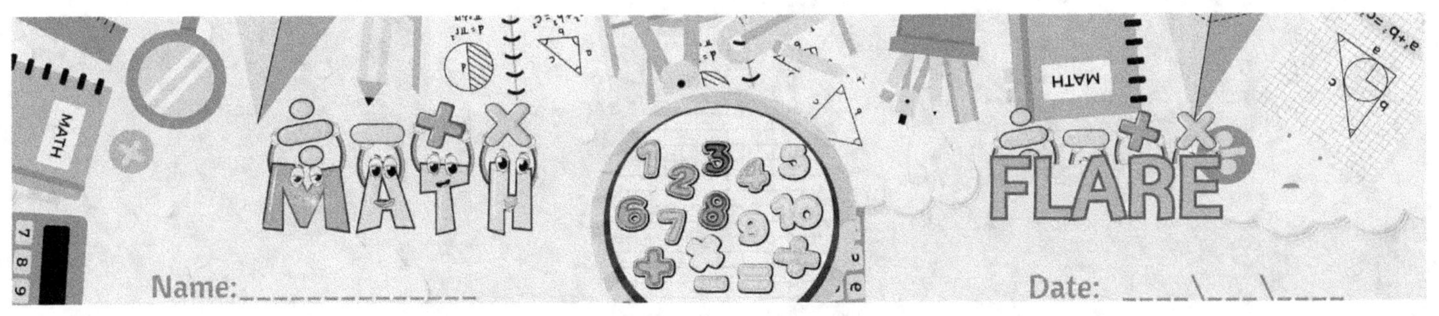

Evaluate Equations

Solve for the variable.

1) $5(5 - x) = 5$

$$= 25-5x=5$$
$$= 25-25-5x=5-25$$
$$= -5x=-20$$
$$= \frac{-5x}{-5} = \frac{-20}{-5}$$
$$= x = 4$$

2) $162 = 6(3x)$

3) $7 + (5y + 2) - 4 + (y) = 11$

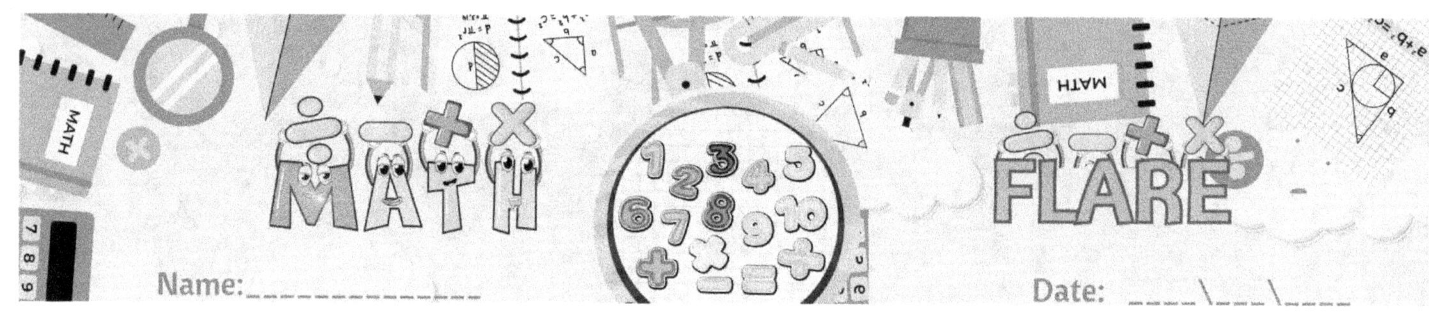

4) $28 = 8z - z$

5) $5.333 = 8 \div z + 4$

6) $71 = 8y - 1$

7) $8 + (3z + 6) = 35$

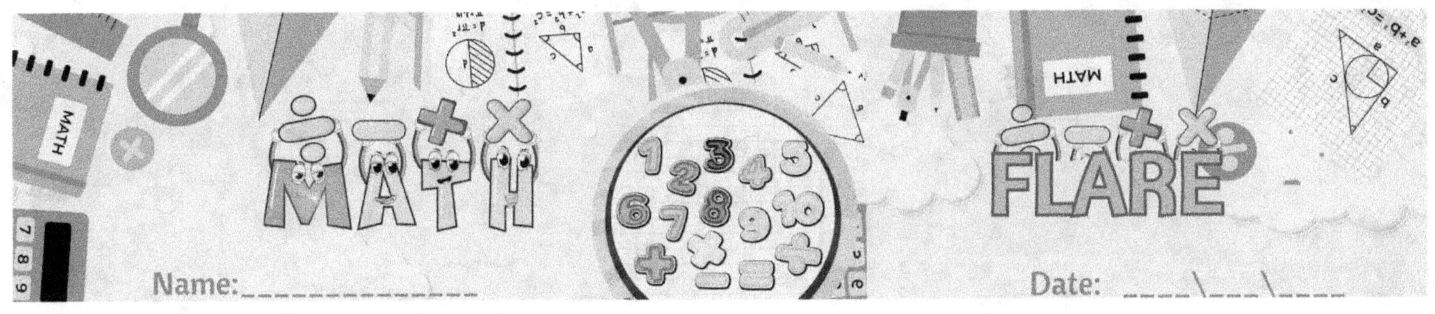

8) $144 = 9x + 8x - 9$

9) $6 + (7z + 2) = 43$

10) $14 = z + 8z - 4$

11) $1 = 1 \div z$

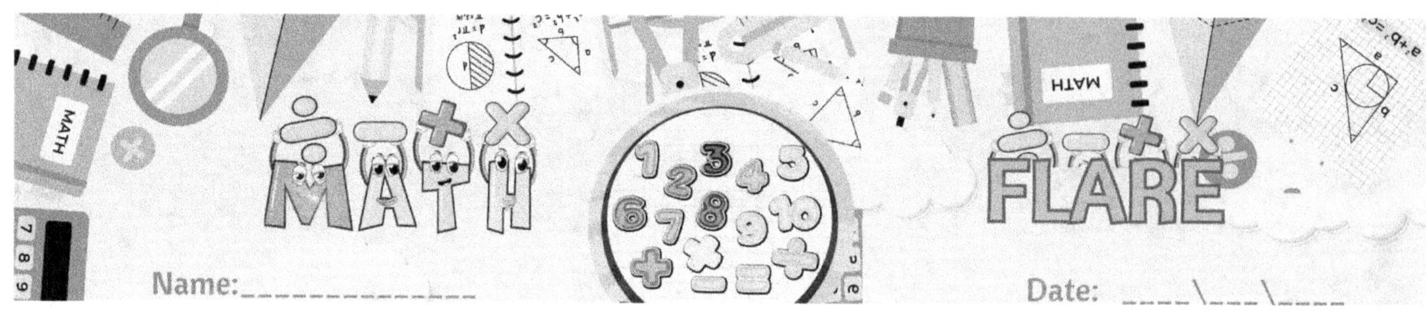

12) $2y + 1 = 15$

13) $15 = 4y - 6 + 3y$

14) $0.125 = 1 \div x$

15) $7z - 1 = 20$

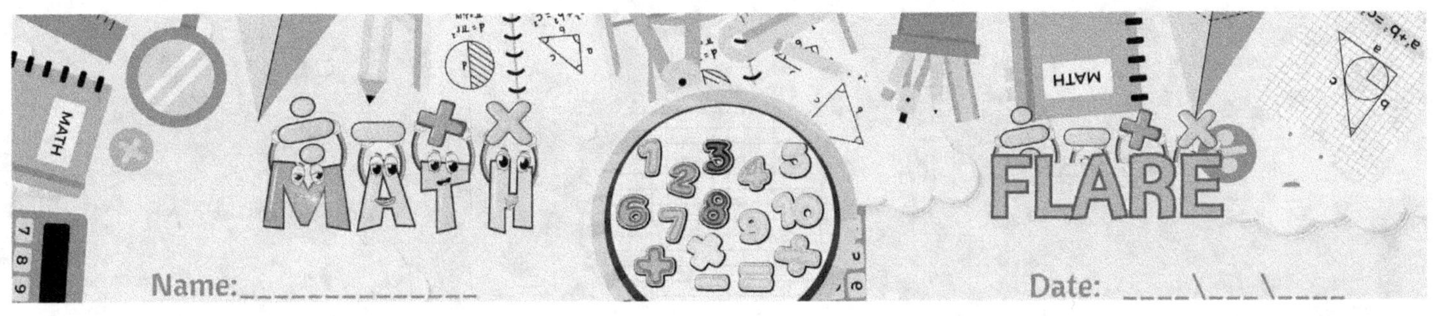

16) $9 = \dfrac{x}{8} + 8$

17) $23 = 4 + \dfrac{9}{z} + 4^2$

18) $6^2 + x^2 = 40$

19) $x + 5 + 4x = 35$

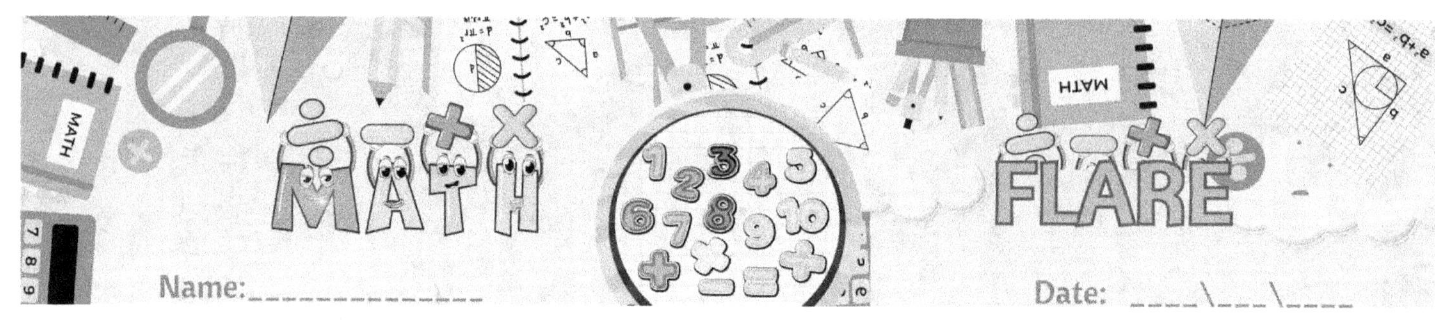

20) $6y + 1 = 7$

21) $(z + 8) \div 8 = 1.75$

22) $30 = 5(3z)$

23) $-4 = (2 + 7x) + (x - 6) - (6 + 2x)$

24) $-12 = (x^2 + 8) - 4(8 + x)$

25) $0.706 = \dfrac{4 + 8}{x + 9}$

26) $-6 = (8 + 2y) + (5y - 9) - (7 + 5y)$

27) $48 = 6(1 + x)$

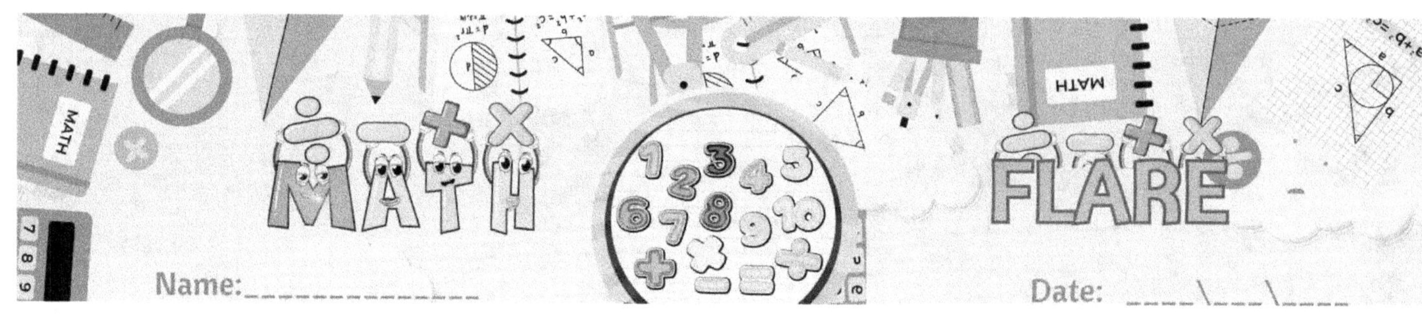

28) $5 + (3x + 2) - 9 + (x) = 26$

29) $0.889 = z \div 9$

30) $33 = 7x + 5$

31) $(7x + 5) + (3x + 2) = 17$

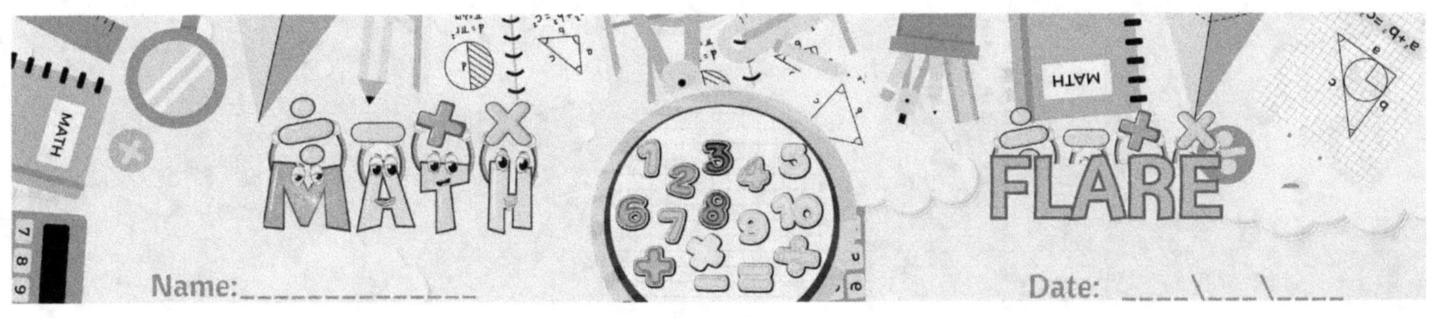

32) $1(8x - 2) + 3(6 + x) = 82$

33) $78 = y(7 + y)$

34) $6 \div (x + 4) = 0.6$

35) $\dfrac{9 + x}{x + 8} = 1.111$

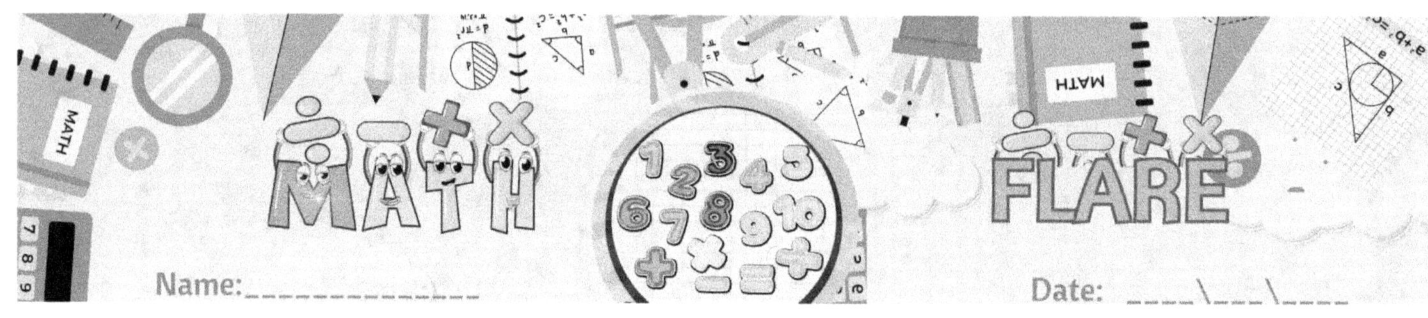

36) $-6 = 2(5 - y)$

37) $7z + 3 = 38$

38) $37 = (4x + 6) + (3x + 3)$

39) $\dfrac{9 + x}{x + 1} = 1.889$

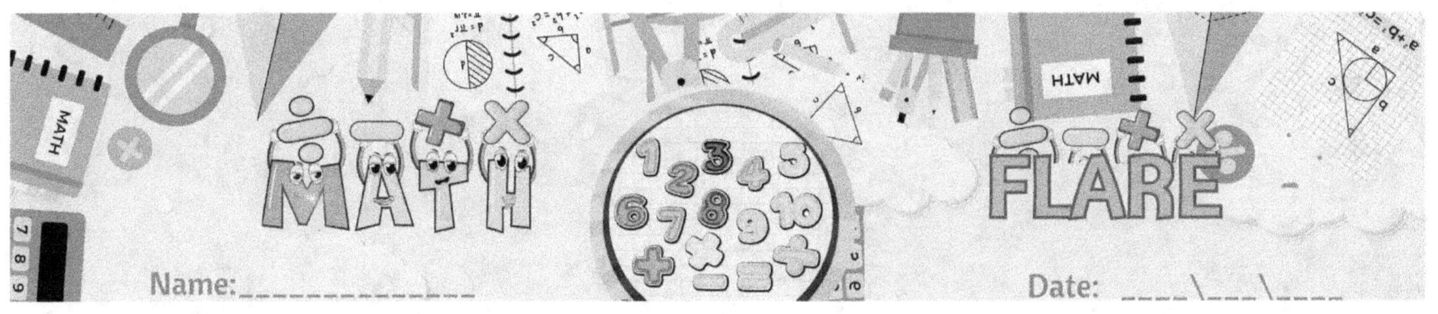

Find Numbers

Think Algebraically and find the numbers.

1) __________ One-fourth of a number increased by 6 is 10. What is the number?

2) __________ One number is ten times another. Their sum is 55. Find the numbers.

3) __________ The greater of two numbers is 6 less than four times the smaller number. Their sum is 34. Find the numbers.

4) __________ One-fourth of a number increased by 1 is 2. What is the number?

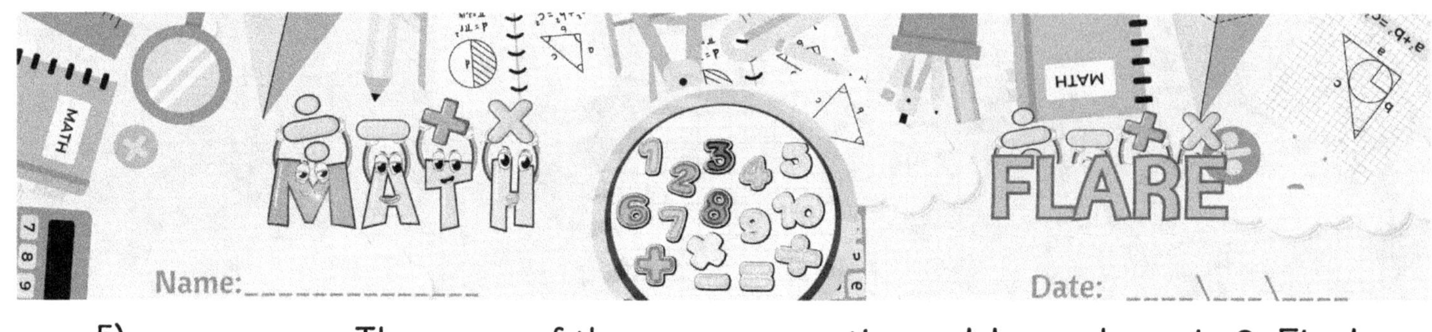

5) __________ The sum of three consecutive odd numbers is 9. Find the numbers.

6) __________ The sum of two numbers is 66. The larger number is ten times the smaller number. What are the numbers?

7) __________ A number decreased by 6 is 2. Find the number.

8) __________ One more than a number is 8. What is the number?

9) __________ One number is seven times another. Their sum is 40. Find the numbers.

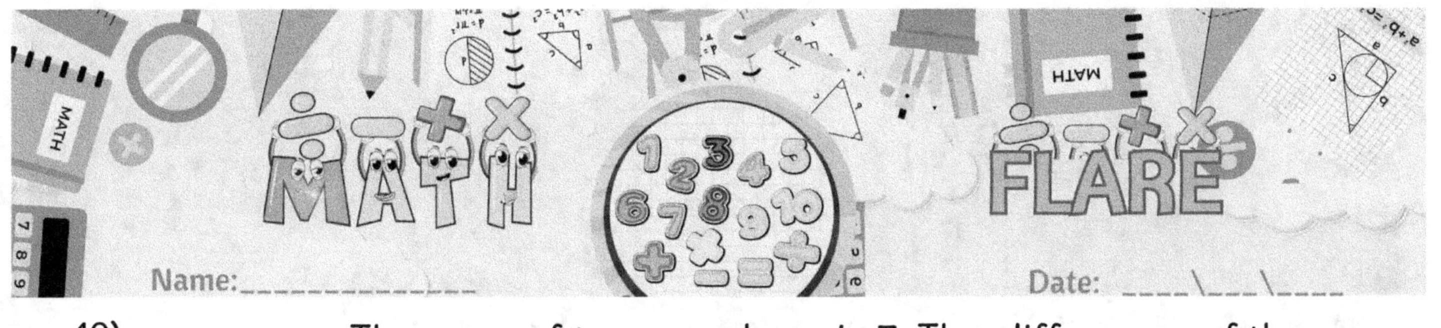

10) __________ The sum of two numbers is 7. The difference of the same two numbers is five. Find the numbers.

11) __________ The product of two numbers is 5. One number is four less than the other. What are the numbers?

12) __________ Four more than eight times a number is equal to the number increased by 18. What is the number?

13) __________ Five times a number increased by 7 is 67. Find the number.

14) __________ Eight times the difference of 10 minus a number is 16. What is the number?

15) __________ Five times the sum of a number and four times the number is 25. Find the number.

16) __________ Six times the difference of 17 minus a number is 48. What is the number?

17) __________ The sum of four consecutive odd numbers is 32. Find the numbers.

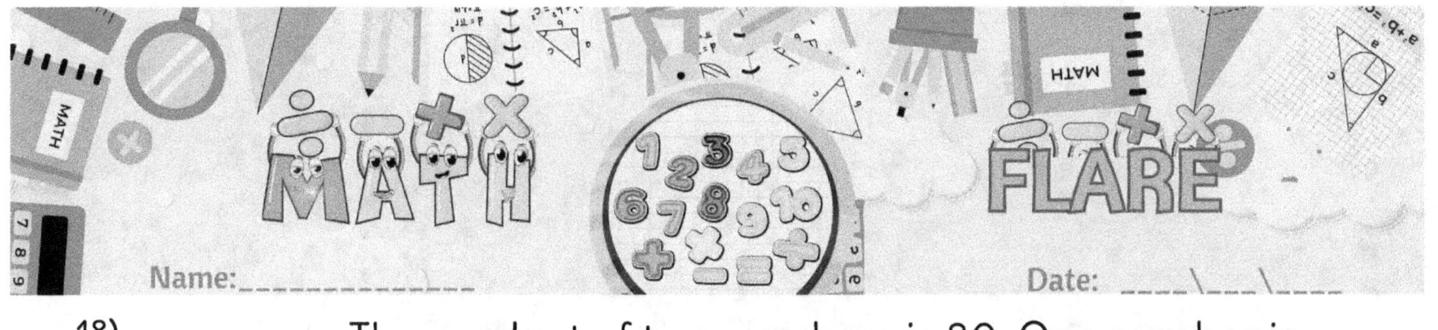

18) _________ The product of two numbers is 80. One number is two less than the other. What are the numbers?

19) _________ The sum of two numbers is 16. The difference of the same two numbers is two. Find the numbers.

20) _________ Seven more than eight times a number is equal to the number increased by 70. What is the number?

21) _________ Seven less than a number is 7. Find the number.

22) _________ One less than four times a number is 31. Find the number.

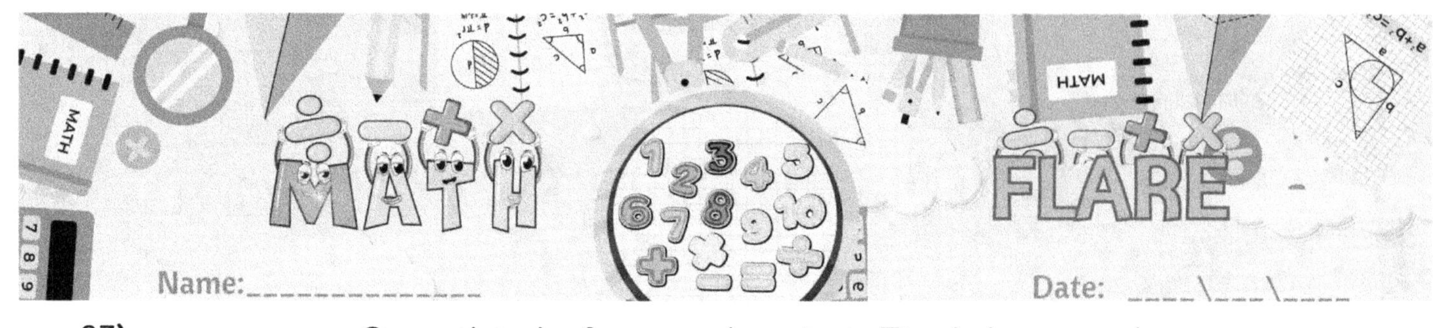

23) __________ One-third of a number is 1. Find the number.

24) __________ The sum of three consecutive odd numbers is 21. Find the numbers.

25) __________ Four more than a number is 5. What is the number?

26) __________ Four more than a number is 8. What is the number?

27) __________ The difference of a number and four is equal to 5. What is the number?

28) __________ The greater of two numbers is 2 less than seven times the smaller number. Their sum is 38. Find the numbers.

29) __________ Four times a number is 8. What is the number?

30) __________ Seven more than eight times a number is equal to the number increased by 49. What is the number?

31) __________ One of two numbers is one-half of the other number. The sum of the numbers is 6. Find the numbers.

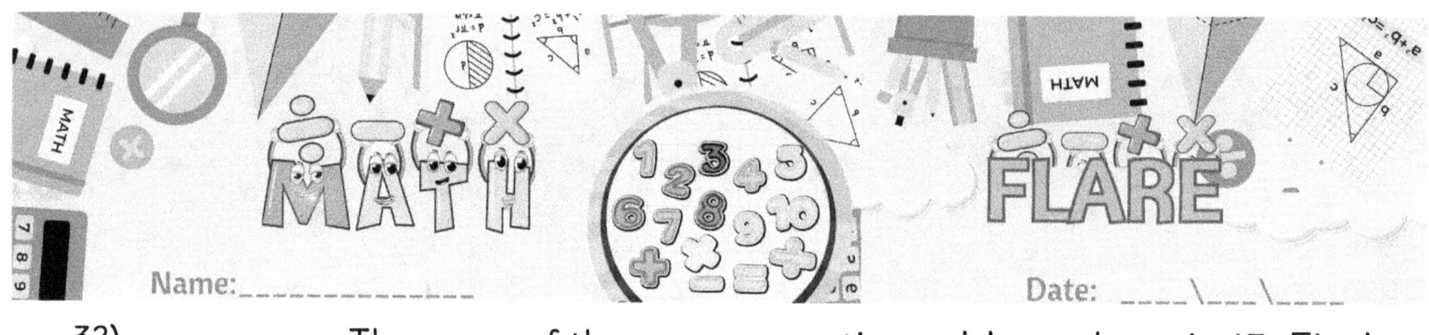

32) __________ The sum of three consecutive odd numbers is 15. Find the numbers.

33) __________ A number increased by two is 3. Find the number.

34) __________ A number diminished by 3 is 7. Find the number.

35) __________ One-third of a number is 0. Find the number.

36) __________ The difference of a number and two is equal to 5. What is the number?

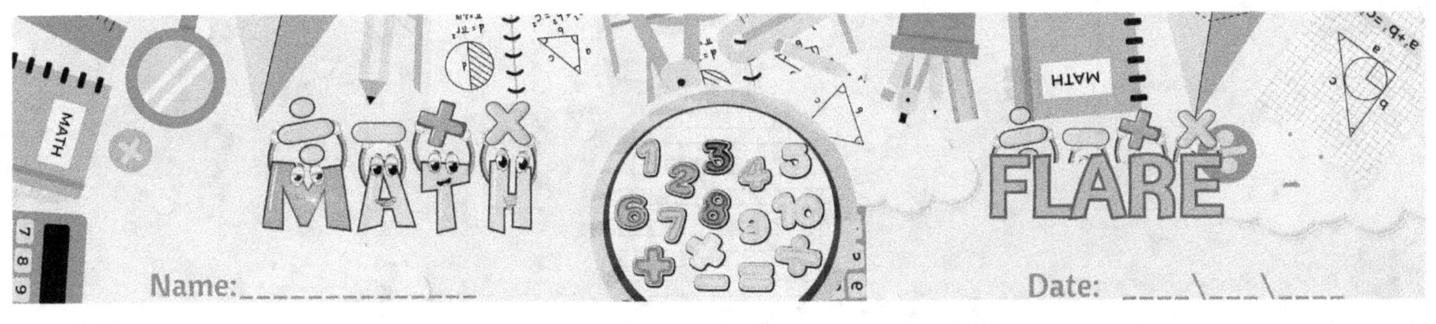

37) __________ Six less than a number is 6. Find the number.

38) __________ One of two numbers is eight more than the other. The sum of the numbers is 10. Find the numbers.

39) __________ The sum of two numbers is 11. One number is seven less than the other. Find the numbers.

40) __________ The quotient of a number and six is 9. Find the number.

41) __________ The product of two and a number is 8. What is the number?

42) __________ Seven is equal to the quotient of a number and 2. Find the number.

43) __________ A number decreased by 8 is 1. Find the number.

44) __________ Eight more than five times a number is equal to the number increased by 44. What is the number?

45) __________ Two-thirds of a number increased by 1 is 9. What is the number?

46) __________ The difference of a number and two is equal to 1. What is the number?

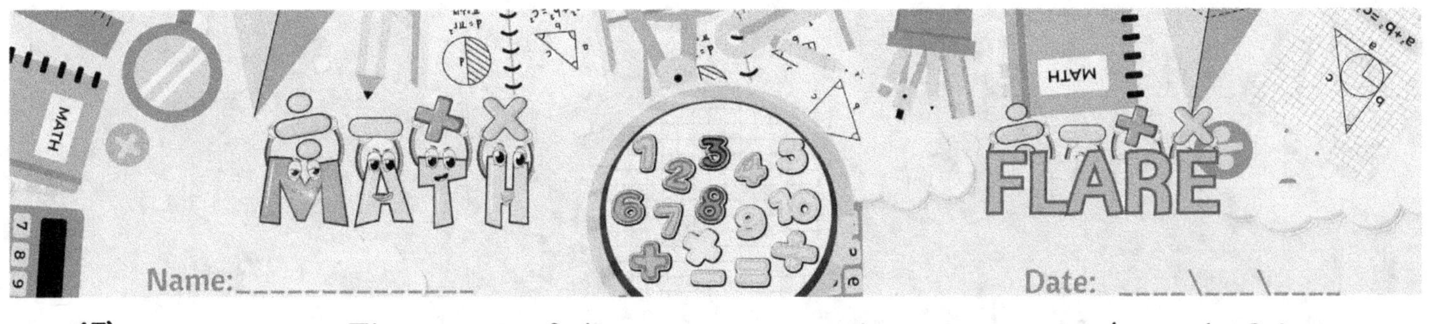

47) __________ The sum of three consecutive even numbers is 24.
What are the numbers?

48) __________ One number is four times another. Their sum is 45.
Find the numbers.

49) __________ One number is nine times another. Their sum is 80.
Find the numbers.

50) __________ The sum of three consecutive even numbers is 36.
What are the numbers?

51) ________ The sum of four consecutive even numbers is 28. What are the numbers?

52) ________ One-third of a number increased by 1 is 2. What is the number?

53) ________ Six times the sum of a number and five times the number is 72. Find the number.

54) ________ One of two numbers is one-half of the other number. The sum of the numbers is 6. Find the numbers.

55) ________ Two more than a number is 7. What is the number?

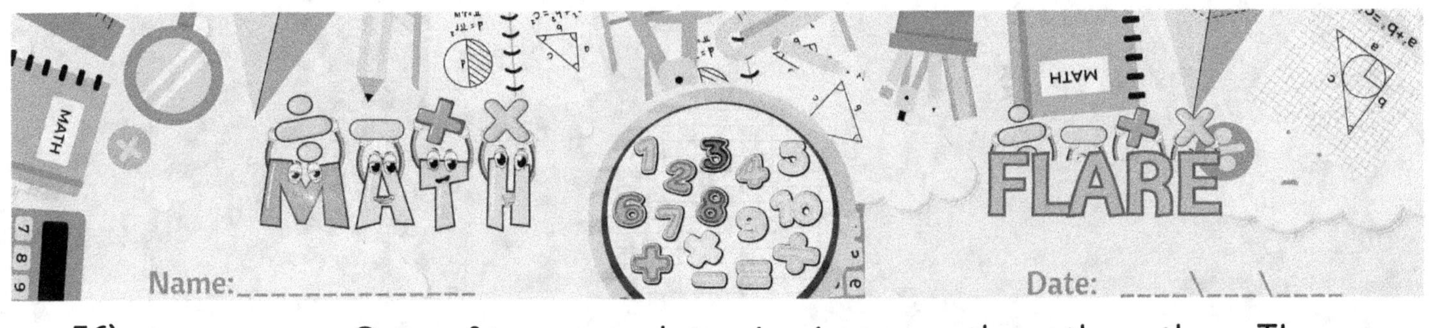

56) __________ One of two numbers is six more than the other. The sum of the numbers is 18. Find the numbers.

57) __________ The sum of two numbers is 25. One number is seven less than the other. Find the numbers.

58) __________ The sum of two numbers is 14. One number is six less than the other. Find the numbers.

59) __________ The sum of two numbers is 8. The larger number is seven times the smaller number. What are the numbers?

Solving Inequalities

1)

$$6\ m \geq -12$$

$$= \quad \frac{6m}{6} \quad \geq \quad \frac{-12}{6}$$

$$= \quad m \quad \geq \quad 6$$

$$m \geq -2$$

2)

$$9 \geq 4 - x$$

3)

$$\frac{z}{-3} < -1$$

4)

$$8 \geq z + 3$$

5)

$$\frac{k}{1} \le -3$$

6)

$$-15 < 6\,m$$

7)

$$9 < y - 2$$

8)

$$2 > x + 3$$

Name:________________   Date: _____________

9)

$$-6 \geq 5y$$

10)

$$y - 2 < 3$$

11)

$$-1 + y < 4$$

12)

$$1 > \frac{m}{2}$$

13)
$$\frac{m}{-3} \geq -3$$

14)
$$m - -7 < 7$$

15)
$$-10 \leq m + 7$$

16)
$$-3 > -5\,k$$

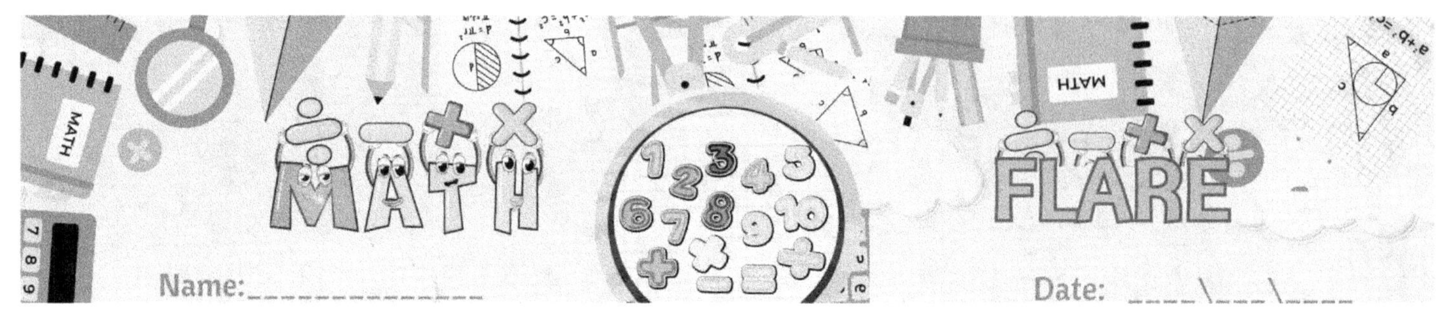

17)

$$-2 > \frac{z}{5}$$

18)

$$-12 \geq 21\,x$$

19)

$$7 > m + -4$$

20)

$$-5 - m \geq -4$$

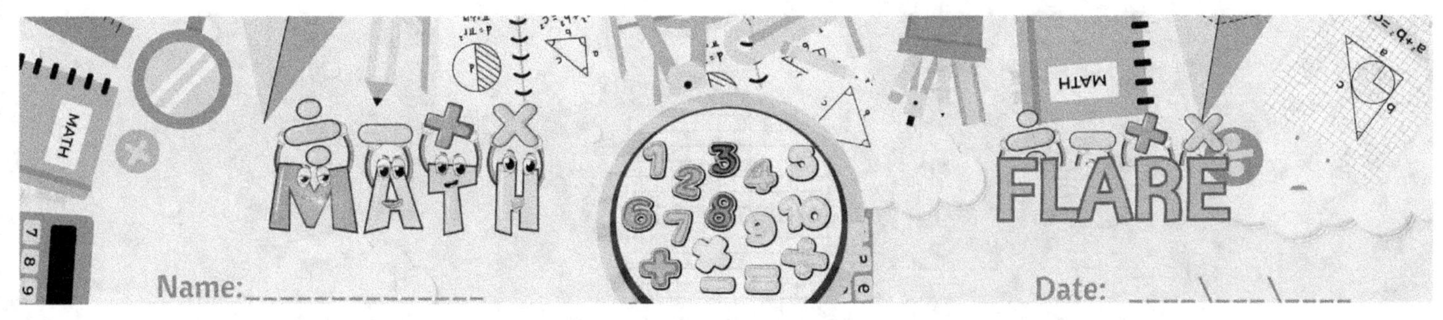

Name:________________   Date: ______________

21) $\dfrac{m}{4} \geq -6$

22) $y - -8 > 5$

23) $4\,m \leq -6$

24) $-1 + y > -6$

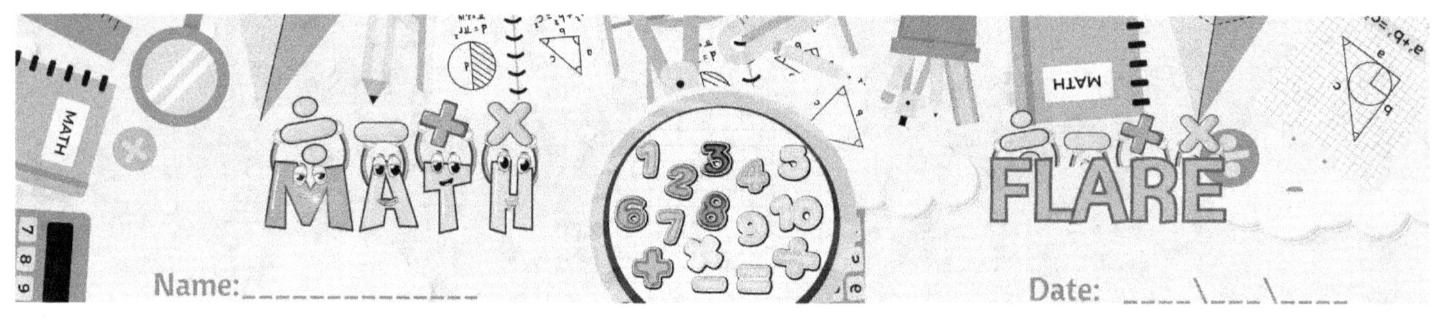

25)

$$-20 > 16\,m$$

26)

$$3 > \dfrac{m}{-9}$$

27)

$$m + 7 > 5$$

28)

$$9 \geq k - 7$$

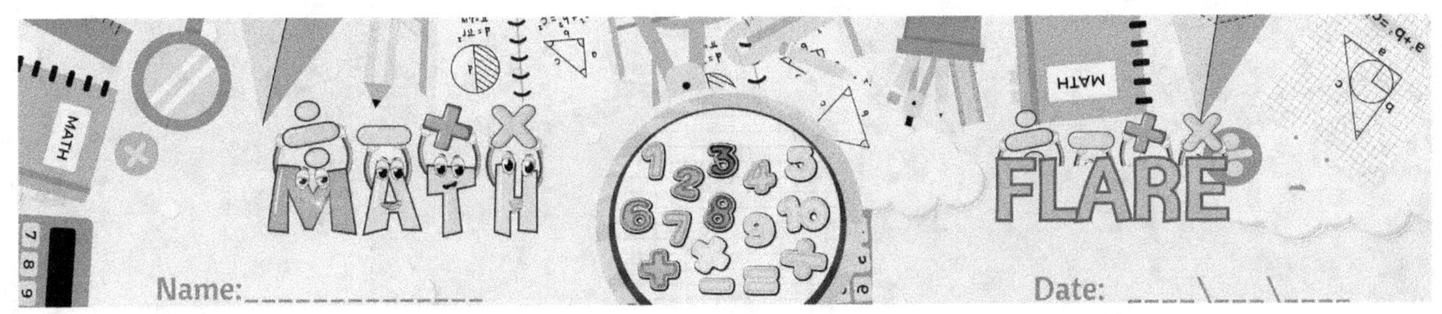

29)

$$-5 < \frac{k}{7}$$

30)

$$x + 6 < -2$$

31)

$$-14\,x \le 12$$

32)

$$-5 - z < 5$$

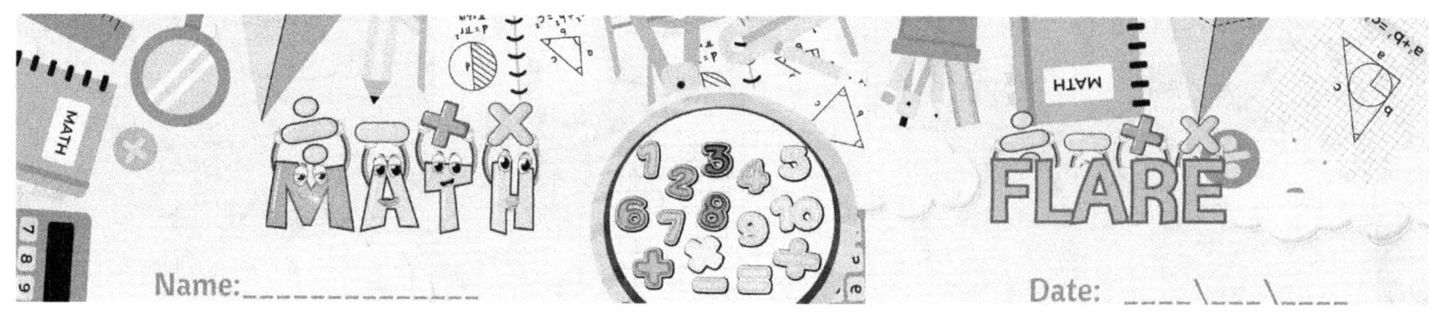

33)

$m - 8 < 9$

34)

$k + -2 \leq 3$

35)

$10 \geq -12\,k$

36)

$4 < \dfrac{k}{7}$

37) $-9 - k > 0$

38) $-15 > 12\,m$

39) $\dfrac{m}{-3} \le -4$

40) $1 < -3 + k$

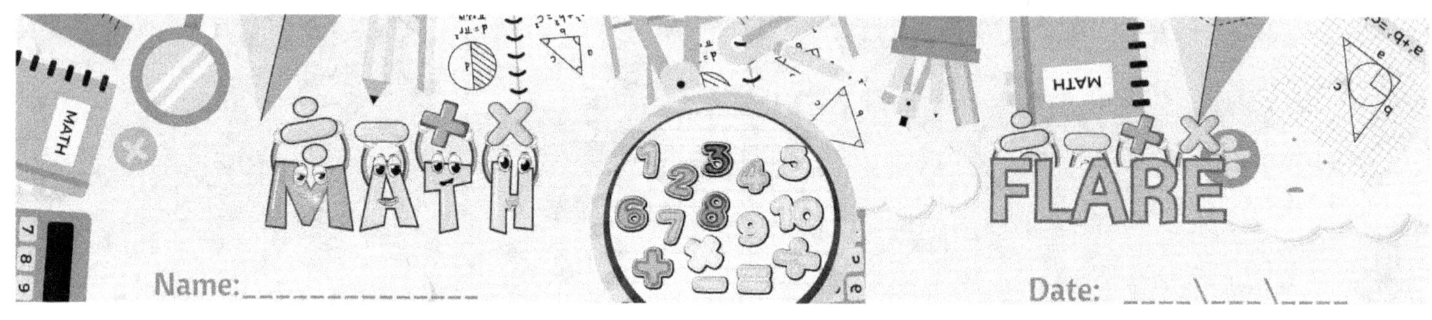

41)
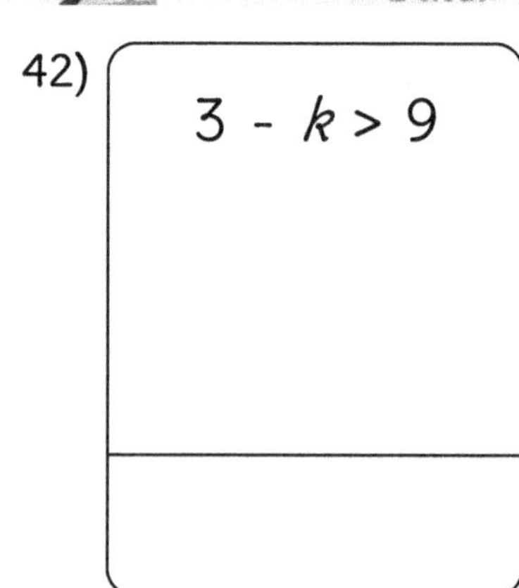

$$2 \geq \frac{x}{8}$$

42)

$$3 - k > 9$$

43)
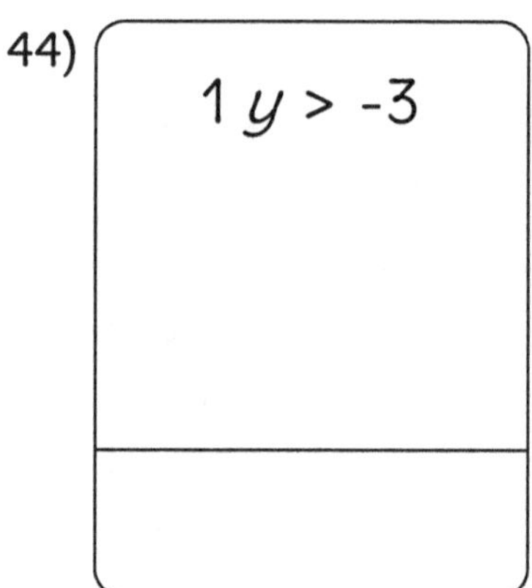

$$7 + y < -1$$

44)

$$1\,y > -3$$

45)

$$5 \leq 3z$$

46)

$$m + -8 \leq 8$$

47)

$$\frac{z}{2} < -6$$

48)

$$1 - x > 8$$

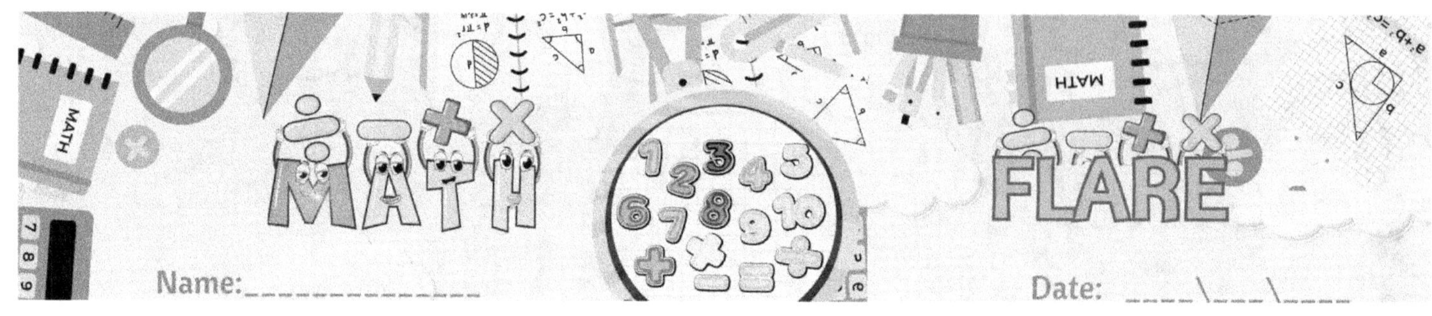

49)

$$-3 \le \frac{y}{-5}$$

50)

$$9 < z - {-2}$$

51)

$$-5 > m + {-3}$$

52)

$$-15 < 3\,m$$

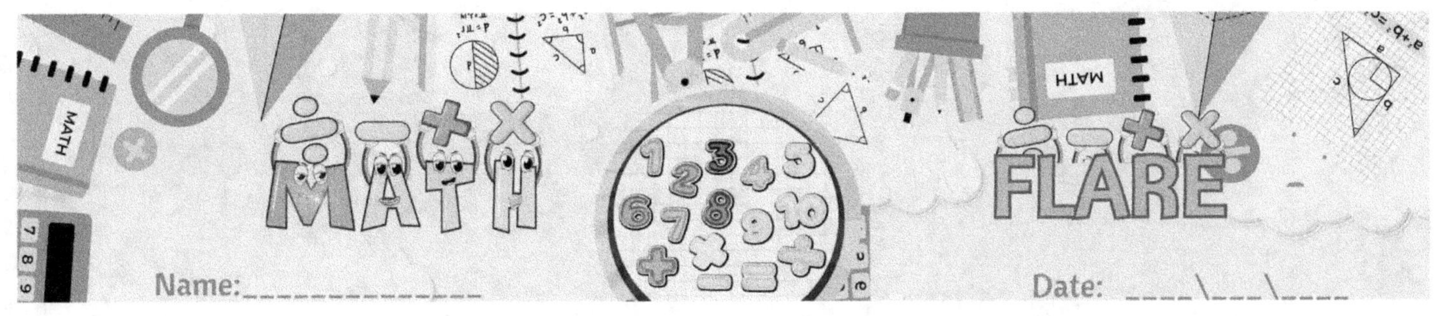

53)

$$-2 \leq \frac{y}{2}$$

54)

$$-2 < -4x$$

55)

$$9 \geq 8 - x$$

56)

$$y + -10 \leq 5$$

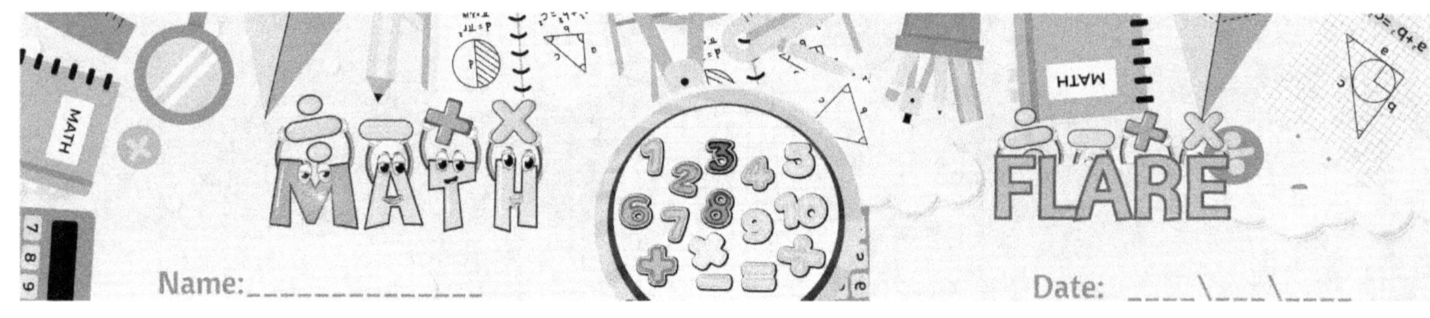

57) $\dfrac{m}{-1} \le 5$

58) $4 \le 2 + k$

59) $6 \le -3\,y$

60) $4 \ge y - {-4}$

61)

$$4z > 12$$

62)

$$6 > \frac{y}{-3}$$

63)

$$-5 \le -8 - m$$

64)

$$5 < -9 + m$$

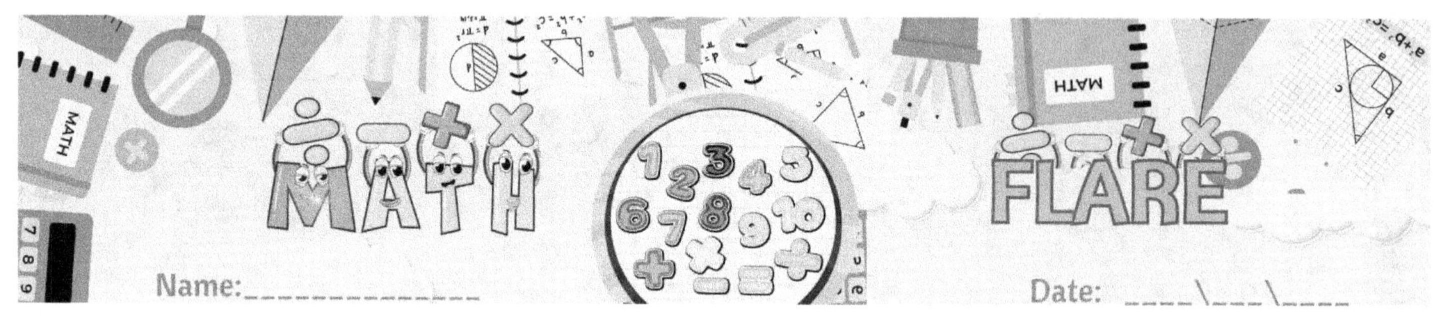

65)
$$-4 > \frac{k}{-6}$$

66)
$$8 > z - 7$$

67)
$$-6 > 7 + z$$

68)
$$12 \leq 6\,k$$

69)

$$1 + m > -6$$

70)

$$7 \geq k - 1$$

71)

$$\frac{z}{-8} \leq -2$$

72)

$$12\,y < 6$$

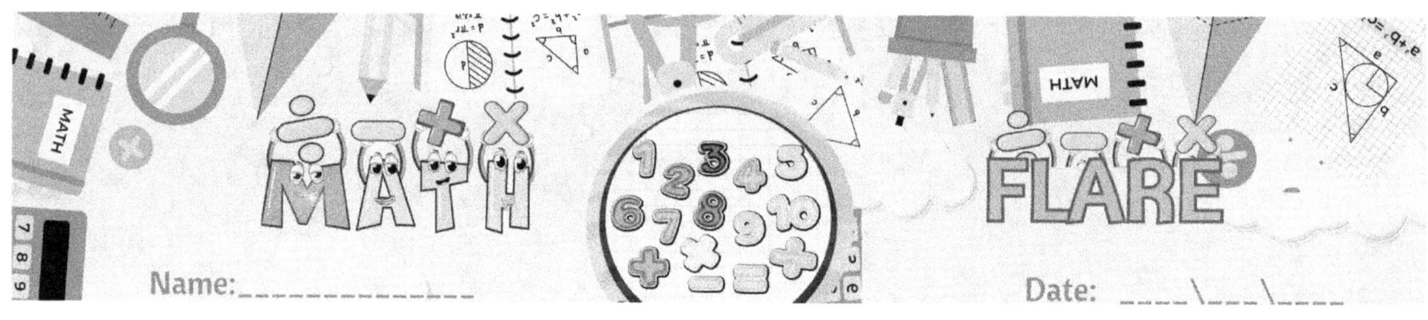

Name:_________________   Date: _______________

73)
$$6 < \frac{k}{2}$$

74)
$$7 \geq k - 4$$

75)
$$-4\,y \geq -12$$

76)
$$-2 + k \geq 4$$

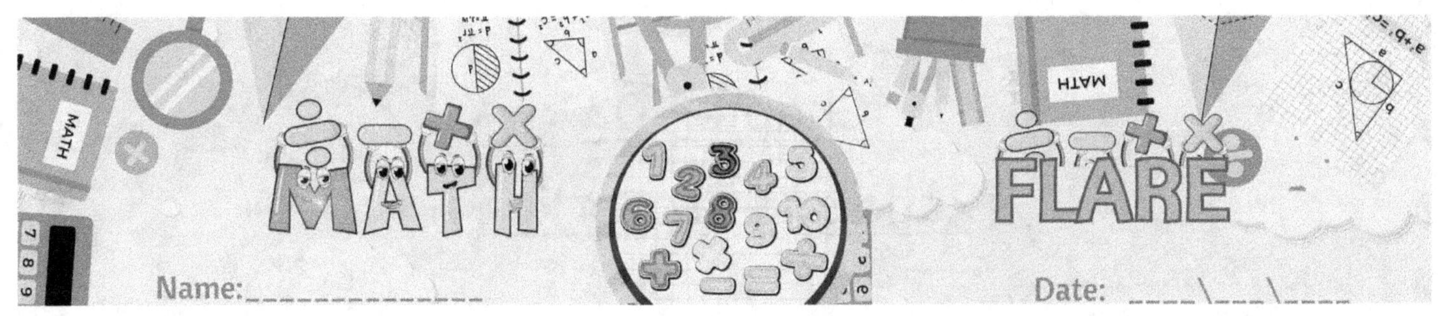

77) $-1 - k \leq 2$

78) $3 \geq \dfrac{x}{-2}$

79) $18 > 15z$

80) $4 \leq z + 5$

Chapter. 02

Ratio and Proportion

A proportional relationship between two quantities exists when they have a constant ratio or when one is a multiple of the other. In other words, if we increase one quantity, the other quantity will increase or decrease by the same factor. For example, if we double one quantity, the other quantity will also double.

Let's solve a problem:

$$\frac{x}{9} = \frac{8}{18}$$

Step 1: Cross Multiply: Cross multiply by multiplying the numerator of one fraction by the denominator of the other, and vice versa:

$$x \times 18 = 9 \times 8$$

Step 2: Solve for the Unknown: Perform the multiplication on both sides of the equation:

$$18x = 72$$

Step 3: Divide Both Sides by the Coefficient of the Unknown: To isolate x, divide both sides of the equation by the coefficient of x, which is 18:

$$\frac{18x}{18} = \frac{72}{18}$$

$$x = 4$$

Step 4: Verify Check your solution by substituting x = 4 back into the original equation:

$$\frac{4}{9} = \frac{8}{18}$$

Since both sides are equal, the solution x = 4 is correct.

Ratio and Proportion Word Problems

We can use the concept of proportionality in solving many word problems, for example:

If a car travels 620 miles in six hours, how far can it travel in 12 hours?

Since the car travels a certain distance in a certain amount of time, we can assume that the distance traveled is directly proportional to the time taken.

Let d be the distance the car can travel in 12 hours.

We can set up a proportion:

$$\frac{\text{Distance1}}{\text{Time1}} = \frac{\text{Distance2}}{\text{Time2}}$$

Substituting the given values:

$$\frac{620 \text{ miles}}{6 \text{ hours}} = \frac{d}{12 \text{ hours}}$$

Now, let's solve for d.

$$d = \frac{620 \times 12}{6} = \frac{7440}{6} = 1240$$

So, the car can travel 1240 miles in 12 hours.

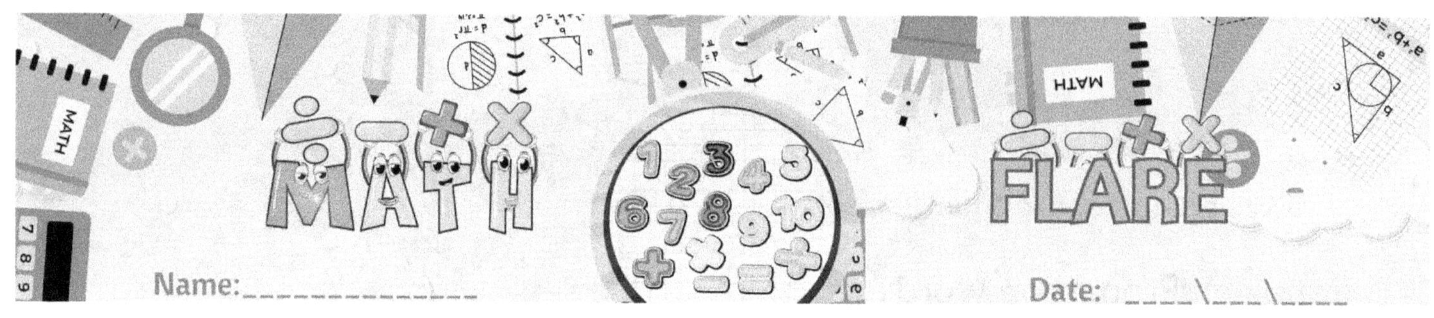

Proportion Relationship

Solve each Ratio and Proportion.

1) $\dfrac{2}{3} = \dfrac{14}{21}$

$= 2 \times 21 = 3 \times x$

$= 42 = 3x$

$= \dfrac{42}{3} = \dfrac{3x}{3}$

$= x = 14$

2) $\dfrac{}{18} = \dfrac{72}{162}$

3) $\dfrac{1}{} = \dfrac{4}{8}$

4) $\dfrac{1}{11} = \dfrac{3}{}$

5) $\dfrac{}{3} = \dfrac{7}{21}$

6) $\dfrac{1}{} = \dfrac{8}{64}$

7) $\dfrac{1}{} = \dfrac{5}{35}$

8) $\dfrac{}{20} = \dfrac{40}{100}$

9) $\dfrac{3}{9} = \dfrac{6}{}$

10) $\dfrac{1}{6} = \dfrac{}{18}$

11) $\dfrac{1}{10} = \dfrac{}{40}$

12) $\dfrac{1}{5} = \dfrac{}{20}$

13) $\dfrac{2}{15} = \dfrac{16}{}$

14) $\dfrac{}{16} = \dfrac{36}{144}$

15) $\dfrac{9}{} = \dfrac{81}{153}$

16) $\dfrac{1}{} = \dfrac{3}{36}$

17) $\dfrac{}{13} = \dfrac{27}{39}$

18) $\dfrac{13}{} = \dfrac{130}{140}$

19) $\dfrac{5}{11} = \dfrac{40}{}$

20) $\dfrac{12}{19} = \dfrac{}{38}$

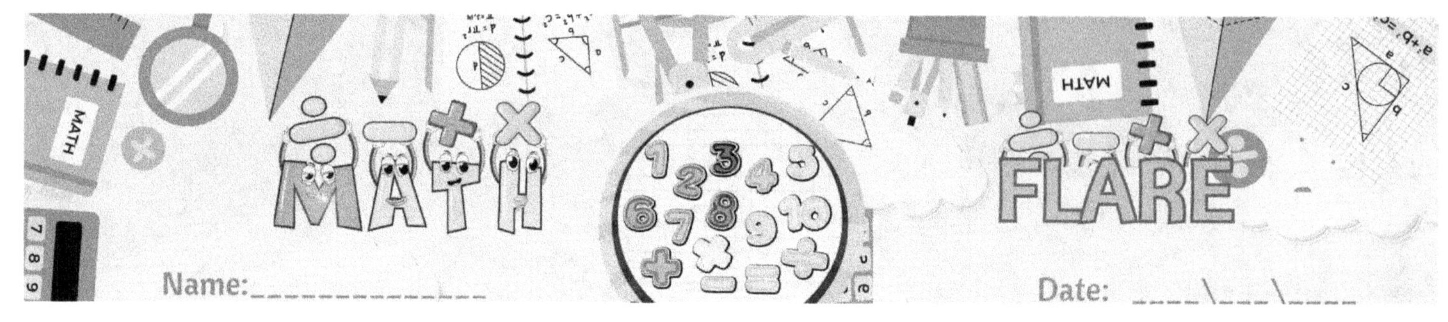

21) $\dfrac{6}{} = \dfrac{36}{48}$

22) $\dfrac{2}{20} = \dfrac{}{100}$

23) $\dfrac{9}{10} = \dfrac{27}{}$

24) $\dfrac{2}{} = \dfrac{14}{35}$

25) $\dfrac{}{14} = \dfrac{28}{98}$

26) $\dfrac{}{18} = \dfrac{14}{36}$

27) $\dfrac{}{14} = \dfrac{40}{112}$

28) $\dfrac{7}{10} = \dfrac{}{100}$

29) $\dfrac{10}{} = \dfrac{70}{84}$

30) $\dfrac{}{20} = \dfrac{44}{80}$

31) $\dfrac{3}{\quad} = \dfrac{15}{40}$

32) $\dfrac{1}{\quad} = \dfrac{5}{10}$

33) $\dfrac{4}{\quad} = \dfrac{32}{40}$

34) $\dfrac{1}{\quad} = \dfrac{7}{119}$

35) $\dfrac{\quad}{6} = \dfrac{25}{30}$

36) $\dfrac{6}{16} = \dfrac{\quad}{144}$

37) $\dfrac{5}{7} = \dfrac{50}{\quad}$

38) $\dfrac{6}{15} = \dfrac{30}{\quad}$

39) $\dfrac{2}{\quad} = \dfrac{20}{30}$

40) $\dfrac{3}{\quad} = \dfrac{12}{36}$

MathFlare - Math Workbook 7th Grade

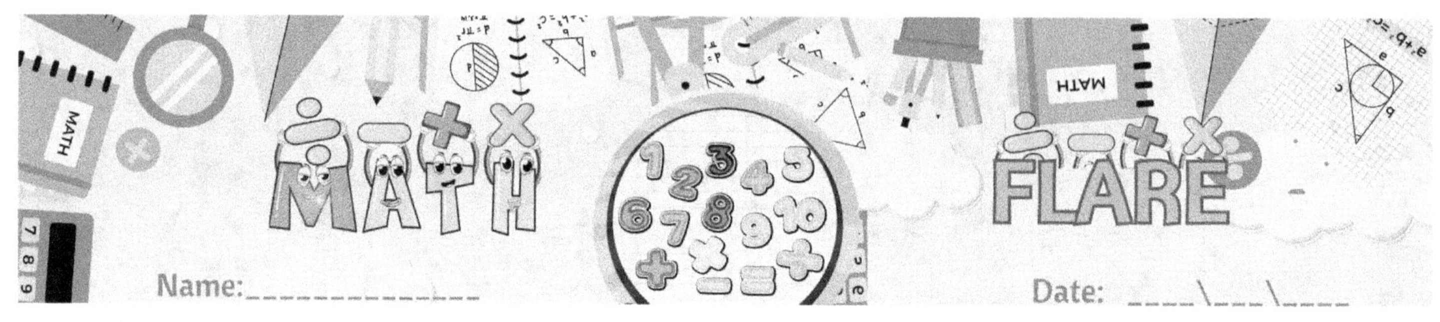

41) $\dfrac{11}{19} = \dfrac{77}{}$

42) $\dfrac{10}{13} = \dfrac{}{39}$

43) $\dfrac{1}{4} = \dfrac{2}{}$

44) $\dfrac{13}{18} = \dfrac{}{72}$

45) $\dfrac{2}{11} = \dfrac{}{88}$

46) $\dfrac{8}{12} = \dfrac{64}{}$

47) $\dfrac{}{17} = \dfrac{36}{102}$

48) $\dfrac{1}{2} = \dfrac{9}{}$

49) $\dfrac{}{18} = \dfrac{44}{72}$

50) $\dfrac{14}{16} = \dfrac{}{64}$

51) $\dfrac{5}{9} = \dfrac{25}{}$

52) $\dfrac{}{10} = \dfrac{21}{30}$

53) $\dfrac{1}{6} = \dfrac{}{30}$

54) $\dfrac{16}{} = \dfrac{144}{180}$

55) $\dfrac{4}{} = \dfrac{24}{66}$

56) $\dfrac{8}{19} = \dfrac{}{57}$

57) $\dfrac{9}{15} = \dfrac{}{105}$

58) $\dfrac{5}{7} = \dfrac{10}{}$

59) $\dfrac{}{13} = \dfrac{56}{91}$

60) $\dfrac{6}{8} = \dfrac{}{56}$

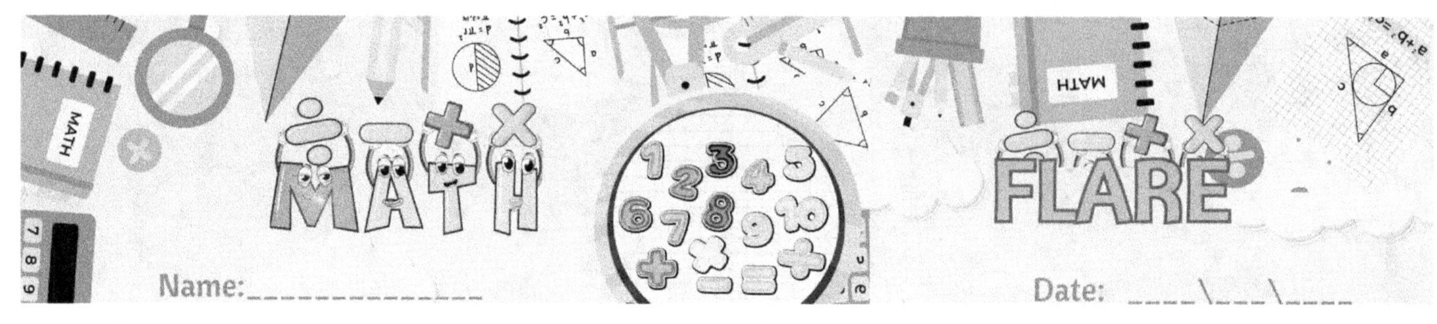

61) $\dfrac{9}{14} = \dfrac{}{84}$

62) $\dfrac{2}{5} = \dfrac{}{30}$

63) $\dfrac{13}{} = \dfrac{117}{171}$

64) $\dfrac{11}{13} = \dfrac{}{130}$

65) $\dfrac{1}{3} = \dfrac{2}{}$

66) $\dfrac{}{18} = \dfrac{12}{54}$

67) $\dfrac{3}{5} = \dfrac{15}{}$

68) $\dfrac{10}{} = \dfrac{40}{56}$

69) $\dfrac{10}{11} = \dfrac{30}{}$

70) $\dfrac{2}{} = \dfrac{12}{24}$

71) $\dfrac{3}{15} = \dfrac{}{60}$

72) $\dfrac{1}{7} = \dfrac{}{42}$

73) $\dfrac{}{20} = \dfrac{6}{120}$

74) $\dfrac{10}{12} = \dfrac{40}{}$

75) $\dfrac{13}{17} = \dfrac{}{85}$

76) $\dfrac{3}{8} = \dfrac{}{72}$

77) $\dfrac{6}{} = \dfrac{54}{90}$

78) $\dfrac{}{16} = \dfrac{30}{160}$

79) $\dfrac{1}{} = \dfrac{4}{36}$

80) $\dfrac{2}{6} = \dfrac{}{12}$

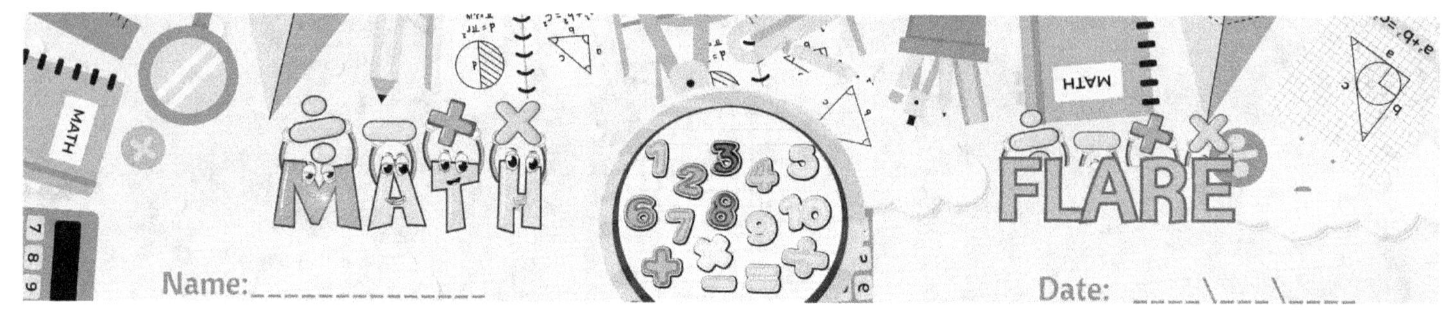

Ratio and Proportion Word Problems

1) If two workers can build a wall in 17 hours, how many workers are needed to build the wall in 10 hours?

Total worker-hours required to build the wall

$$2 \times 17 = 34$$

Workers × Hours = Total Worker-Hours

$$x \times 10 = 34$$

$$x = \frac{34}{10} \qquad x = 3.4, \text{ or } 4 \text{ rounded}$$

2) If it takes six students 14 hours to complete a science project, how many students are needed to finish the project in seven hours?

3) If six workers can build a house in 14 hours, how many workers are needed to build the house in six hours?

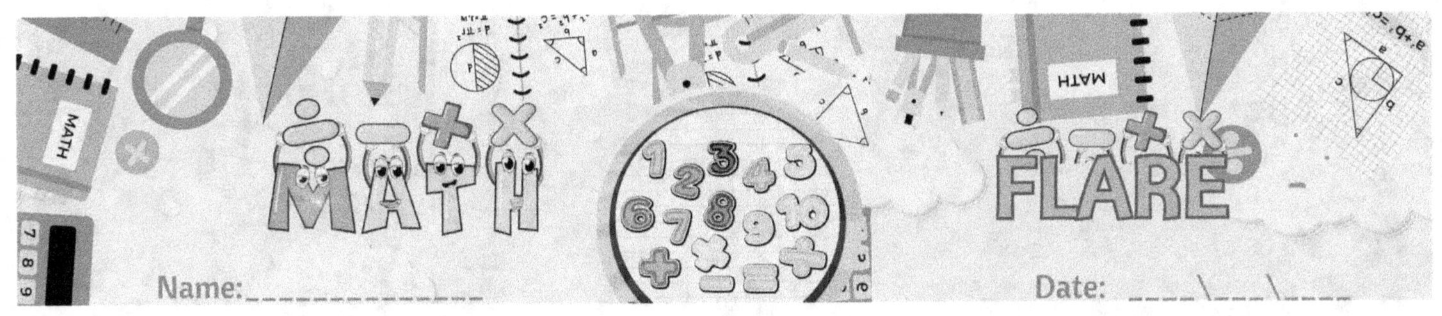

Name:_________________________   Date: ____________

4) A farmer has a ratio of four sheep to every nine cows in his pasture. If there are 37 cows in the pasture, how many sheep are there?

5) A bike travels at a speed of 24 miles per hour. How long will it take to travel 44 miles?

6) A charity received a donation of $1,135 from a company. If the donation was divided among five charities in the ratio 2:3:4:5:6, how much did the fifth charity receive?

Name:________________   Date: _______________

7) If a car travels 340 miles in four hours, how far can it travel in nine hours?

8) If seven painters can paint a house in eight days, how many painters are needed to paint the same house in six days?

9) A zoo has a ratio of four monkeys to every six lions. If there are 41 lions in the zoo, how many monkeys are there?

10) In a bag of candies, the ratio of chocolate candies to fruit candies is four:eight. If there are 13 fruit candies, how many chocolate candies are there?

11) A road is 119 miles long and it takes a car three hour to travel the entire length. What is the speed of the car in miles per hour?

12) If a recipe calls for six eggs for every eight cups of flour, how many eggs are needed for 16 cups of flour?

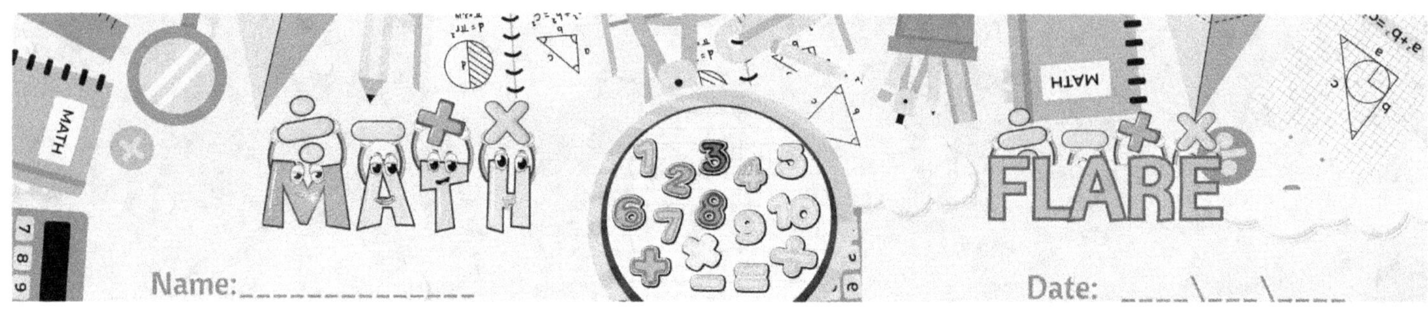

13) If a square has an area of 77 square meters, what is the length of each side of the square?

14) A car travels 166 miles in two hours. How far can it travel in 10 hours?

15) If three chefs can bake 100 cakes in 11 hours, how many chefs are needed to bake the same number of cakes in 10 hours?

16) If nine workers can complete a job in 12 days, how many workers are needed to complete the job in seven days?

17) A bus travels at a speed of 73 miles per hour. How long will it take to travel 200 miles?

18) A machine can produce 187 units of a product in 10 hours. How long will it take to produce 323 units?

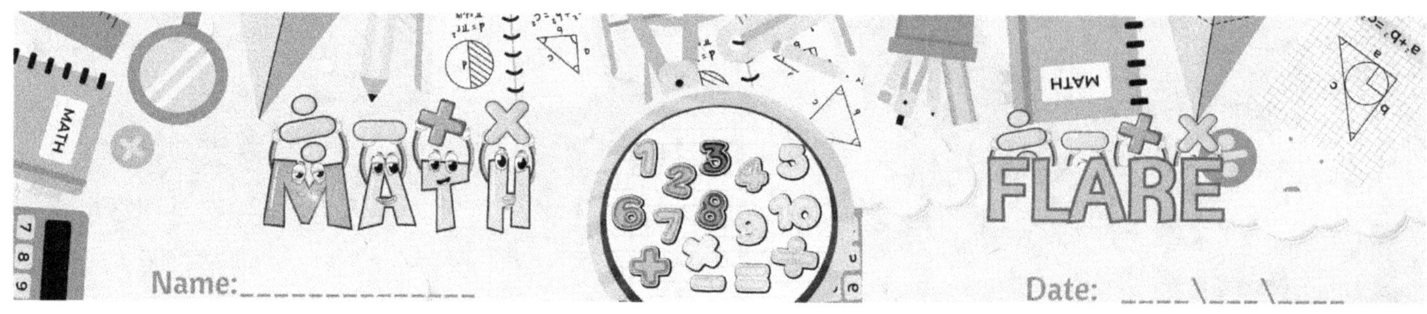

19) A train travels 148 miles in three hours. How far can it travel in 13 hours?

20) A company has a ratio of three female employees to every seven male employees. If there are 23 male employees, how many female employees are there?

21) A school has a teacher-student ratio of 1:37. If there are 932 students, how many teachers are needed?

22) If a team of two construction workers can build a road in 19 days, how many workers are required to complete the road in 10 days?

23) Mila sells five calendars for every eight violins. If there are 55 calendars, how many violins are there?

24) If a car travels 110 miles using 14 gallons of gas, how far can it travel using 20 gallons of gas?

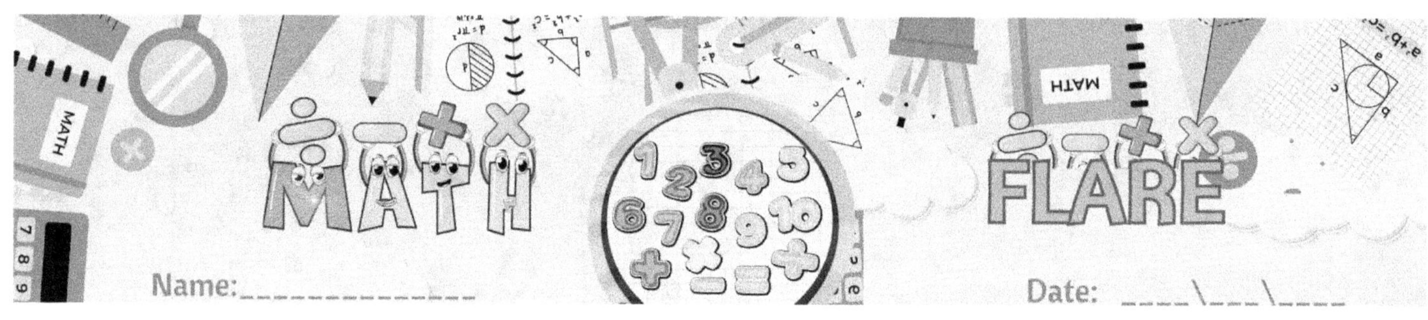

25) If a recipe calls for two cups of water for every six cups of rice, how much water is needed for eight cups of rice?

26) A school has a ratio of four female teachers to every 10 male teachers. If there are 22 male teachers, how many female teachers are there?

27) If a recipe calls for two eggs for every eight cups of flour, how many eggs are needed for nine cups of flour?

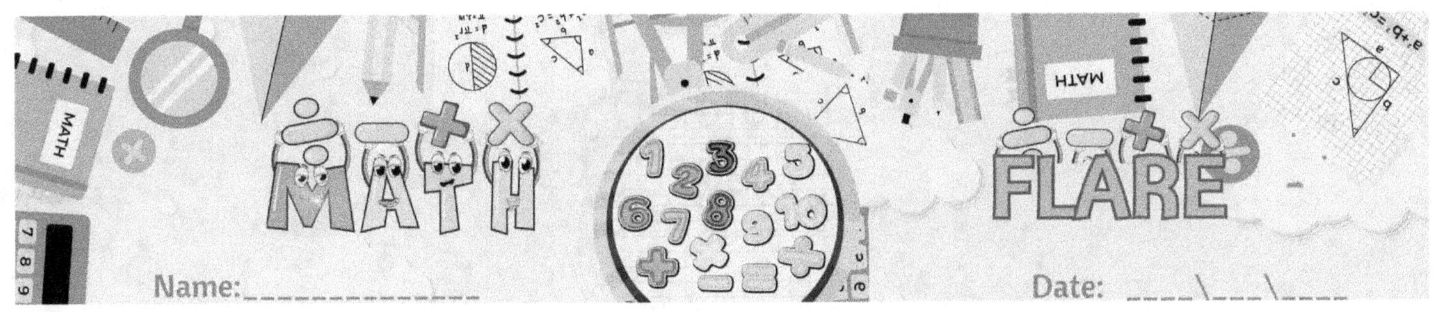

28) Nicholas drives 271 miles in five hours. How far can he travel in 14 hours?

29) A class has a ratio of three girls to every six boys. If there are 27 boys, how many girls are there?

30) If a recipe calls for three teaspoon of salt for every four cups of flour, how much salt is needed for 11 cups of flour?

Chapter. 03

Percentage

Percentage is a way of expressing a number as a fraction of 100. It is commonly used to represent proportions, rates, and comparisons. The symbol "%" is used to denote percentages.

To calculate a percentage, we multiply the given number by the appropriate fraction or decimal equivalent.

How to calculate a percentage:

Convert Percentage to Decimal: If the percentage is given as a percentage value (e.g., 25%), convert it to its decimal equivalent by dividing by 100.

$$\text{For example, 25\% as a decimal is } \frac{25}{100} = 0.25$$

Multiply: Multiply the decimal equivalent of the percentage by the given number. This gives us the portion of the number that represents the percentage.

$$100 \times 0.25 = 25\%$$

Result: The result is the calculated percentage value.

For example, to calculate 25% of 80:

Convert 25% to a decimal: 25% = 0.25.

Multiply 0.25 by 80: $0.25 \times 80 = 20$. The result is 20.

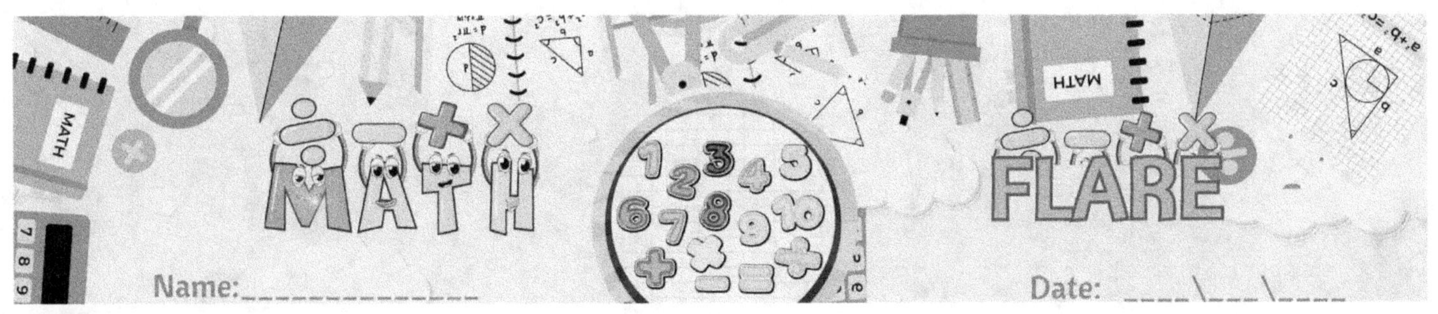

Percentage

Find the percentage of given numbers.

1) __75%__ of 500 = 375

2) _______ of 800 = 640

3) 90% of ____ = 360

4) 30% of ____ = 90

5) _______ of 300 = 45

6) 300% of ____ = 600

7) 5% of 100 = _______

8) _______ of 80 = 20

9) _______ of 90 = 6.3

10) _______ of 200 = 2

11) 8% of ____ = 40

12) 2% of 10 = _______

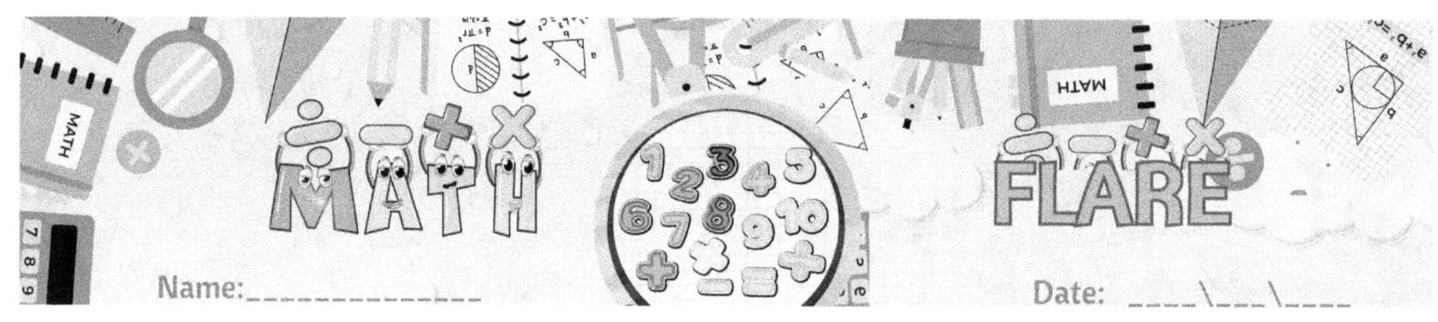

13) 40% of ____ = 280

14) ____ of 500 = 1000

15) 9% of 400 = ____

16) 35% of ____ = 315

17) 25% of 300 = ____

18) ____ of 600 = 1800

19) 35% of ____ = 35

20) 100% of ____ = 100

21) 200% of ____ = 14

22) 20% of 300 = ____

23) 9% of ____ = 45

24) 60% of ____ = 180

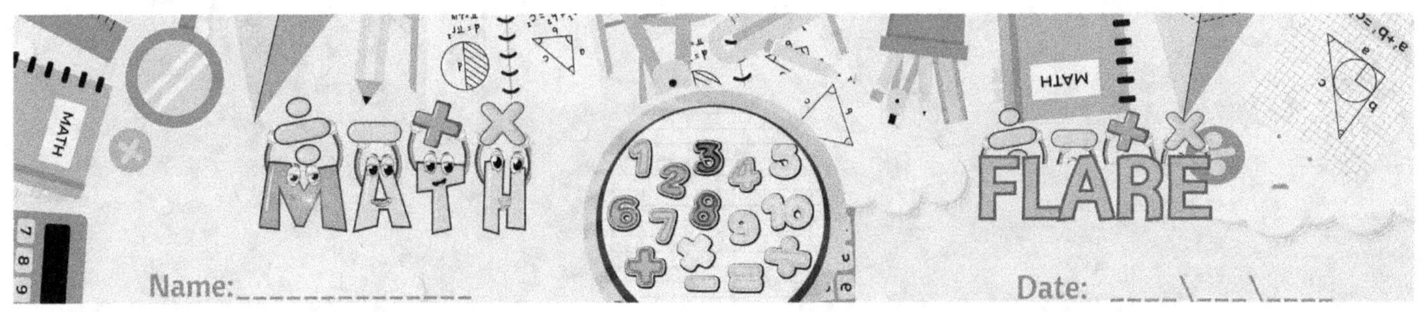

25) 40% of 500 = _____

26) 8% of _____ = 24

27) _____ of 300 = 9

28) 50% of 400 = _____

29) 75% of _____ = 75

30) 10% of 900 = _____

31) _____ of 200 = 8

32) 6% of 700 = _____

33) 1% of 600 = _____

34) 70% of 500 = _____

35) 2% of 500 = _____

36) 5% of 800 = _____

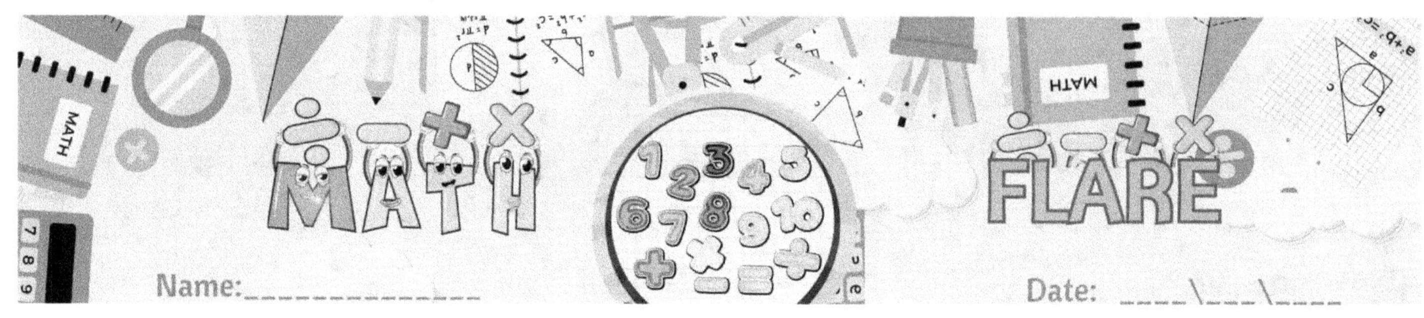

37) 90% of _____ = 450

38) 15% of 600 = _____

39) 7% of _____ = 42

40) 30% of 30 = _____

41) _____ of 50 = 2.5

42) 70% of 400 = _____

43) _____ of 400 = 60

44) 200% of 800 = _____

45) 50% of _____ = 400

46) 40% of _____ = 80

47) _____ of 600 = 36

48) 35% of 600 = _____

49) _______ of 600 = 360

50) 100% of 500 = _______

51) _______ of 100 = 9

52) 25% of _______ = 125

53) 80% of _______ = 720

54) 30% of 900 = _______

55) 2% of 400 = _______

56) 7% of _______ = 56

57) 90% of _______ = 810

58) _______ of 700 = 2100

59) 4% of _______ = 32

60) 1% of 800 = _______

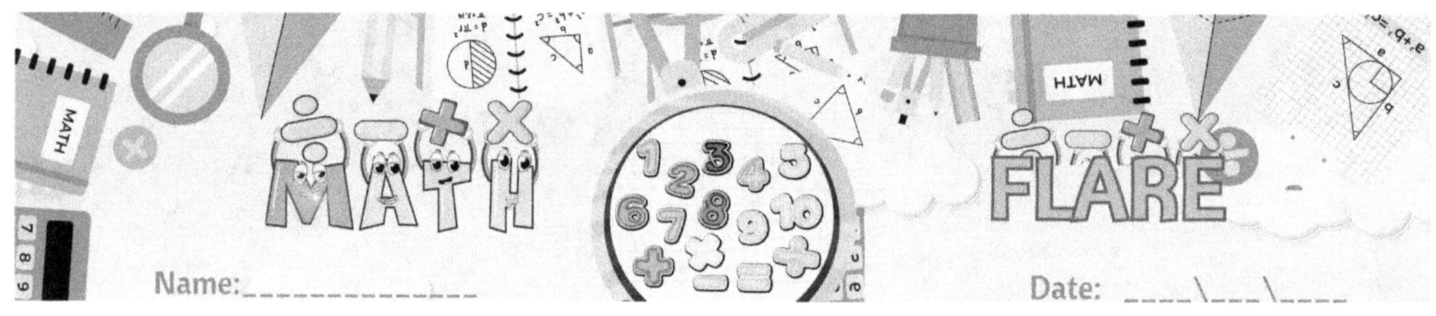

1) 0.2% of 47 = ☐

2) 0.8% of ☐ = 0.024

3) ☐ of 86 = 7.568

4) 8.9% of ☐ = 0.089

5) 0.5% of ☐ = 2.34

6) 2.1% of 860 = ☐

7) 1.9% of 53 = ☐

8) ☐ of 30 = 0.03

9) 0.4% of 45 = ☐

10) 4.8% of 7 = ☐

11) 0.6% of 129 = ☐

12) 2.0% of ☐ = 1

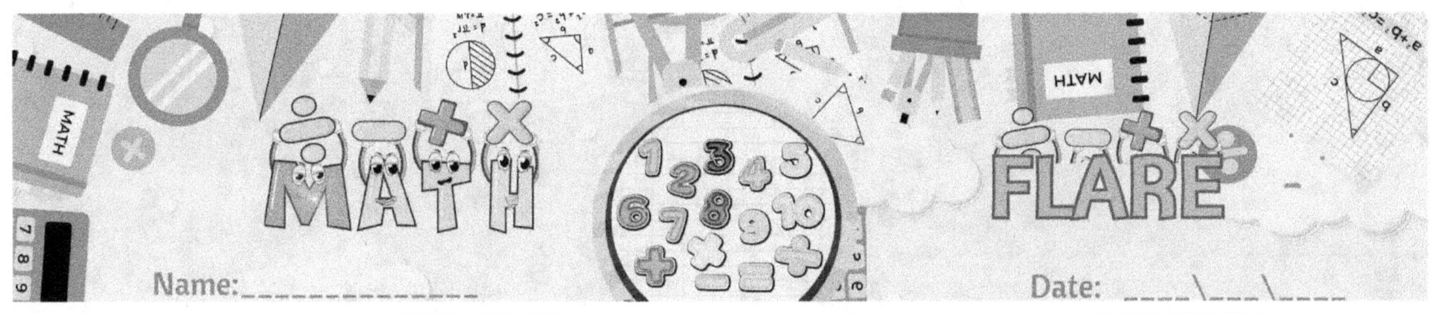

13) 0.9% of 4 = ________

14) 8.8% of 153 = ________

15) 0.6% of ________ = 5.424

16) 0.1% of 70 = ________

17) 8.8% of ________ = 0.44

18) 0.7% of ________ = 0.028

19) ________ of 21 = 1.533

20) 3.8% of ________ = 26.98

21) ________ of 854 = 76.006

22) 3.4% of ________ = 26.248

23) 0.2% of ________ = 1.424

24) 9.8% of ________ = 0.196

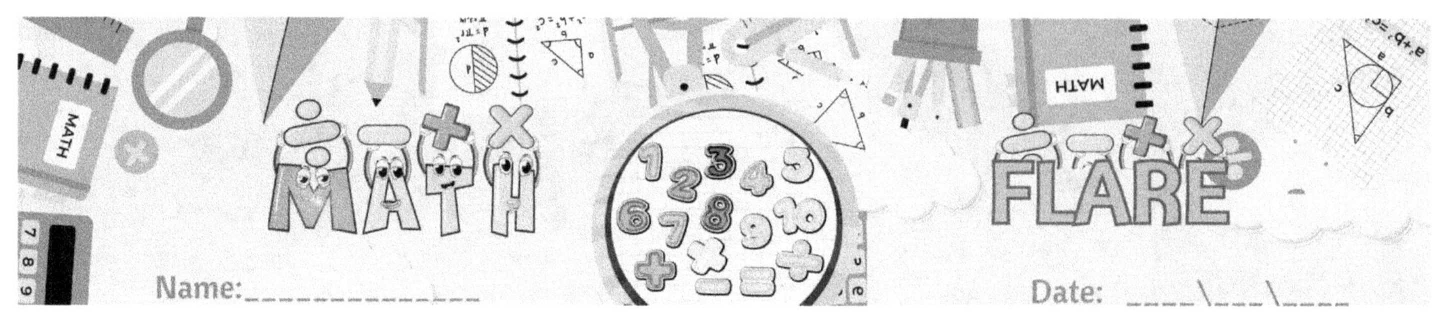

25) 0.3% of ⬚ = 2.847

26) 0.5% of ⬚ = 0.03

27) 0.9% of ⬚ = 1.368

28) ⬚ of 5 = 0.03

29) ⬚ of 661 = 41.643

30) ⬚ of 3 = 0.18

31) 5.7% of ⬚ = 0.057

32) ⬚ of 1 = 0.071

33) 3.7% of 186 = ⬚

34) 0.2% of 866 = ⬚

35) 0.8% of ⬚ = 0.016

36) 8.8% of ⬚ = 38.984

37) 8.9% of 41 = ________

38) 0.5% of 2 = ________

39) 2.1% of ________ = 0.168

40) ________ of 473 = 8.987

41) 0.1% of 6 = ________

42) 0.4% of ________ = 0.328

43) 4.8% of ________ = 6.576

44) 0.6% of ________ = 0.738

45) 2.0% of ________ = 0.12

46) 0.9% of 87 = ________

47) 8.8% of 723 = ________

48) 0.6% of ________ = 0.414

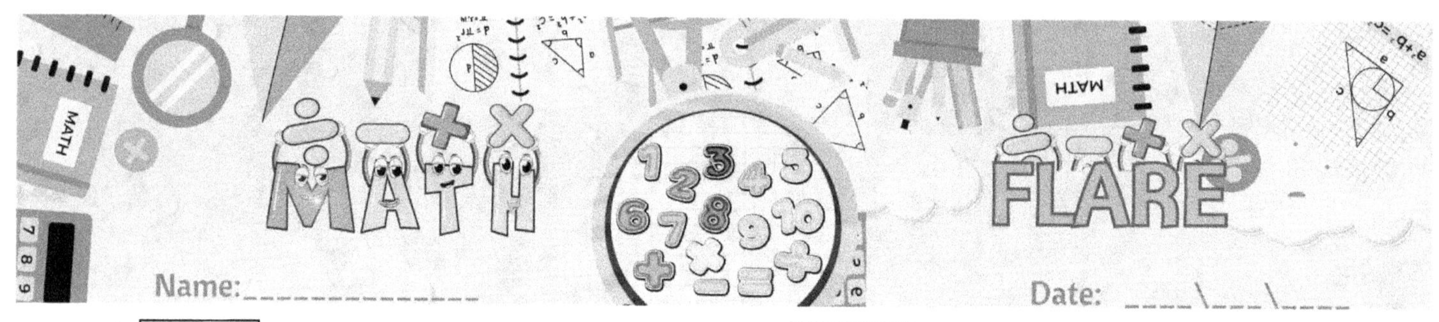

49) [ ] of 74 = 0.074

50) [ ] of 633 = 55.704

51) [ ] of 338 = 2.366

52) 7.3% of [ ] = 44.238

53) 3.8% of 7 = [ ]

54) [ ] of 5 = 0.445

55) [ ] of 3 = 0.102

56) [ ] of 1 = 0.002

57) 9.8% of 779 = [ ]

58) 0.3% of 461 = [ ]

59) [ ] of 546 = 2.73

60) [ ] of 7 = 0.063

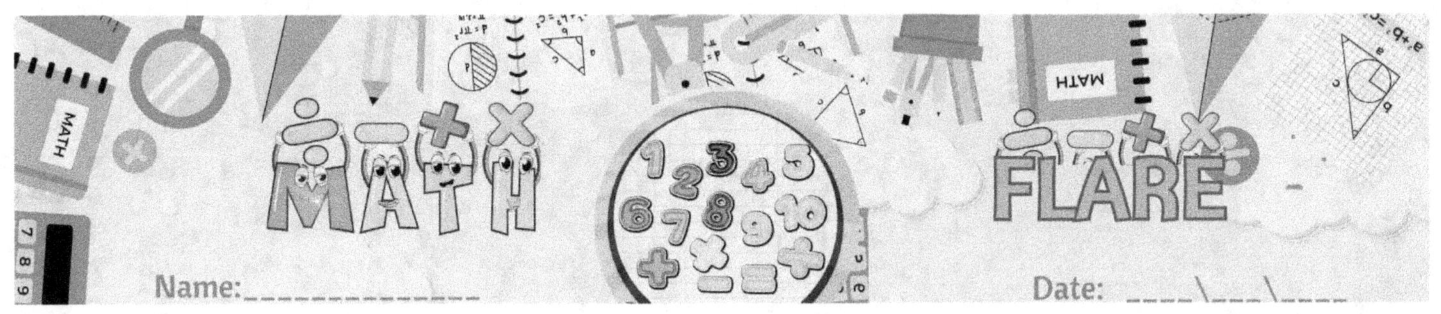

61) 0.6% of ☐ = 0.042

62) 6.3% of ☐ = 43.911

63) 6.0% of 87 = ☐

64) 5.7% of 76 = ☐

65) ☐ of 425 = 30.175

66) 3.7% of ☐ = 2.183

67) 0.2% of ☐ = 0.504

68) ☐ of 11 = 0.088

69) 8.8% of ☐ = 69.872

70) ☐ of 15 = 1.335

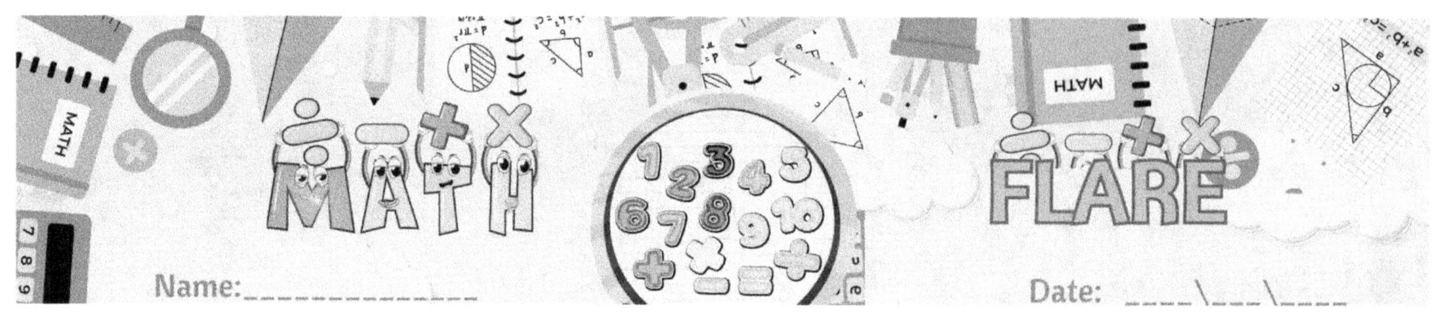

Convert: Ratio, Fraction, Percent, and Decimals

1)

	Ratio	Fraction	Percent	Decimal
a.	3:4	3/4	75%	0.75
b.	16:17	16/17	94.1%	0.941
c.	9:14			
d.	2:2			
e.				0.471
f.		11/14		
g.			33.3%	
h.			25%	
i.		1/8		
j.			92.3%	
k.	9:17			
l.			50%	
m.				0.571
n.			16.7%	
o.				0.5

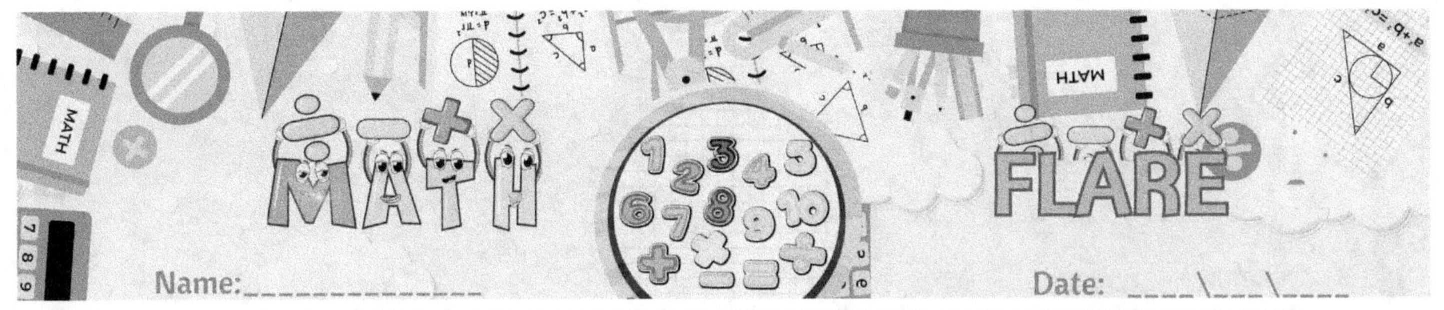

2)

	Ratio	Fraction	Percent	Decimal
a.			100%	
b.		13/18		
c.			90.9%	
d.	7:8			
e.				0.25
f.				0.65
g.				0.857
h.		4/5		
i.		10/18		
j.		3/9		
k.		6/17		
l.			83.3%	
m.		5/20		
n.				0.312
o.	1:8			

Name:_________________   Date: ______________

3)

	Ratio	Fraction	Percent	Decimal
a.		11/15		
b.	7:11			
c.	11:18			
d.			21.1%	
e.	1:4			
f.	1:6			
g.		3/8		
h.	1:1			
i.			50%	
j.			58.3%	
k.	4:18			
l.			21.4%	
m.			66.7%	
n.				0.3
o.				0.154

Name:________________ Date: _______________

4)

	Ratio	Fraction	Percent	Decimal
a.		20/20		
b.			16.7%	
c.		2/6		
d.	12:13			
e.				0.625
f.				0.333
g.		17/19		
h.	2:4			
i.			12.5%	
j.	4:14			
k.		12/14		
l.		3/5		
m.				0.5
n.				0.312
o.	2:12			

5)

	Ratio	Fraction	Percent	Decimal
a.				0.5
b.				0.375
c.	1:1			
d.		5/17		
e.		13/18		
f.			40%	
g.			16.7%	
h.				0.222
i.				0.5
j.		6/8		
k.				0.5
l.	14:17			
m.	4:5			
n.	4:11			
o.				0.706

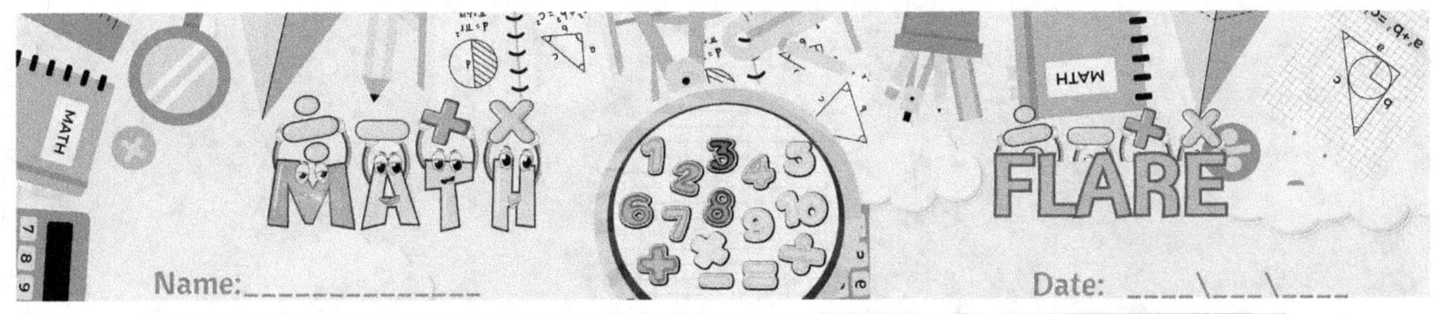

6)

	Ratio	Fraction	Percent	Decimal
a.			100%	
b.				0.167
c.				0.5
d.				0.083
e.			55.6%	
f.		15/17		
g.				0.2
h.	7:15			
i.	1:2			
j.		3/11		
k.	2:10			
l.			56.2%	
m.		10/18		
n.				0.727
o.				0.6

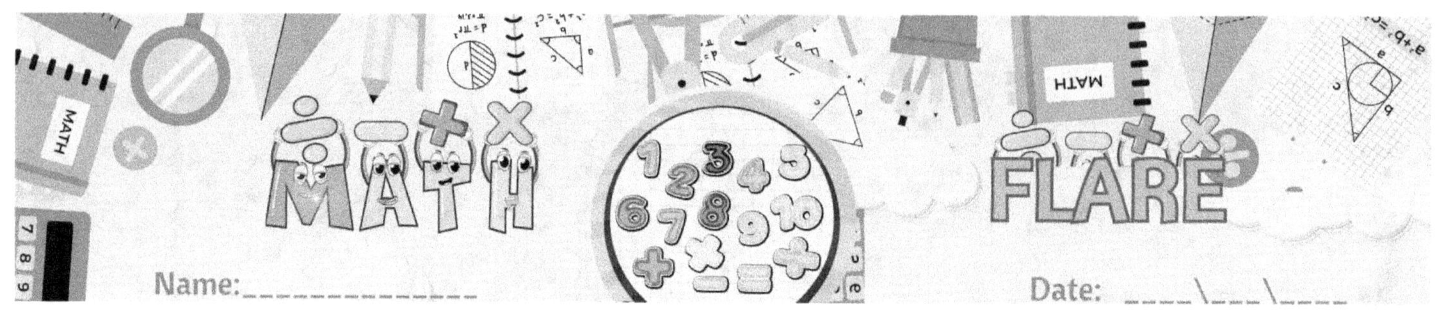

7)

	Ratio	Fraction	Percent	Decimal
a.			42.1%	
b.				1
c.		2/7		
d.				0.833
e.		6/7		
f.		11/13		
g.				0.714
h.				0.818
i.	2:12			
j.				0.923
k.				0.5
l.	7:17			
m.				0.4
n.				0.25
o.	16:19			

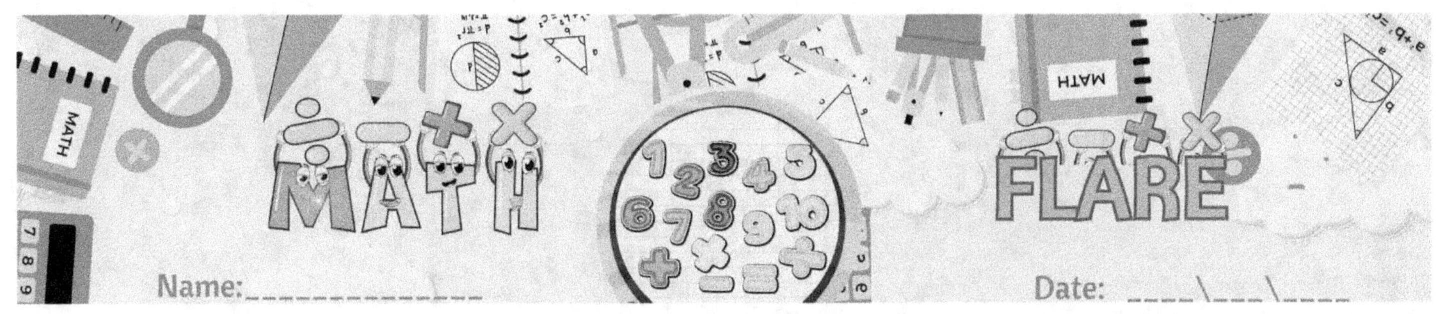

Name:______________________ Date: _______________

8)

	Ratio	Fraction	Percent	Decimal
a.		13/18		
b.		3/3		
c.	8:10			
d.	14:19			
e.		1/2		
f.			93.8%	
g.				0.333
h.			12.5%	
i.			50%	
j.			25%	
k.			81.8%	
l.				0.667
m.	7:11			
n.			16.7%	
o.		11/20		

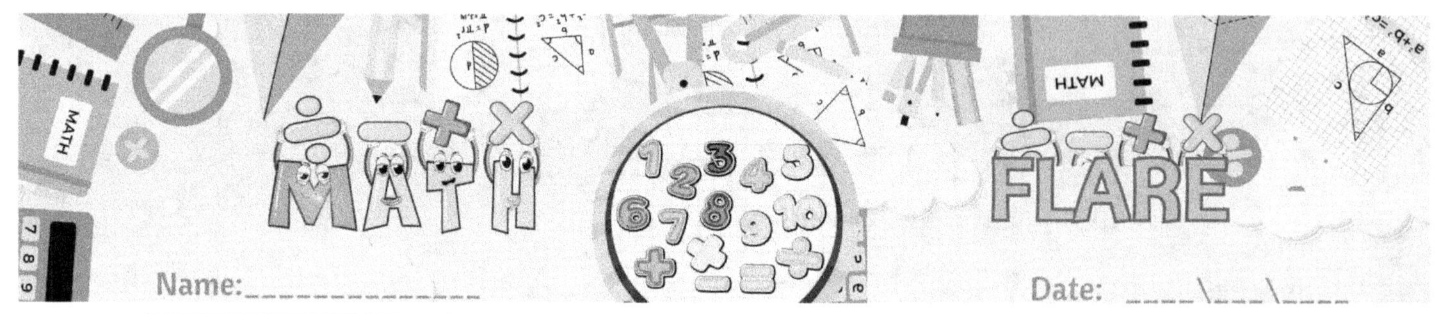

Name:_____________   Date: _______________

9)

	Ratio	Fraction	Percent	Decimal
a.	1:13			
b.				0.667
c.	20:20			
d.	5:7			
e.				0.667
f.			40%	
g.				0.75
h.		9/19		
i.				0.25
j.	4:8			
k.	12:19			
l.			94.4%	
m.				0.833
n.	1:12			
o.	8:16			

10)

	Ratio	Fraction	Percent	Decimal
a.		6/8		
b.			50%	
c.		1/6		
d.			41.7%	
e.	6:6			
f.			75%	
g.				0.158
h.	4:19			
i.		2/13		
j.			60%	
k.	4:8			
l.				0.929
m.				0.385
n.			50%	
o.		5/18		

Chapter. 04

Geometry

Area and Perimeter

The area of a shape represents the amount of space it occupies. The perimeter of a shape is the total distance around its outer edge.

Area of Rectangle

For a square, since all four sides are equal, we only need to know the length of one side to find its area. We can calculate the area of a square by multiplying the length of one side by itself (squared). So, if the length of one side of the square is 's', then the area (A) is given by:

$$A = s \times s$$

4 in

4 in

$$A = 4 \times 4$$

$$A = 16$$

Perimeter of Rectangle

For a square, since all four sides are equal, we can find the perimeter by adding up the lengths of all four sides. If 's' represents the length of one side, then the perimeter (P) is given by:

$$P = 4 \times s$$

$$P = 4 \times 4$$

$$P = 16$$

Area of Triangle:

The area of a triangle represents the amount of space enclosed within its three sides. The formula for calculating the area of a triangle depends on the type of triangle. For a general triangle, we use the formula:

$$A = \frac{1}{2} \times base \times height$$

Where:

- A represents the area of the triangle.

- The base is the length of any one side of the triangle.

- The height is the perpendicular distance from the base to the opposite vertex.

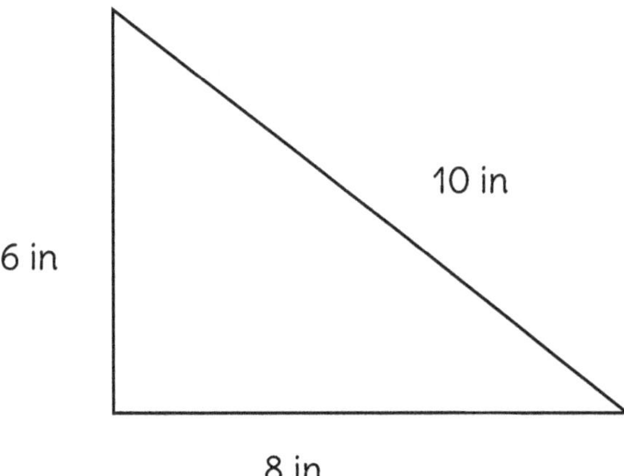

$$A = \frac{1}{2} \times base \times height$$

$$A = \frac{1}{2} \times 6 \times 8$$

$$A = \frac{1}{2} \times 48$$

$$A = 24$$

Perimeter of Triangle:

The perimeter of a triangle is the total length of its three sides. To find the perimeter, we simply add the lengths of all three sides together:

$$P = side1 + side2 + side3$$

$$P = 6 + 8 + 10$$

$$P = 24$$

Equilateral Triangle

An equilateral triangle is a triangle in which all three sides are equal in length. To find the area and perimeter of an equilateral triangle, we can use the following formulas:

- Area (A): $\frac{\sqrt{3}}{4} \times a^2$ where a is the length of one side of the equilateral triangle.

- Perimeter (P): $P = 3a$ where a is the length of one side of the equilateral triangle.

Let's solve a problem:

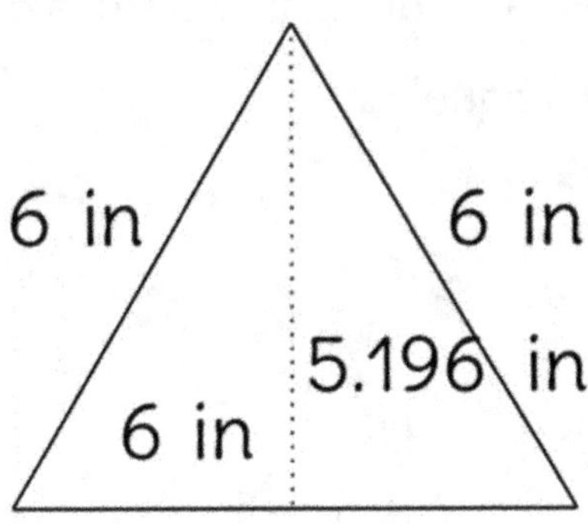

Area of Equilateral Triangle:

$$\text{Area (A): } \frac{\sqrt{3}}{4} \times (6)^2$$

$$\text{Area (A): } \frac{\sqrt{3}}{4} \times 36$$

$$\text{Area (A): } \frac{36\sqrt{3}}{4}$$

$$\text{Area (A): } \frac{36(1.73)}{4}$$

$$\text{Area (A): } \frac{62.35}{4}$$

$$\text{Area (A): } 15.59 \text{ in}^2$$

Perimeter of Equilateral Triangle:

$$P = 3a$$

$$P = 3(6) = 18$$

MathFlare - Math Workbook 7th Grade

Isosceles Triangle

An isosceles triangle is a triangle with at least two sides of equal length. The angles opposite the equal sides are also equal.

Area of Isosceles Triangle

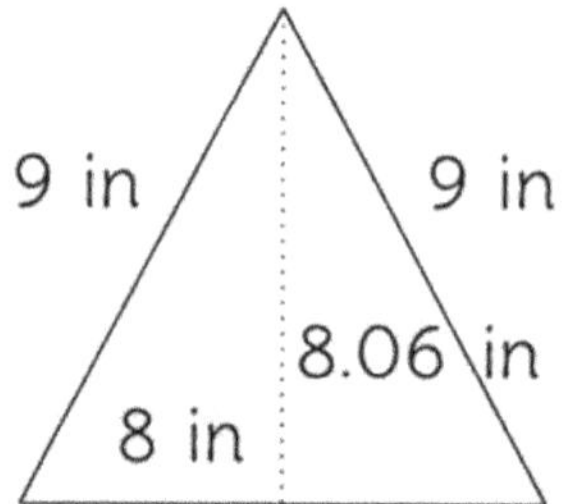

$$A = \frac{1}{2} \times \text{base} \times \text{height}$$

$$A = \frac{1}{2} \times 8 \times 8$$

$$A = \frac{1}{2} \times 64$$

$$A = 32$$

Perimeter of Isosceles Triangle

The perimeter of a triangle is the total length of its three sides. To find the perimeter, we simply add the lengths of all three sides together:

$$P = \text{side1} + \text{side2} + \text{side3}$$

$$P = 9 + 9 + 8$$

$$P = 26$$

Scalene Triangle

A scalene triangle is a triangle with no equal sides and no equal angles. The formula for finding various properties of a scalene triangle is as follows:

Area (A): The area of a scalene triangle can be calculated using Heron's formula, which is given by:

$$A = \sqrt{s(s-a)(s-b)(s-c)}$$

where s is the semi-perimeter of the triangle,

and a, b, and c are the lengths of its three sides.

Perimeter (P): The perimeter of a scalene triangle is the sum of the lengths of its three sides.

$$P = side1 + side2 + side3$$

Let's find the Area and Perimeter of a Scalene Triangle:

15.6 cm   16.6 cm

15.52 cm

7.7 cm

Area (A): First, we calculate the semi-perimeter (s):

$$S = \frac{a+b+c}{2} = \frac{15.6 + 16.6 + 7.7}{2} = \frac{39.8}{2} = 19.9 \text{ cm}$$

Heron's formula to find the area:

$$A = \sqrt{s(s-a)(s-b)(s-c)}$$

$$A = \sqrt{19.9\,(19.9 - 15.6)(19.9 - 16.6)(19.9 - 7.7)}$$

$$A = \sqrt{19.9 \times 4.3 \times 3.3 \times 12.2}$$

$$A = \sqrt{3445} \approx 59$$

Perimeter (P):

$$P = side1 + side2 + side3$$

$$P = 15.6 + 16.6 + 7.7$$

$$P = 39.8$$

Area and Perimeter of an L-shape

The L-shaped figure typically consists of two rectangles joined together to form an L-shape. To find the area and perimeter of an L-shaped figure, we will need to calculate the areas and perimeters of each rectangle and then combine them.

Area=Area of Rectangle 1 + Area of Rectangle 2

Perimeter=Perimeter of Rectangle 1 + Perimeter of Rectangle 2

Let's find the Area and Perimeter of an L-shape:

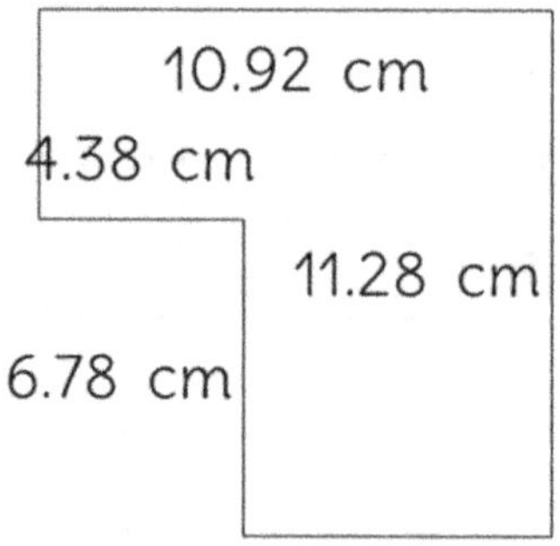

Area of L-Shape

$$\text{Area 1} = 4.38 \times 4.5 = 19.7 \text{ cm}^2$$

$$\text{Area 2} = 11.28 \times 6.54 = 73.7 \text{ cm}^2$$

$$\text{Area} = 19.7 + 73.7$$

$$\text{Area} = 93.481 \text{ cm}^2$$

Perimeter of L-Shape

$$P = 11.28 + 6.54 + 6.78 + 4.38 + 4.5 + 10.92$$

$$P = 44.4 \text{ cm}$$

Area and Perimeter of U-shape

U-shape is basically composed of three rectangles, we'll need to calculate the area and perimeter of each rectangle separately and then sum them up.

Area of the U-shape:

The total area (A) of the U-shape is the sum of the areas of the three rectangles:

$$A = A1 + A2 + A3$$

Perimeter of the U-shape: The total perimeter (P) of the U-shape is the sum of the perimeters of the three rectangles:

$$P = P1 + P2 + P3$$

Let's find the area and perimeter of the following U-shape:

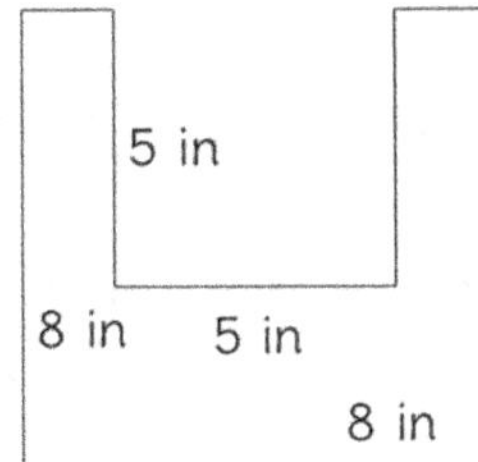

Area:

$$A1 = 8 \times 1.5 = 12 + A2 = 3 \times 5 = 15 + A3 = 8 \times 1.5 = 12$$

$$= 12 + 15 + 12$$

$$= 39 \text{ in}^2$$

Perimeter:

$$2 \times 8 + 2 \times 5 + 2 \times 8$$

$$= 16 + 10 + 16$$

$$= 42$$

Volume and surface Area

Volume refers to the amount of space occupied by a three-dimensional object. For shapes like cubes or rectangular prisms, we calculate volume by multiplying their length, width, and height.

To find the volume V of a rectangular prism, we use the formula:

$$Volume = length \ x \ width \ x \ height$$

Surface Area represents the total area covering all the faces of a three-dimensional object. For shapes like cubes or rectangular prisms, we find the surface area by summing the areas of all its faces.

The formula for surface area SA of a cube or rectangular prism is:

$$Surface \ Area = 2lw + 2lh + 2wh$$

Where: l is the length, w is the width, and h is the height of the object.

For example: Let's find the Volume and Surface Area of following rectangular prisms:

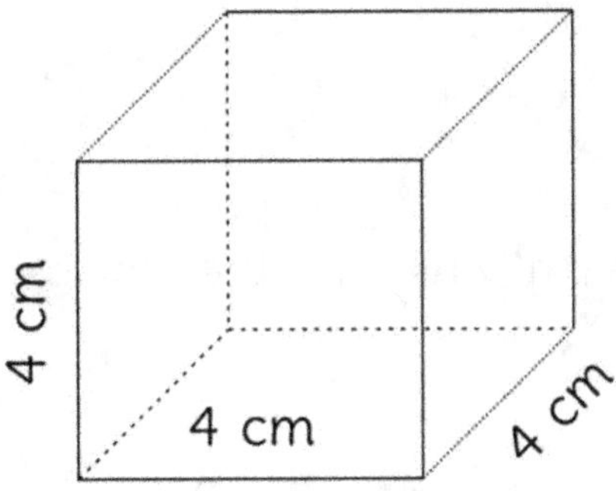

$$Volume \ = \ length \ \times \ width \ \times \ height$$

$$= 4 \times 4 \times 4$$

$$= 64 \ cm^2$$

$$Surface \ Area \ = \ 2lw \ + \ 2lh \ + \ 2wh$$

$$= 2(4 \times 4) + 2(4 \times 4) + 2(4 \times 4)$$

$$= 32 + 32 + 32$$

$$= 96 \ cm2$$

Different 3D objects have unique formulas for finding their volume and surface area. Here are some common ones:

1. Cube:

    - Volume: $V = s^3$ (where s is the length of one side of the cube)

    - Surface area: $SA = 6s^2$

2. Sphere:

    - Volume: $V = (\frac{4}{3})\pi r^3$ (where r is the radius of the sphere)

    - Surface area: $SA = 4\pi r^2$

3. Cone:

- Volume: $V = (\frac{1}{3})\pi r^2 h$ (where r is the radius of the base and h is the height of the cone)

- Surface area: $SA = \pi r^2 + \pi r\sqrt{(r^2 + h^2)}$

4. Cylinder:

- Volume: $V = \pi r^2 h$ (where r is the radius of the base and h is the height of the cylinder)

- Surface area: $SA = 2\pi r^2 + 2\pi rh$

5. Pyramid:

- Volume: $V = (\frac{1}{3})Bh$ (where B is the area of the base and h is the height of the pyramid)

- Surface area: $SA = B + \frac{1}{2}Pl$ (where P is the perimeter of the base and l is the slant height of the pyramid)

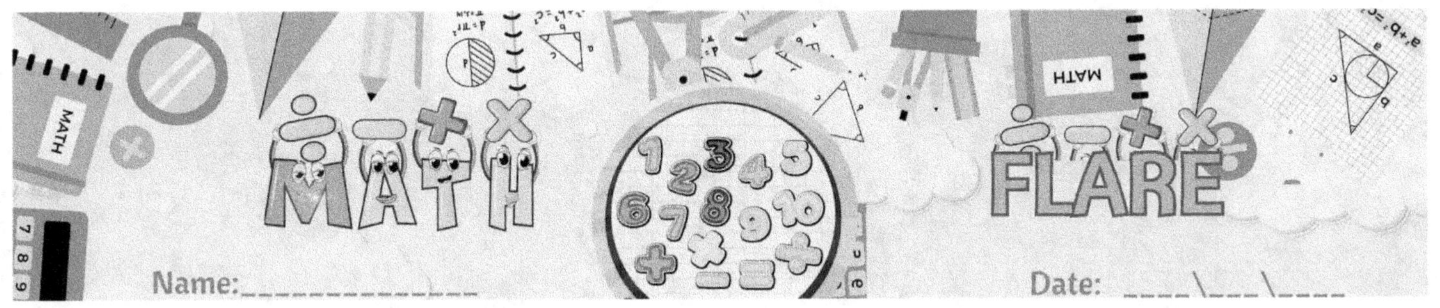

Area and Perimeter

1)

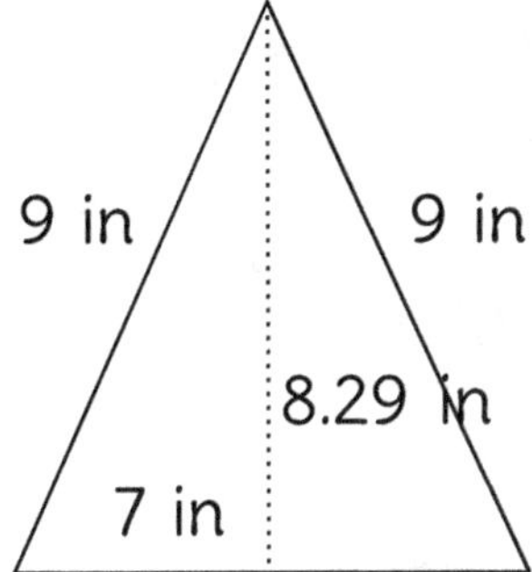

2)

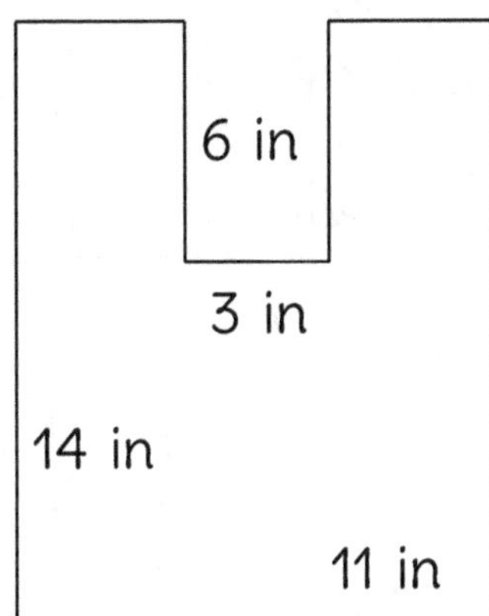

3)

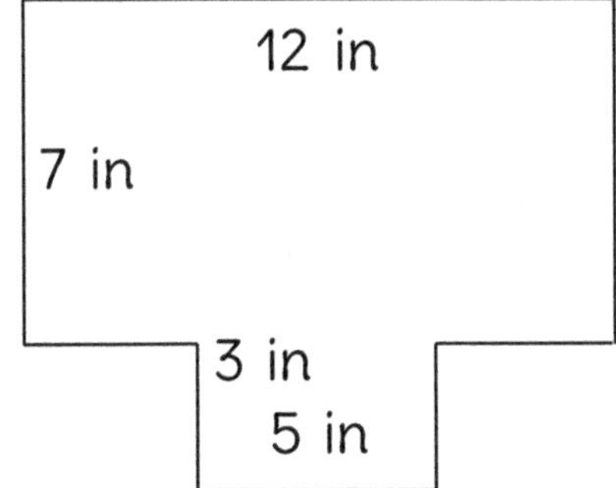

4)

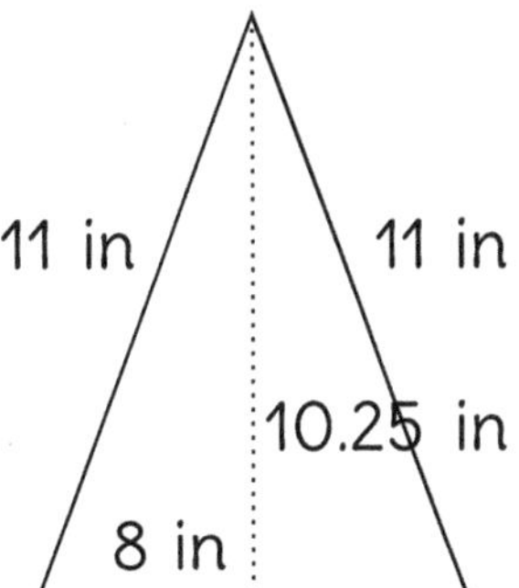

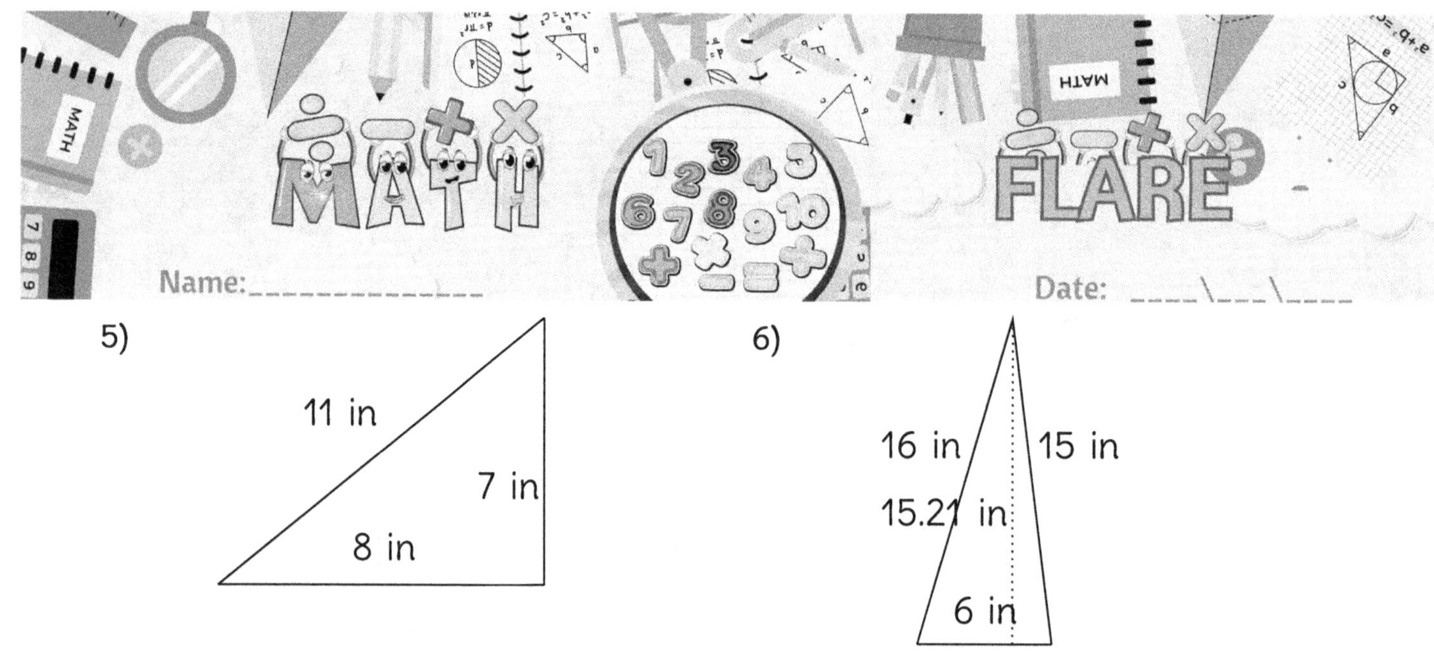

5)

11 in

7 in

8 in

6)

16 in   15 in

15.21 in

6 in

7)

10 in   10 in

10 in   8.660 in

8)

17 in

12 in

11 in

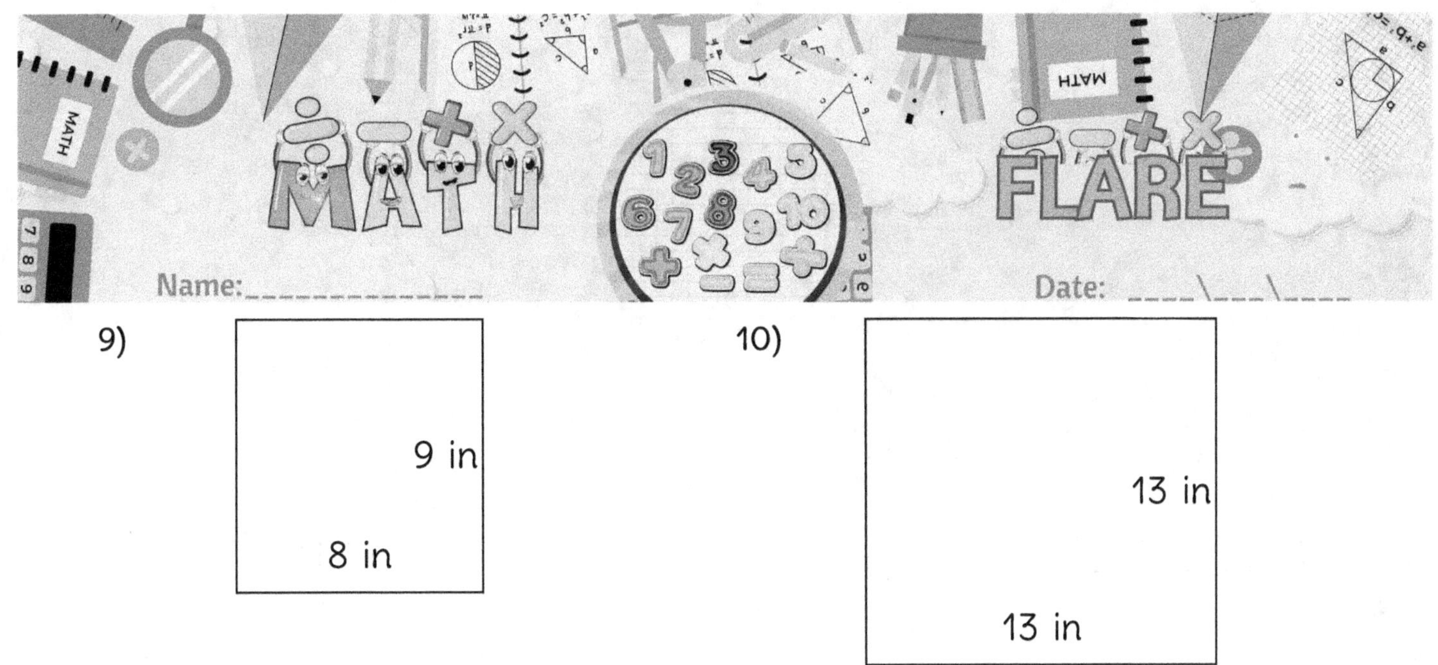

9)

9 in

8 in

10)

13 in

13 in

11)

11 in

10 in

4 in

4 in

12)

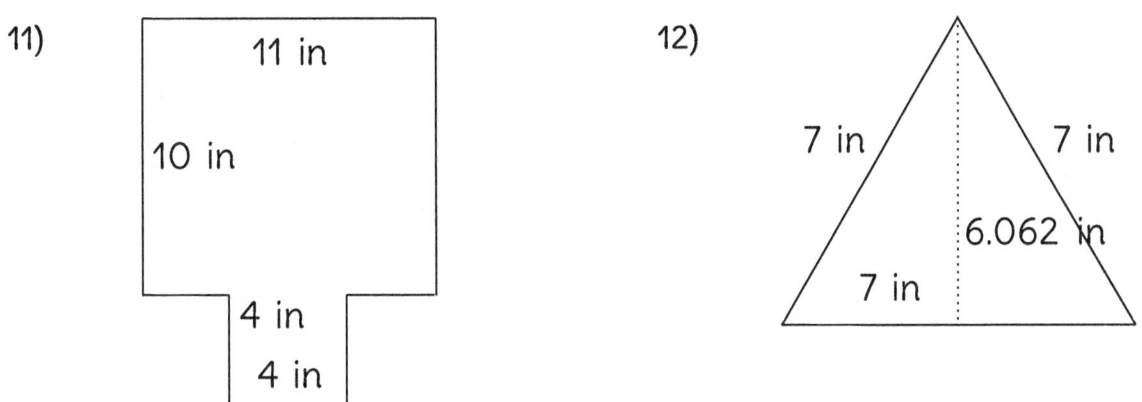

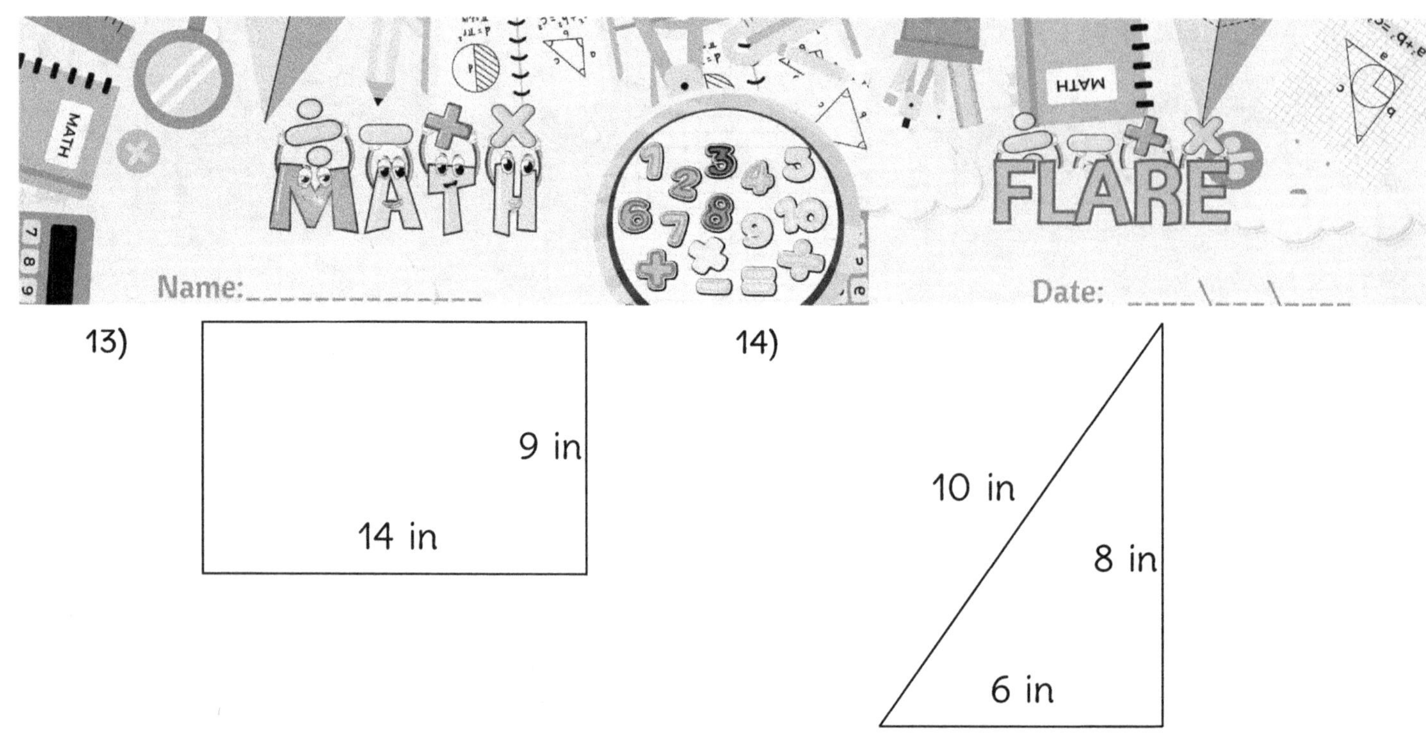
Name:
Date:
13)
9 in
14 in
14)
10 in
8 in
6 in

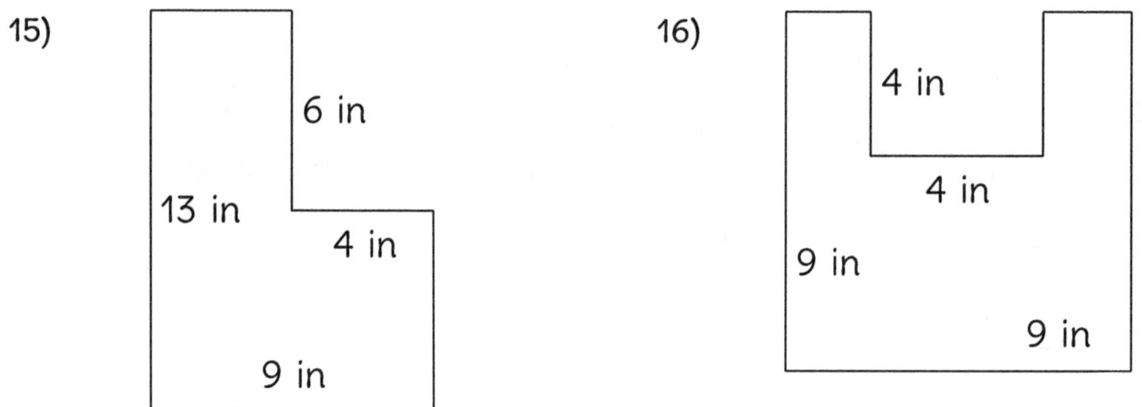
15)
6 in
13 in
4 in
9 in
16)
4 in
4 in
9 in
9 in

Name:
Date:

17)

17 in
12 in
12 in

18)

6 in
6 in
5.45 in
5 in

19)

11 in
8 in
8 in

20)

14 in
12 in

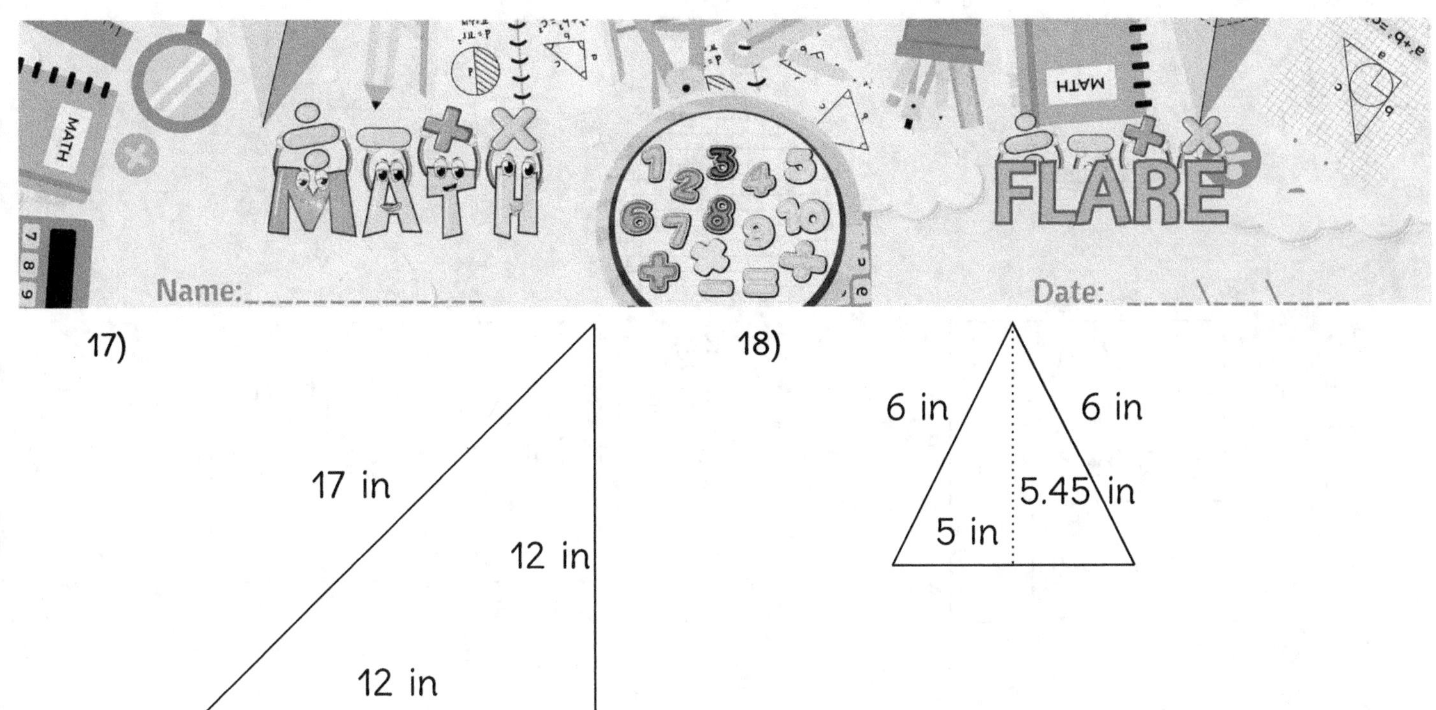

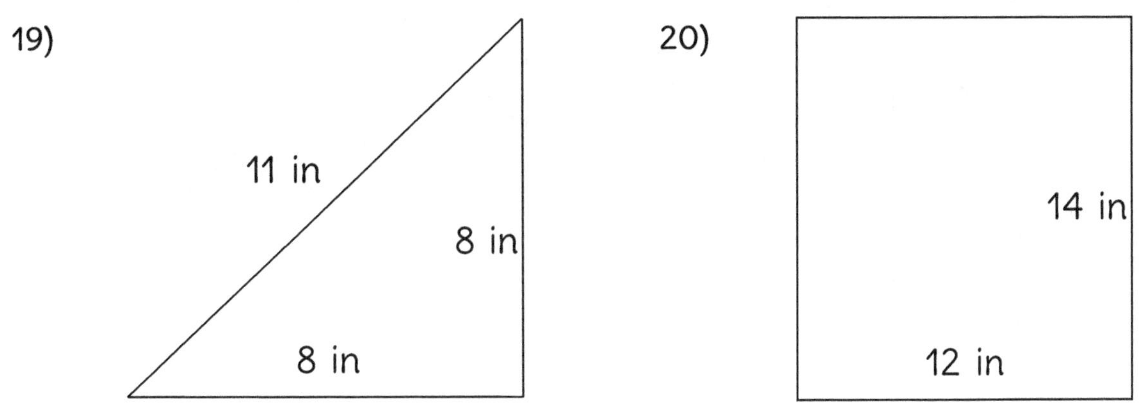

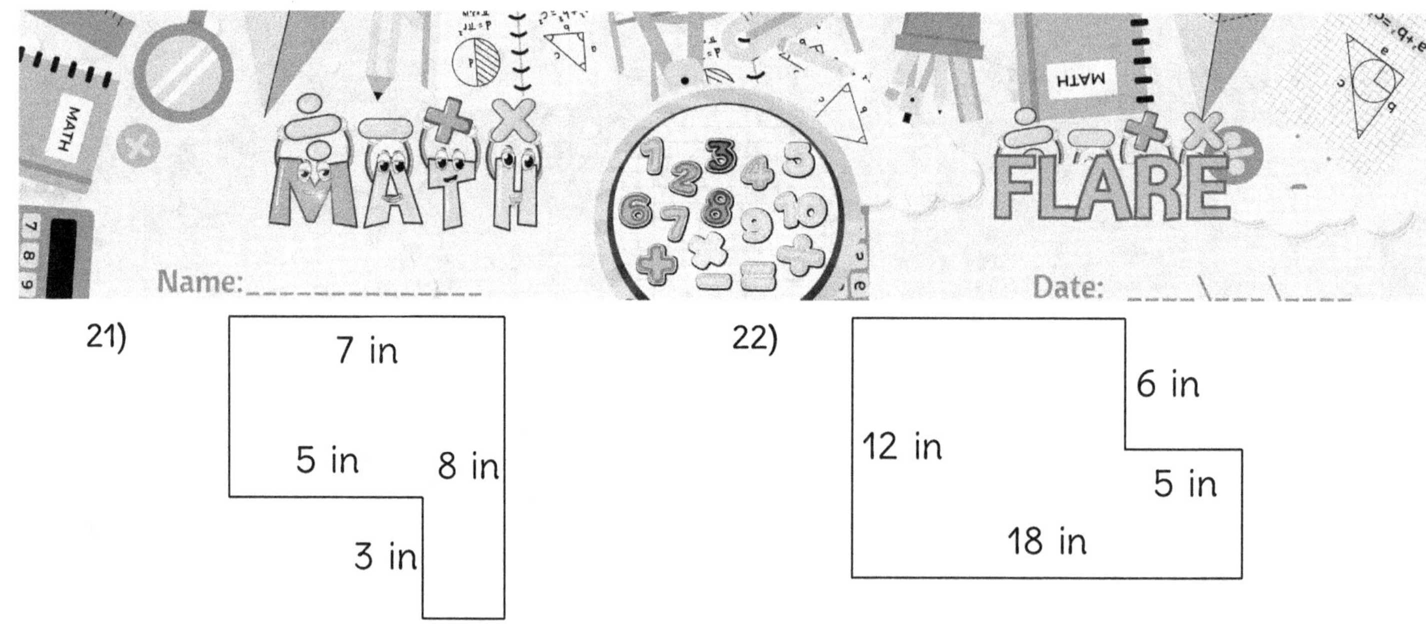

21)

22)

23)
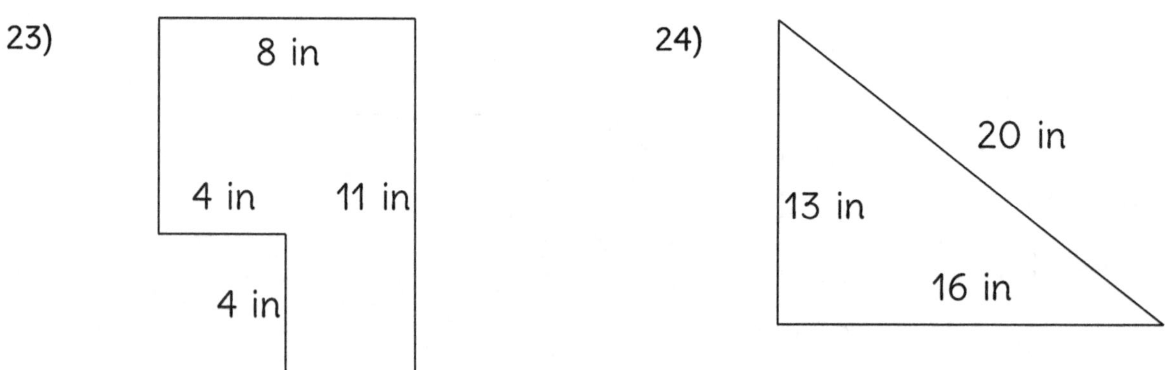

24)

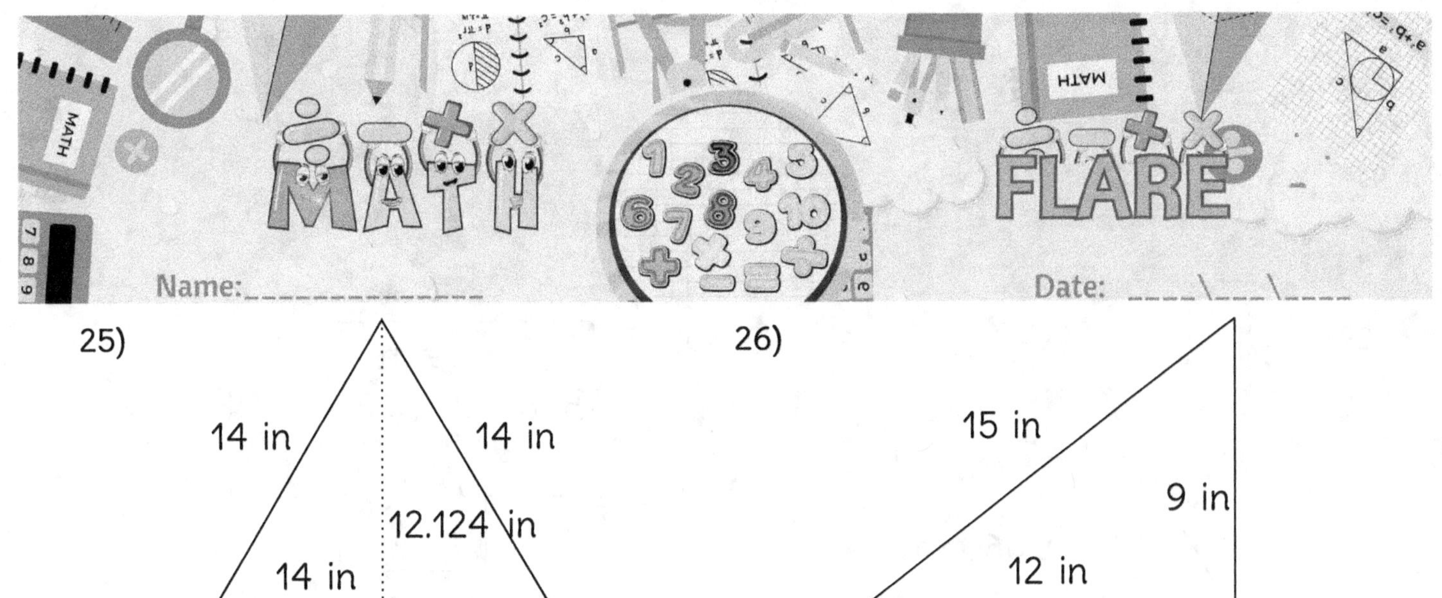

25)

14 in   14 in

12.124 in

14 in

26)

15 in

9 in

12 in

27)

10 in

7 in

8 in

28)

10 in   10 in

8.93 in

9 in

MATH
FLARE
Name:
Date:

29)

10 in
10 in
8.660 in
10 in

30)

9 in
5 in
2 in
4 in

31)

12 in
6 in
14 in
10 in

32)

4 in
9 in
3 in
10 in

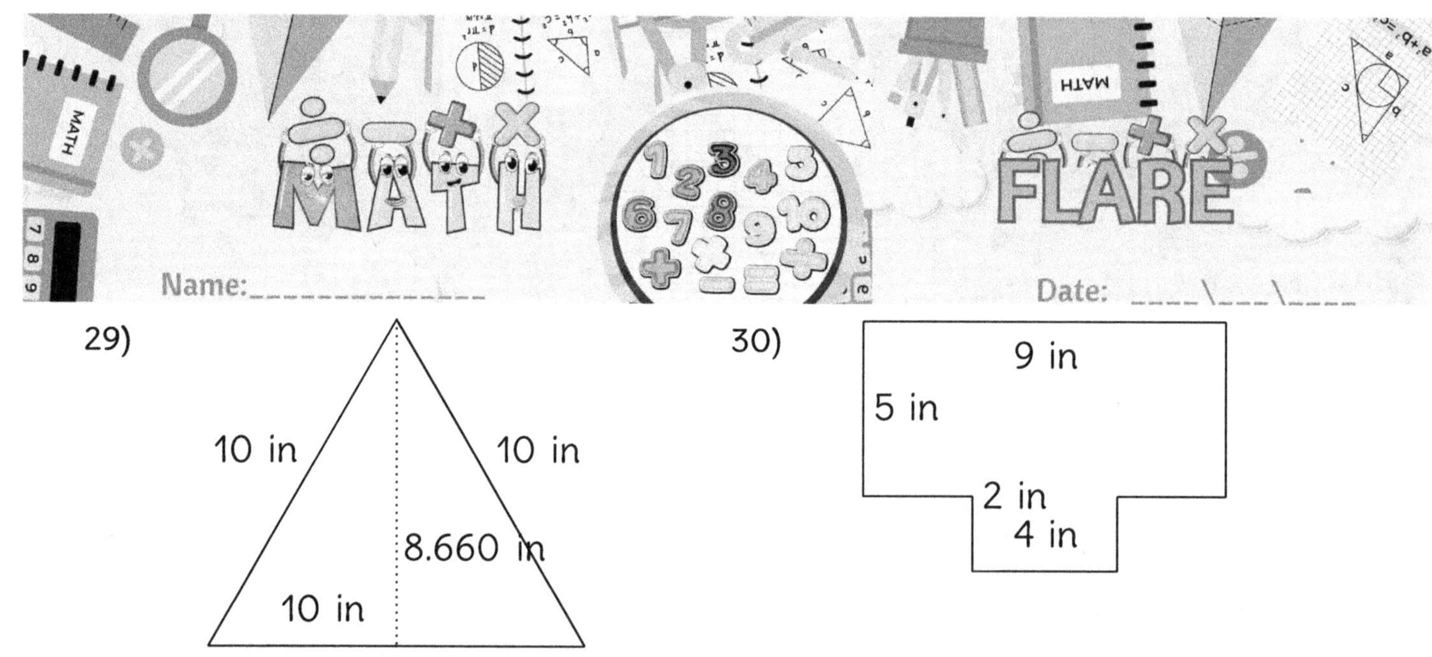

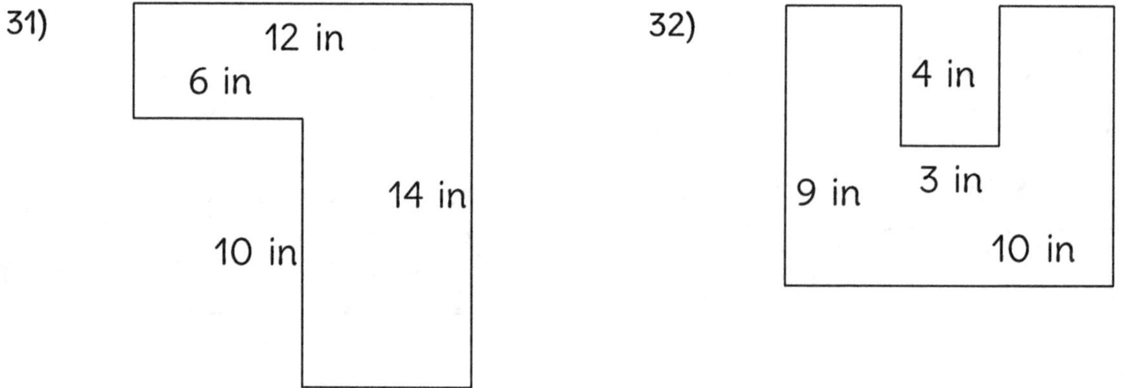

Name:
Date:
MATH FLARE
MATH

33)

11 in
5 in
5 in
4 in

34)

11 in
8 in
8 in

35)

8 in
8 in
6.928 in
8 in

36)

7 in
4 in
5 in
3 in

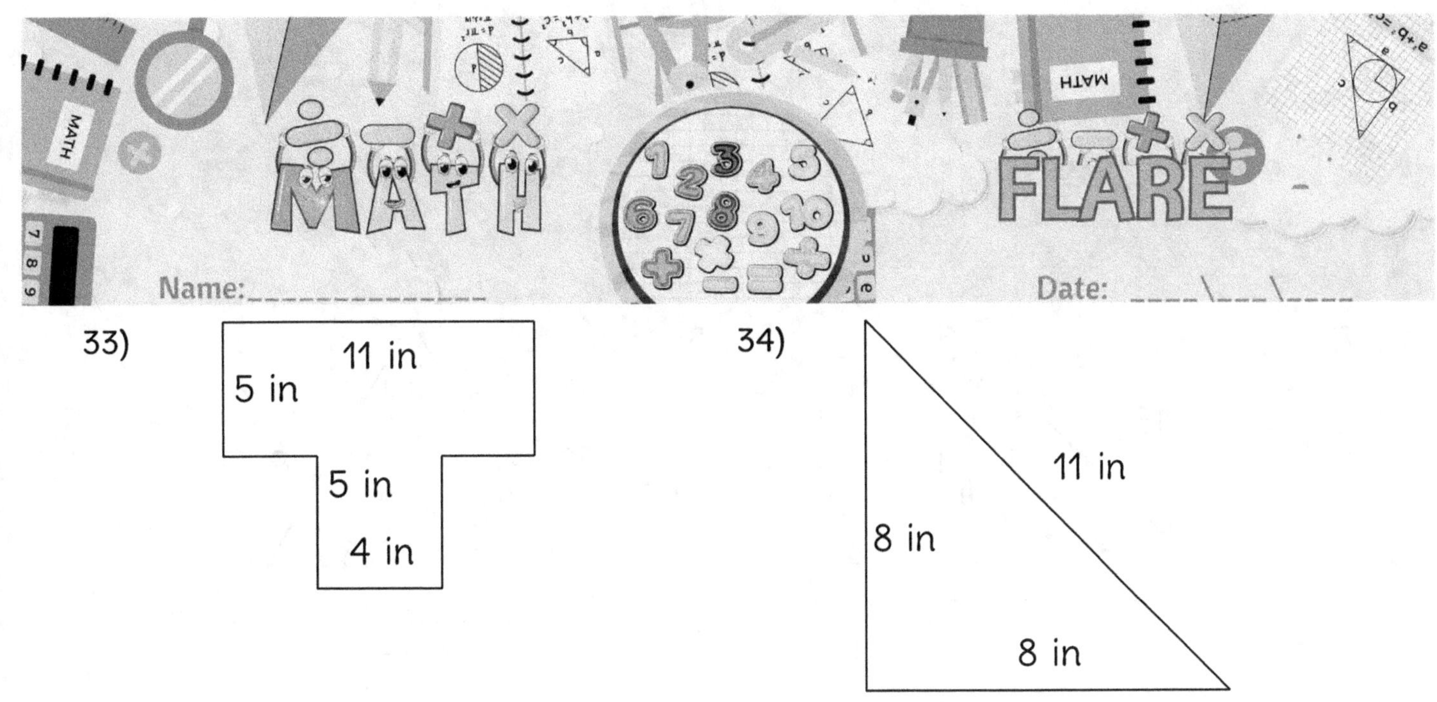

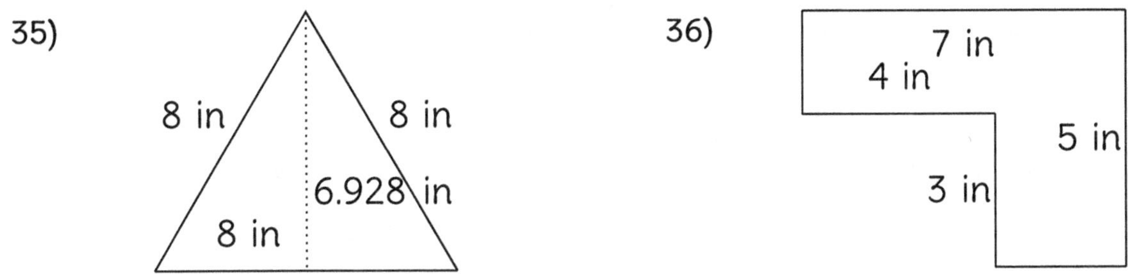

Name:________________
Date: ____________

37)

13 in
9 in
9 in

38)

16 in
16 in
13.856 in
16 in

39)

10 in
14 in

40)

5 in
9 in
7 in
12 in

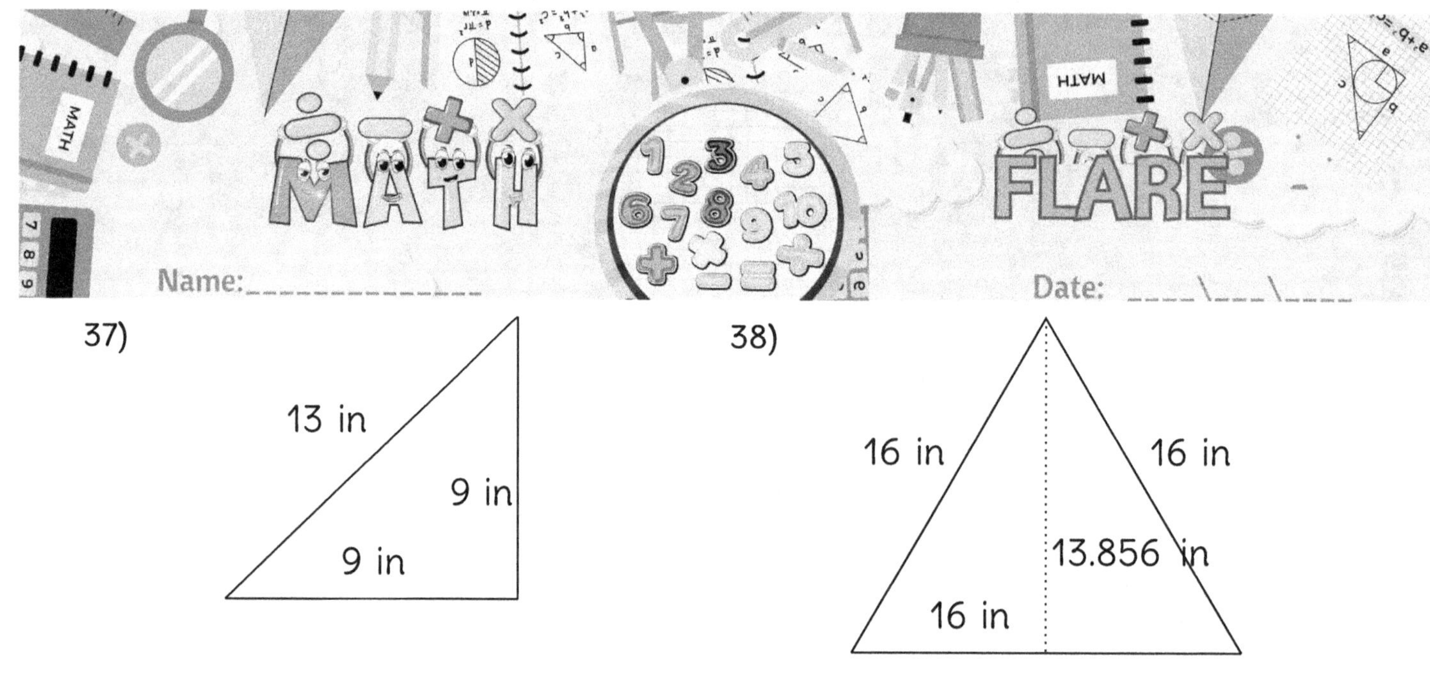

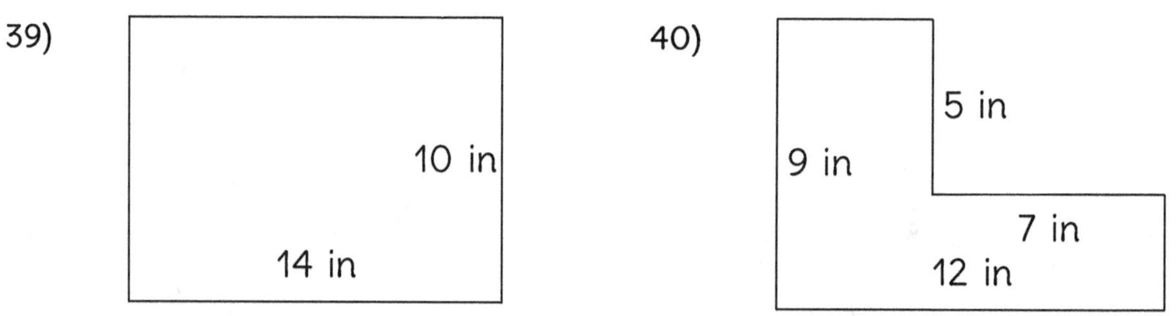

Name:
Date:

41)

6 in
3 in
4 in
2 in

42)

7 in
10 in
4 in
9 in

43)

3 in
3 in
7 in
8 in

44)

15 in
14 in
14.22 in
6 in

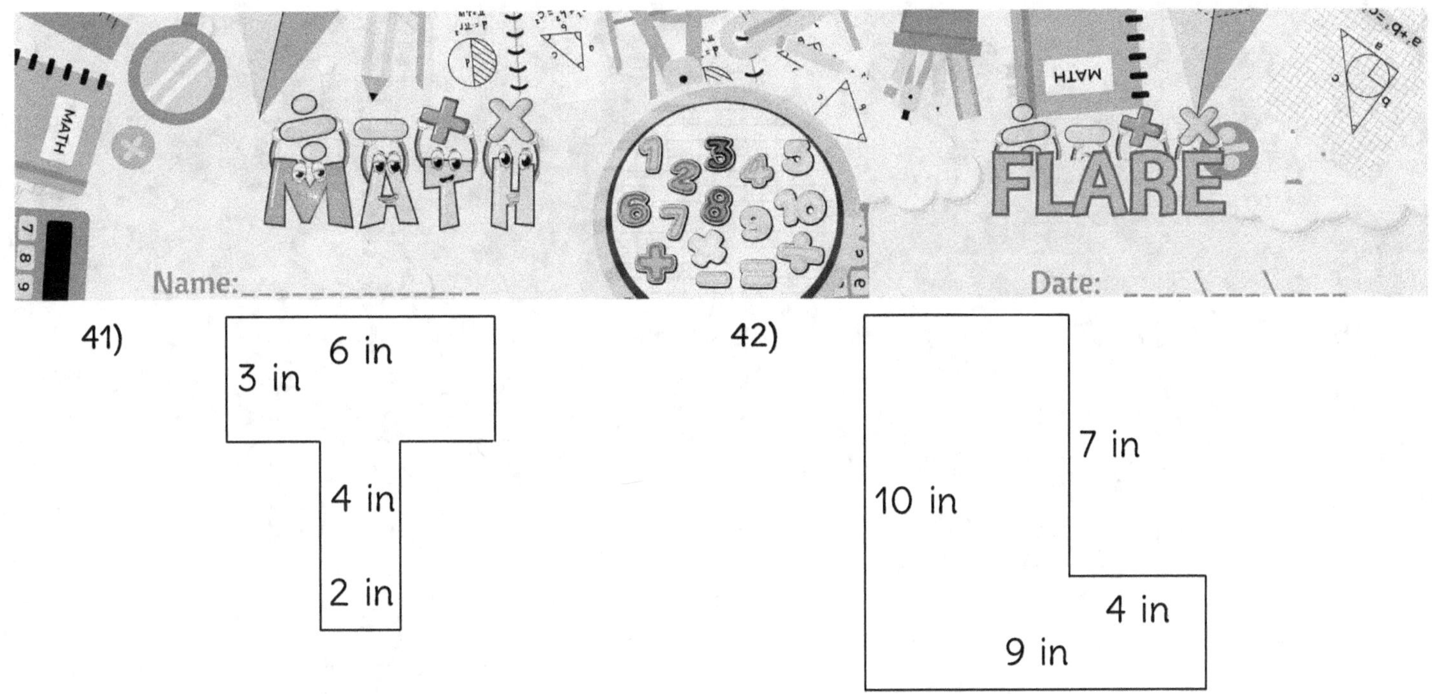

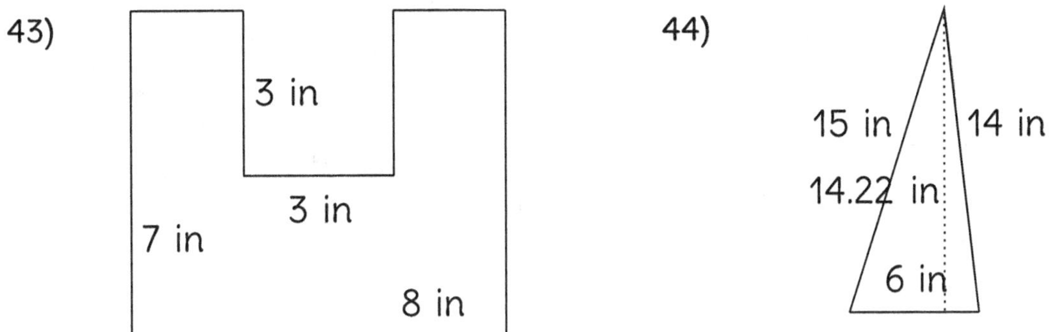

Name:
Date:

45)

13 in
13 in
12 in
10 in

46)

22 in
16 in
14 in

47)

20 in
16 in
12 in

48)

3 in
4 in
7 in
7 in

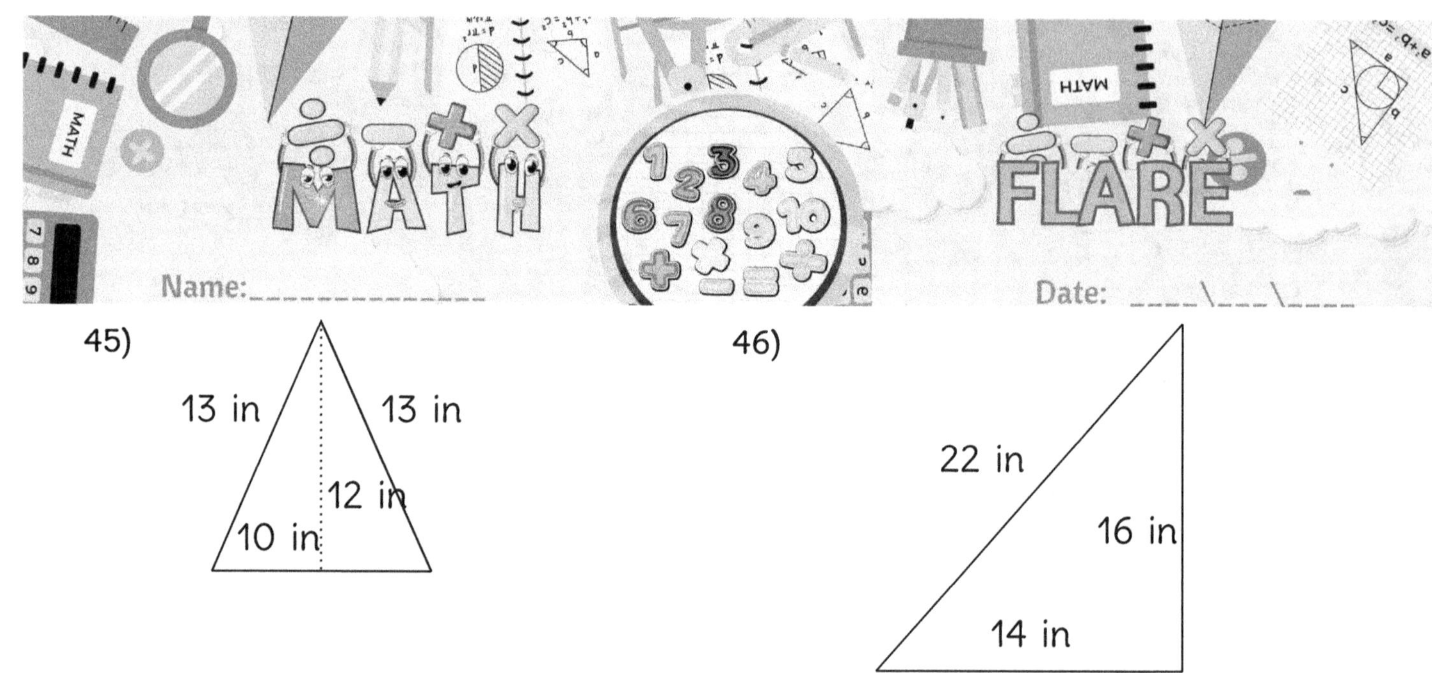

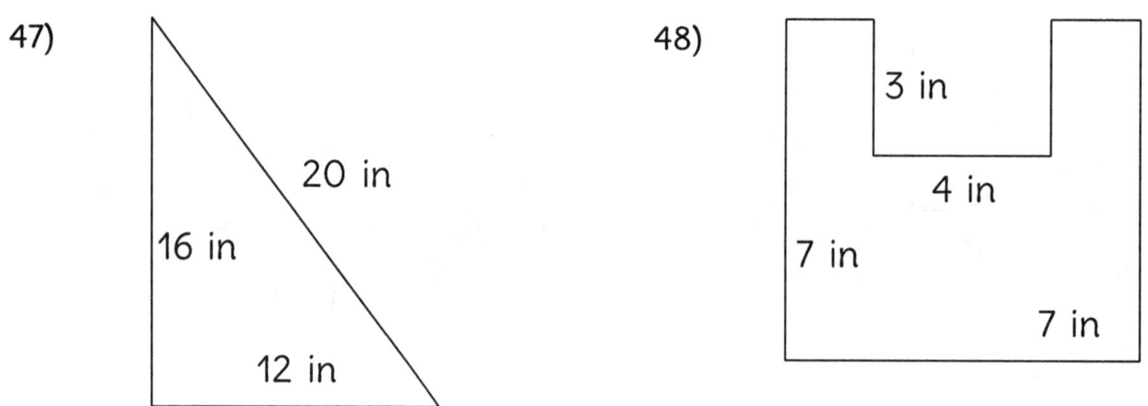

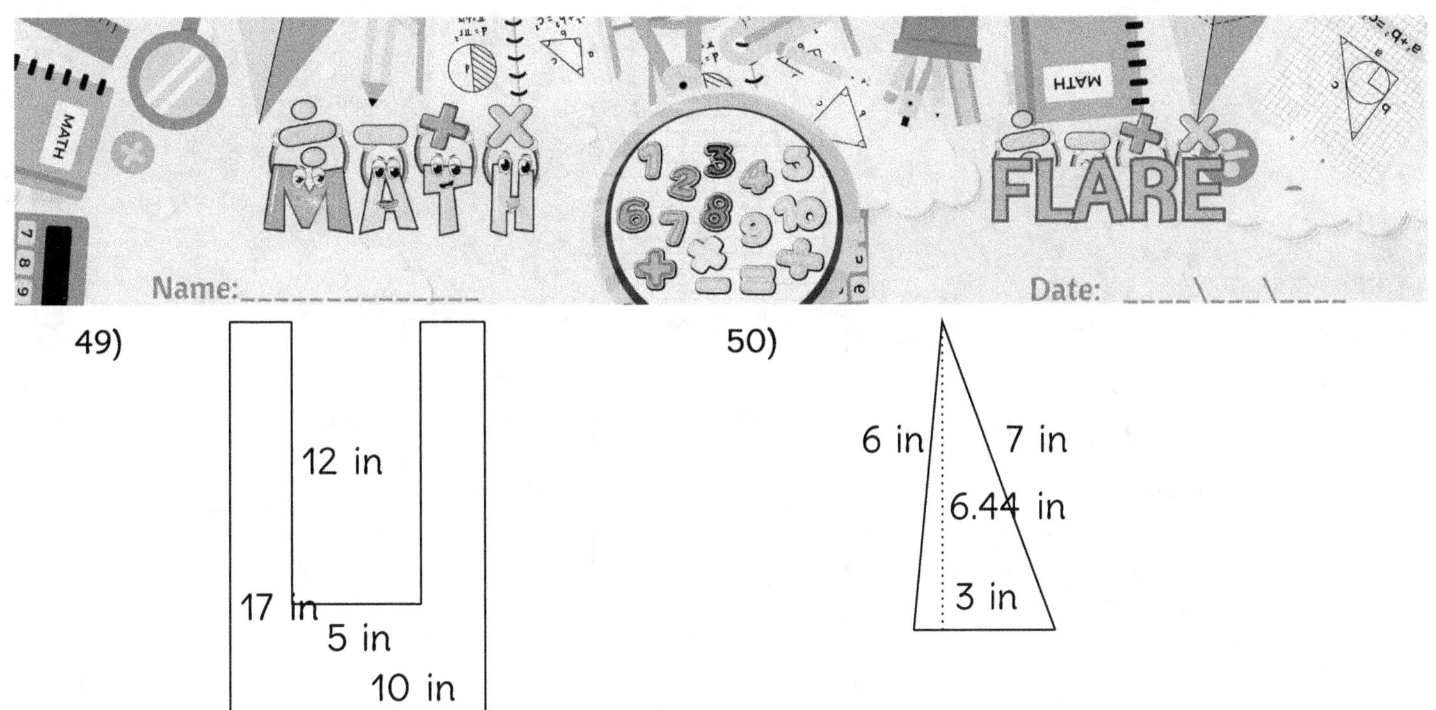

49)

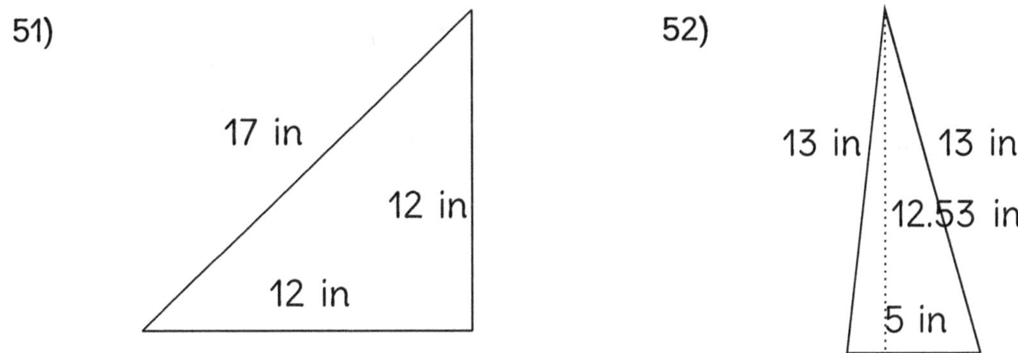

50)

51)

52)

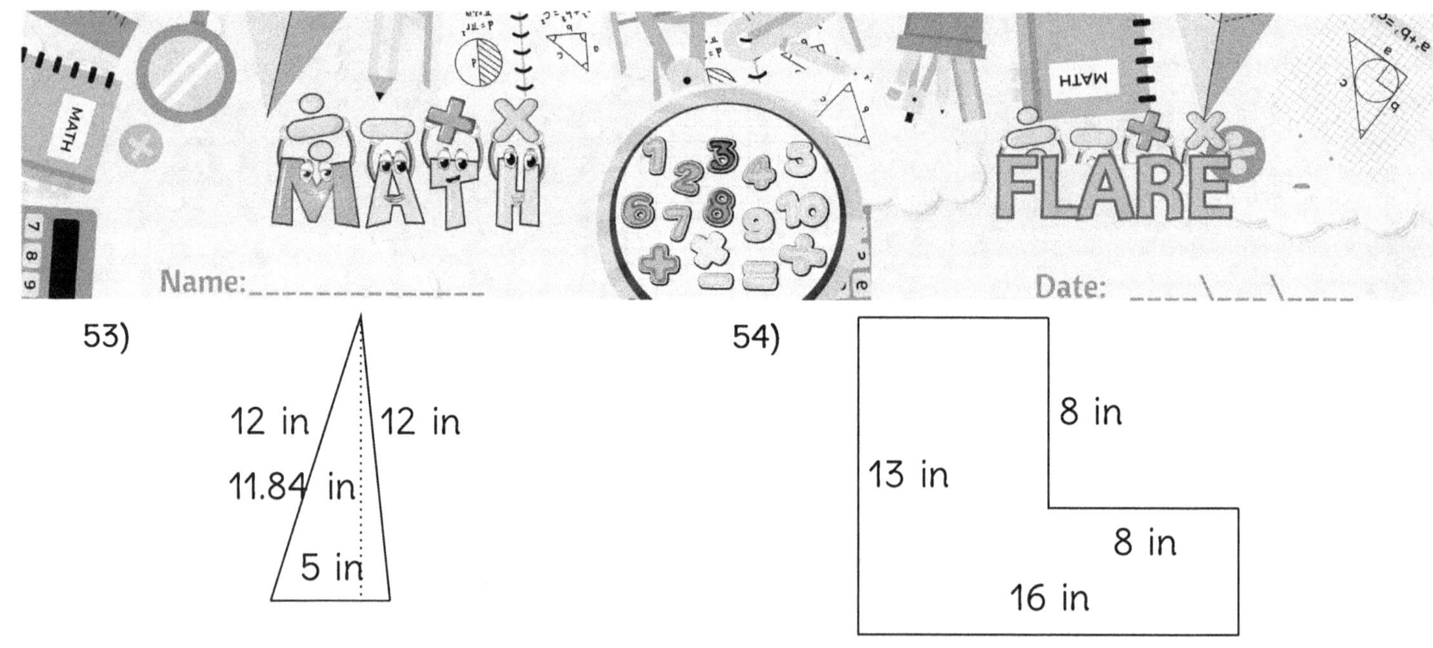

53)

54)

55)

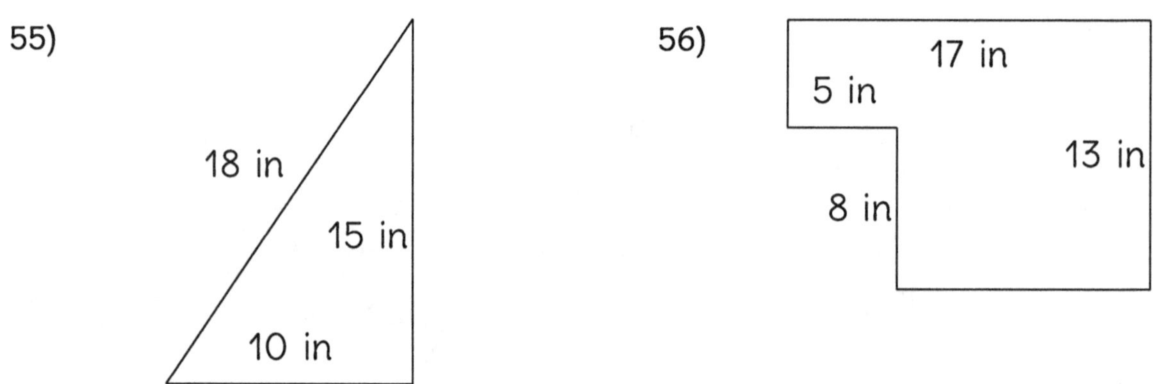

56)

MATH
FLARE
Name:
Date:

57)

23 in
16 in
16 in

58)

10 in
4 in
10 in
5 in

59)

19 in
17 in

60)

5 in
6 in

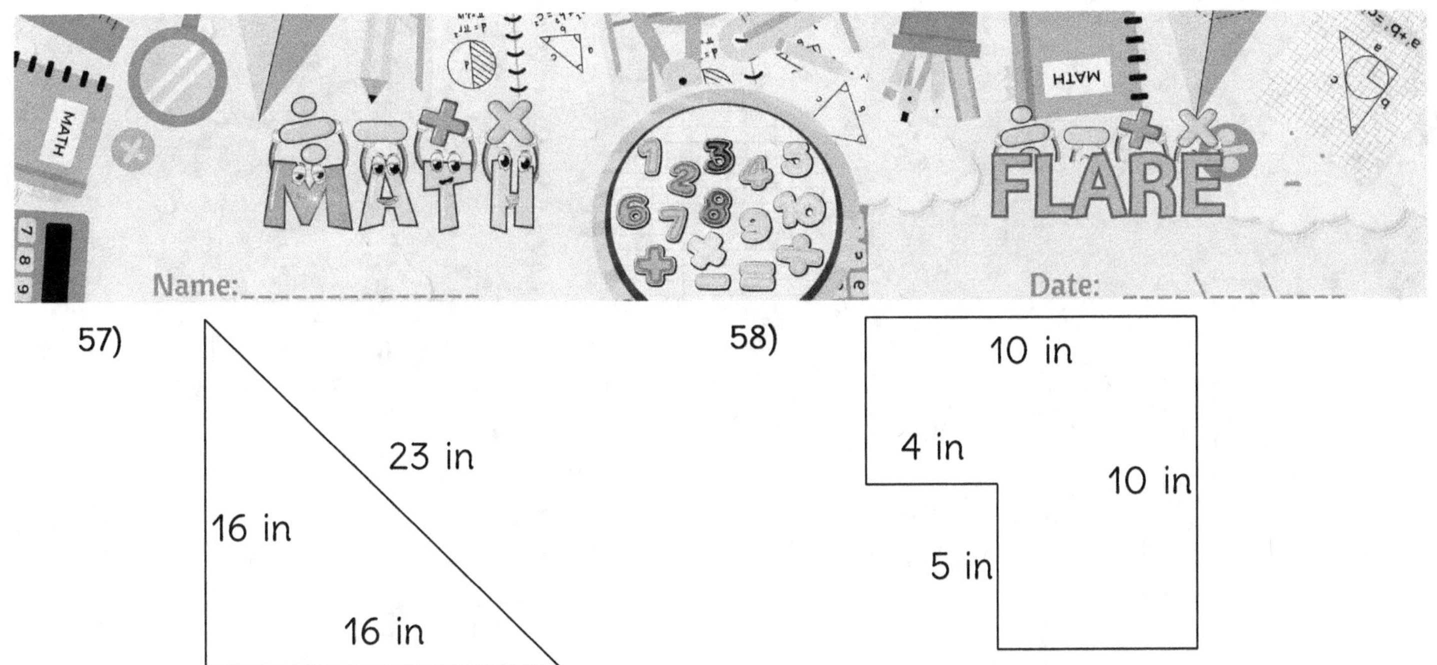

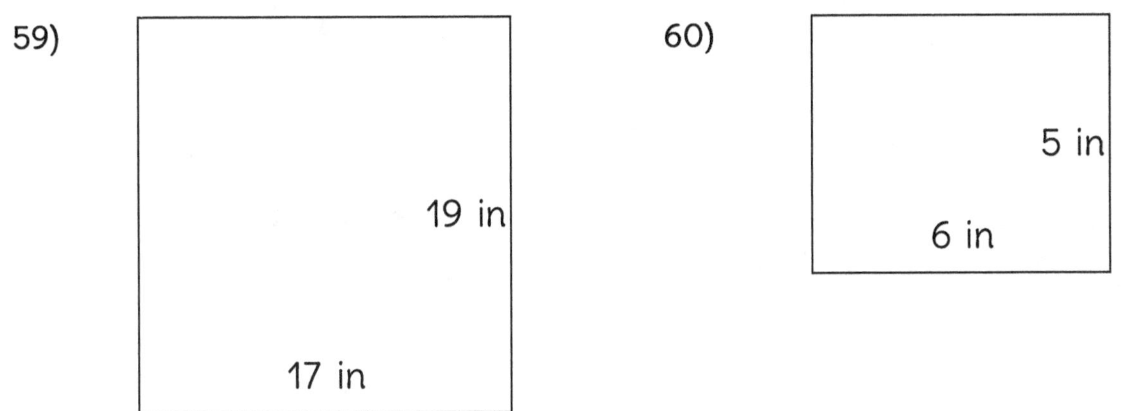

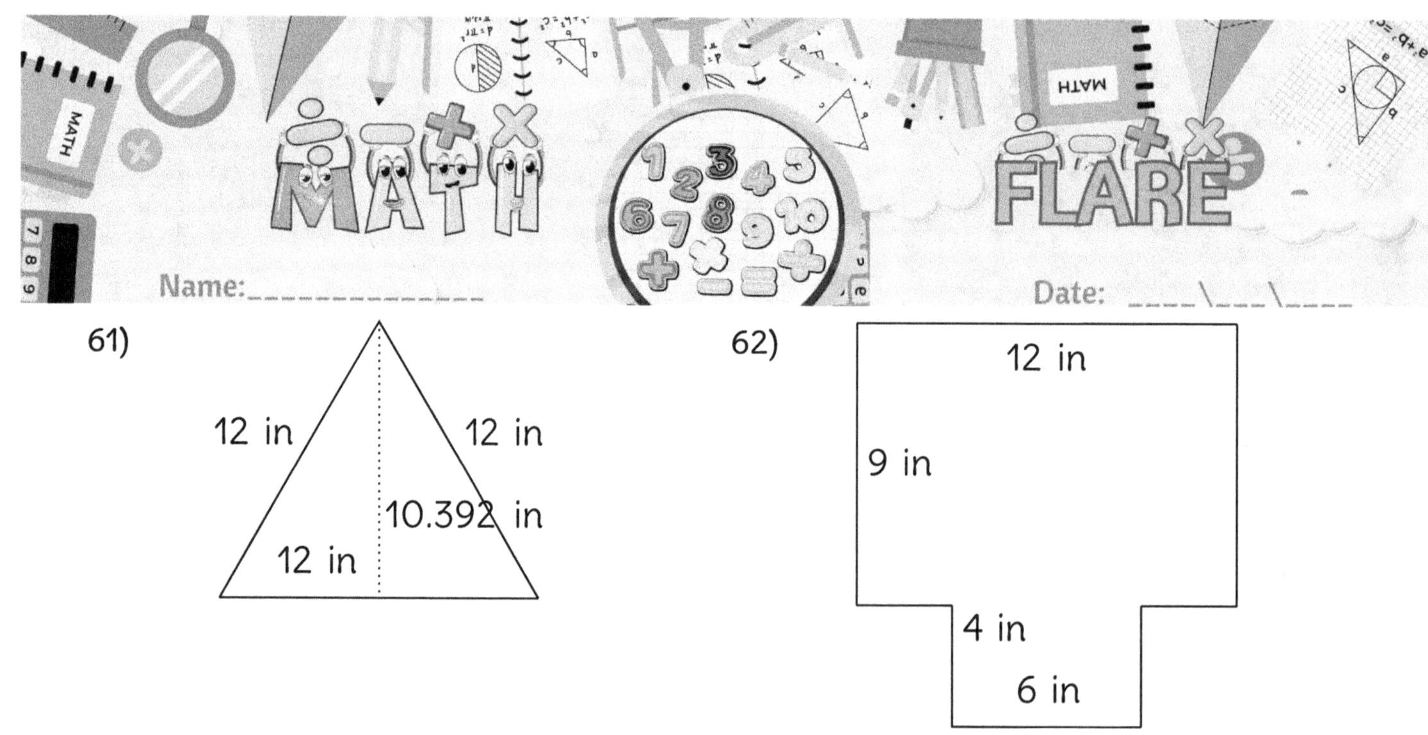
61)
12 in
12 in
10.392 in
12 in
62)
12 in
9 in
4 in
6 in

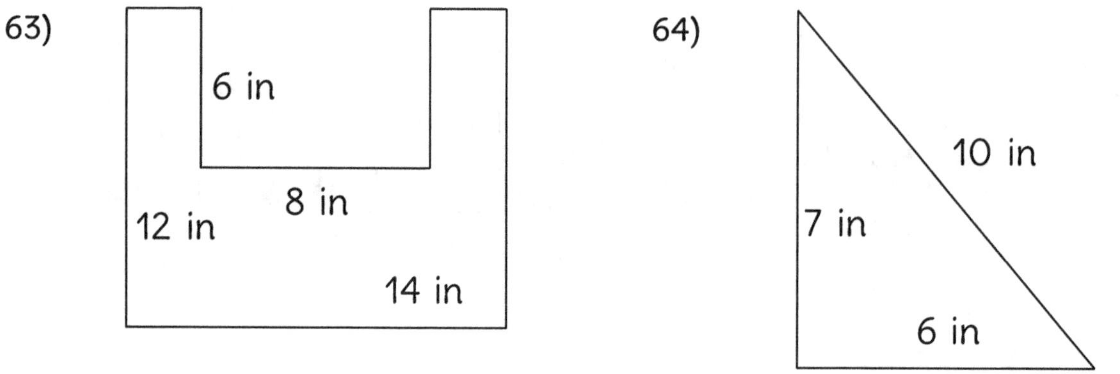
63)
6 in
12 in
8 in
14 in
64)
10 in
7 in
6 in

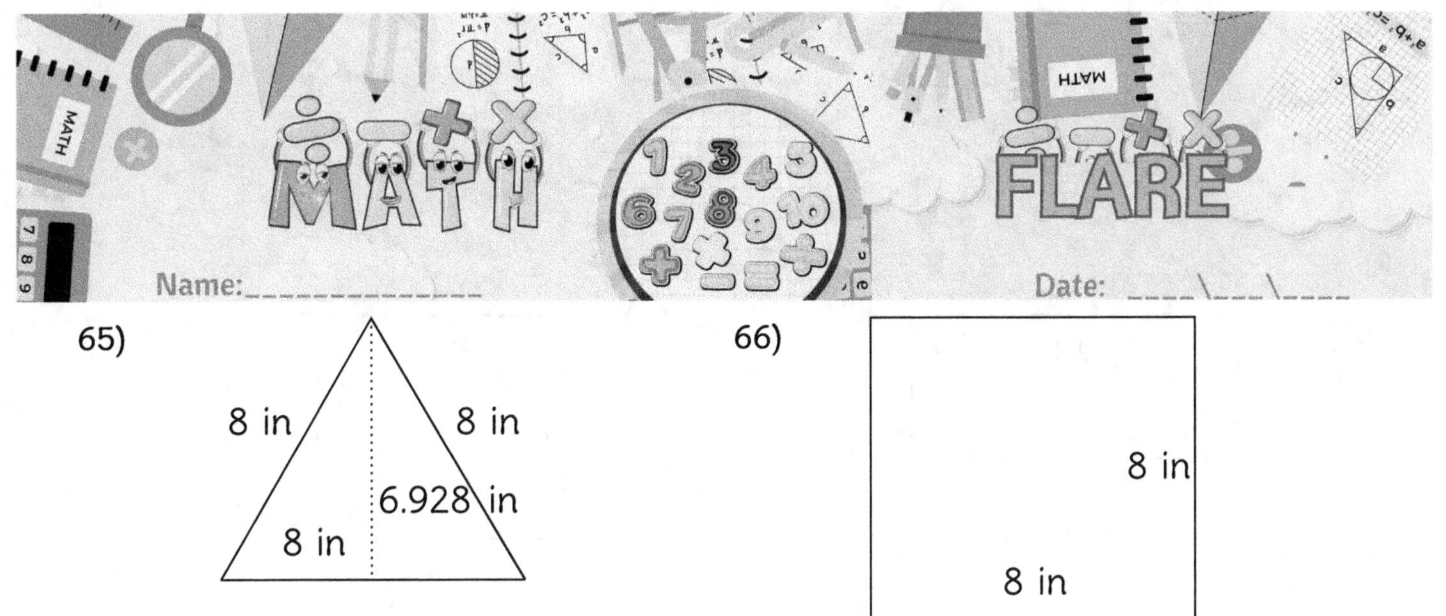

65)

8 in   8 in
6.928 in
8 in

66)

8 in
8 in

67)
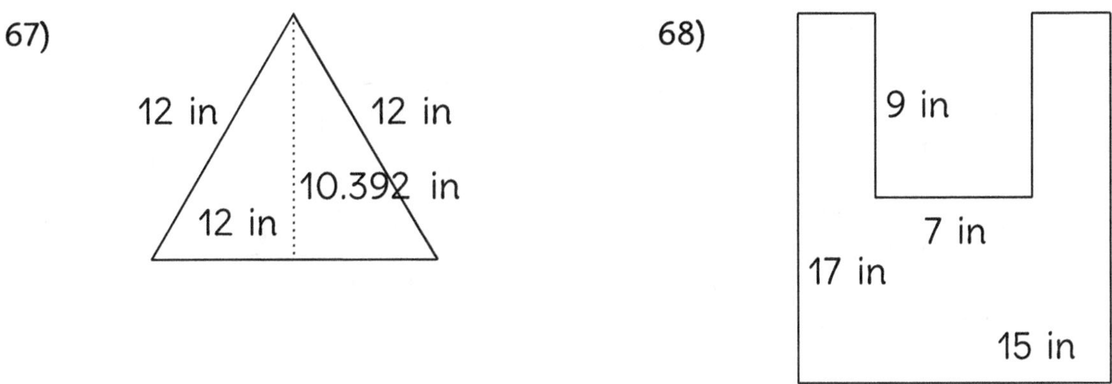

12 in   12 in
10.392 in
12 in

68)

9 in
7 in
17 in
15 in

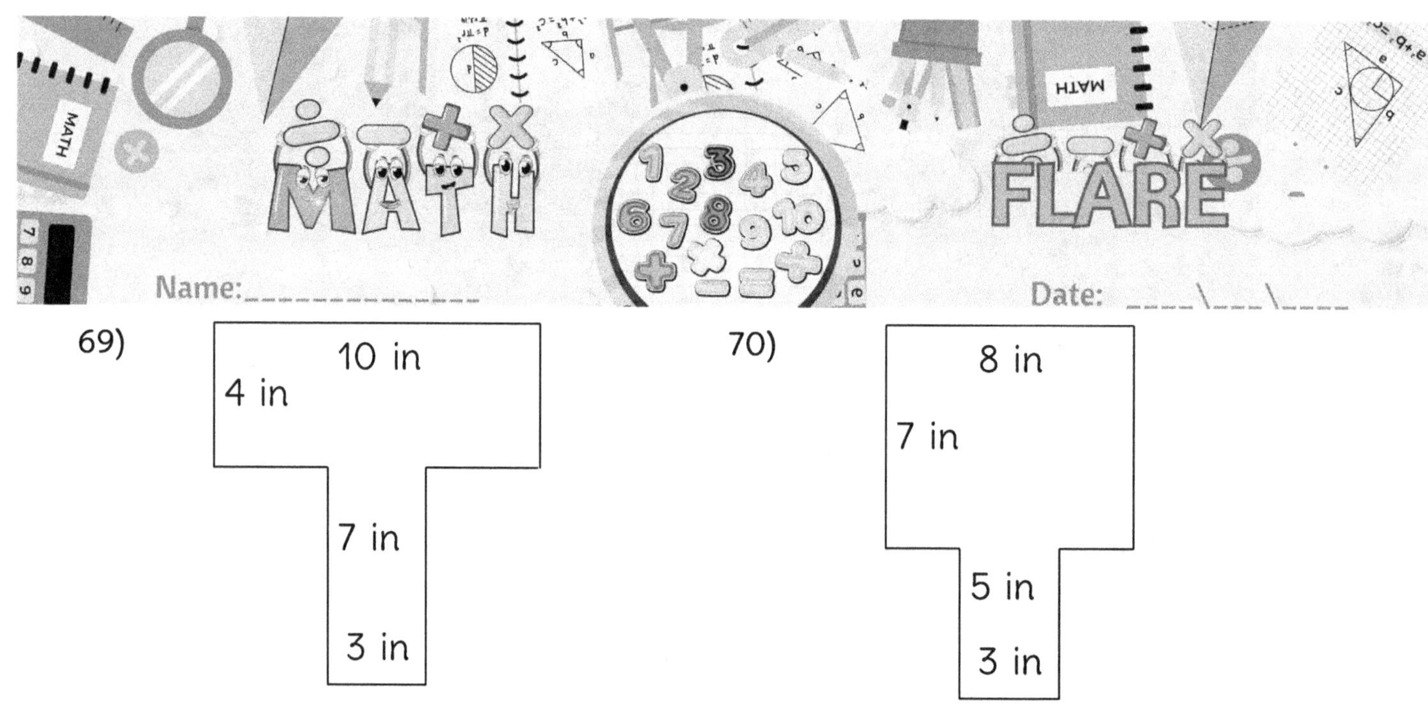

69)

70)

71) 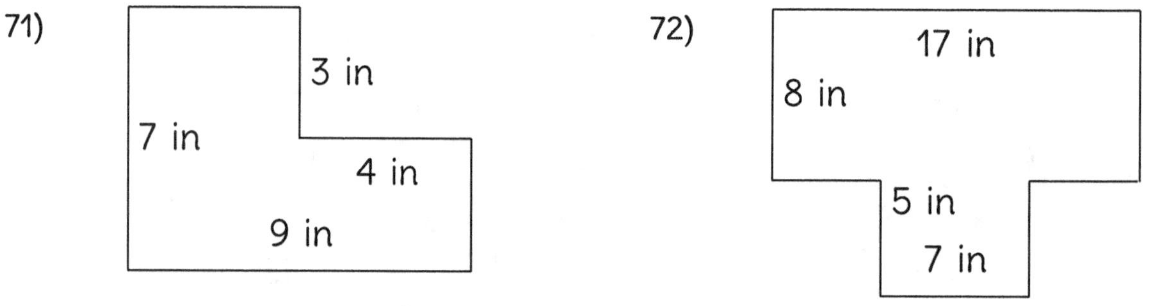

72)

Name:
Date:

73)
13 in
13 in
11.258 in
13 in

74)
8 in
15 in
7.56 in
16 in

75)

8 in
5 in

76)
15 in
11 in
11 in

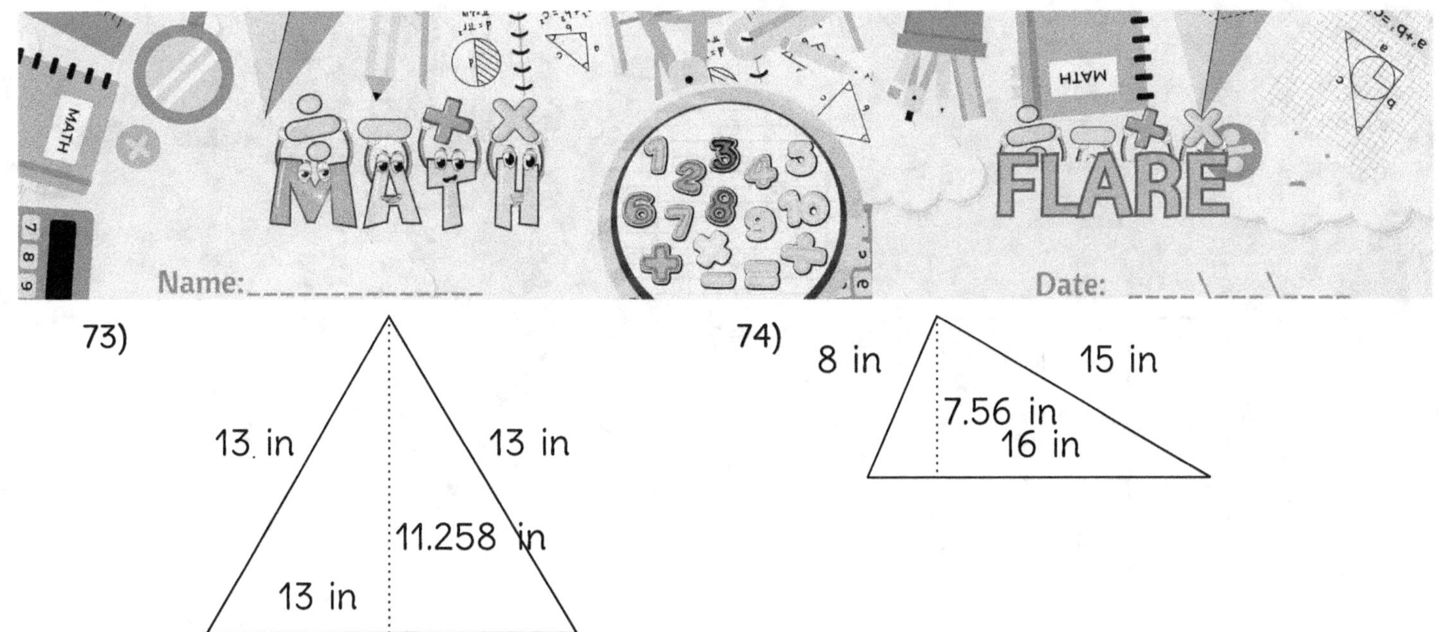

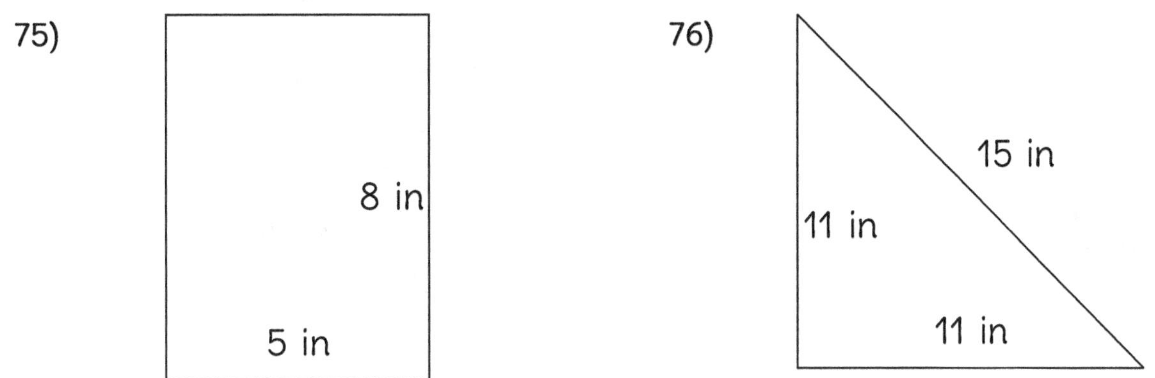

MATH
FLARE
Name:_______________
Date: _____________

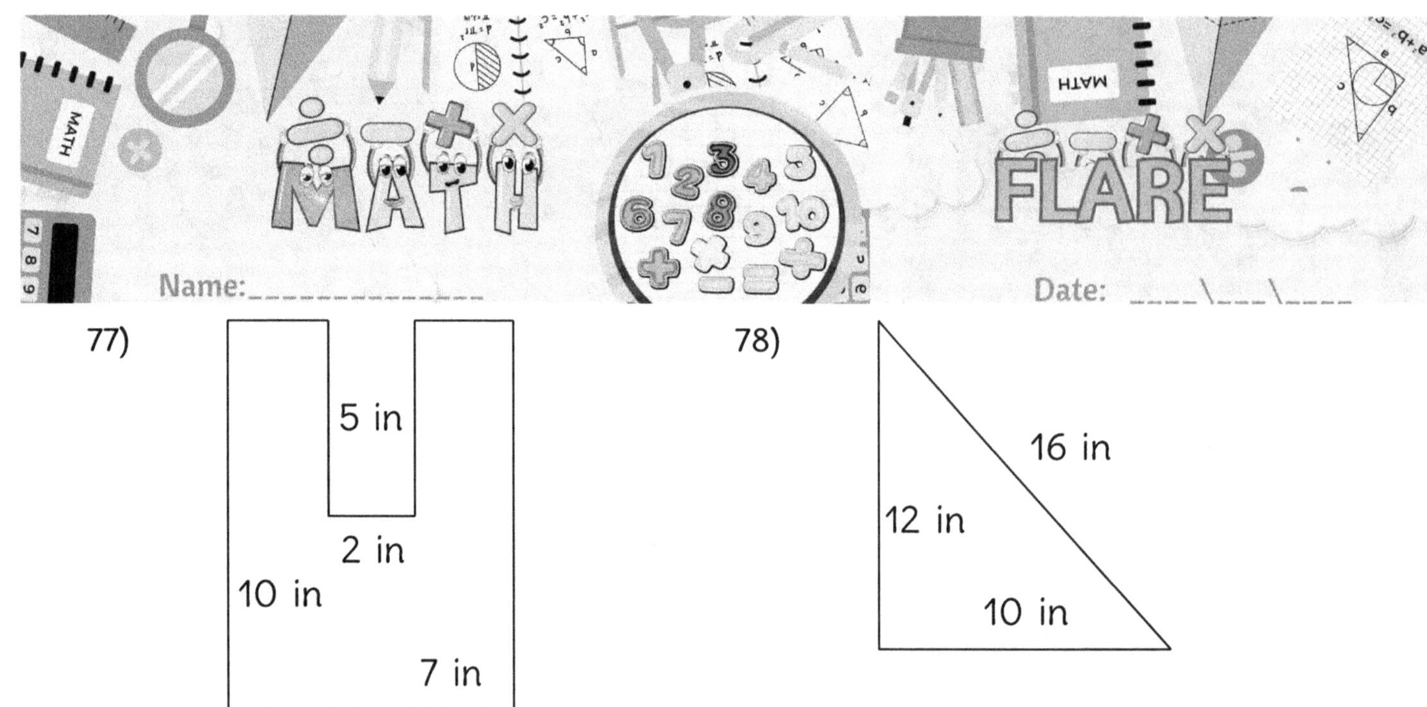

77)
5 in
2 in
10 in
7 in

78)
16 in
12 in
10 in

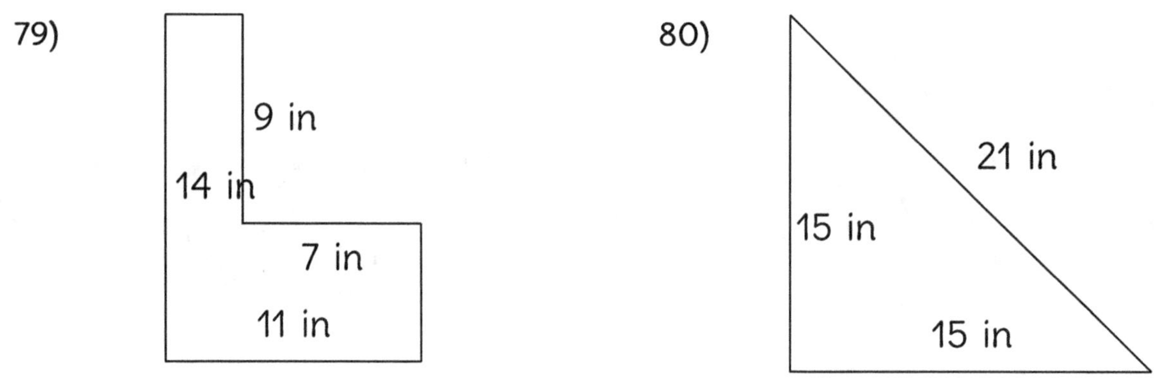

79)
9 in
14 in
7 in
11 in

80)
21 in
15 in
15 in

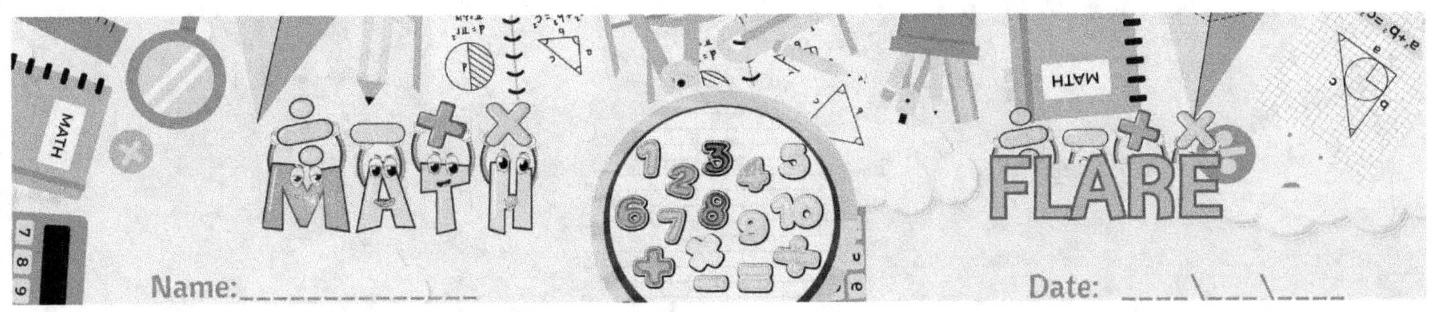

Volume and Surface Area

1)

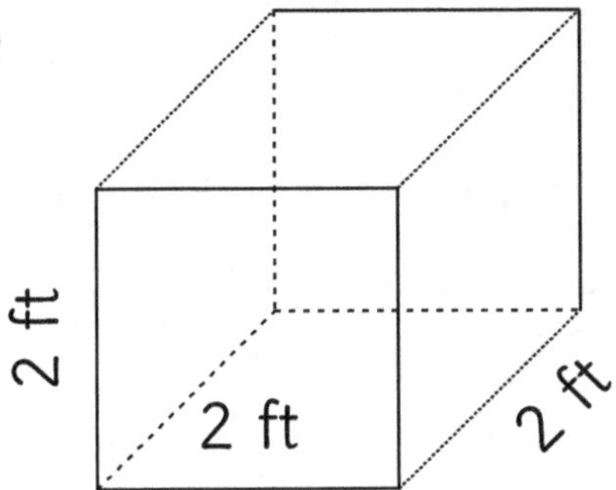

2)

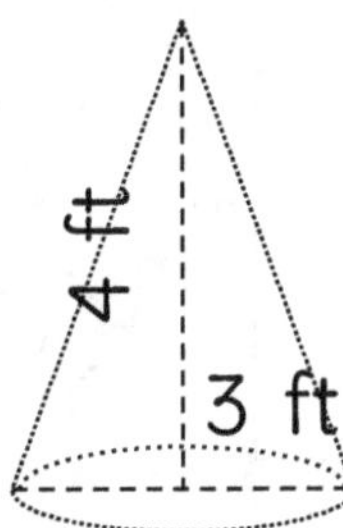

3)

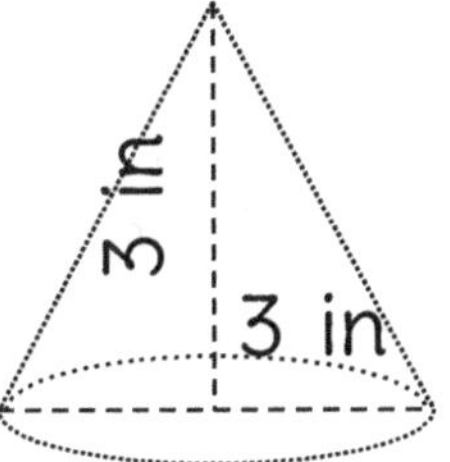

4)

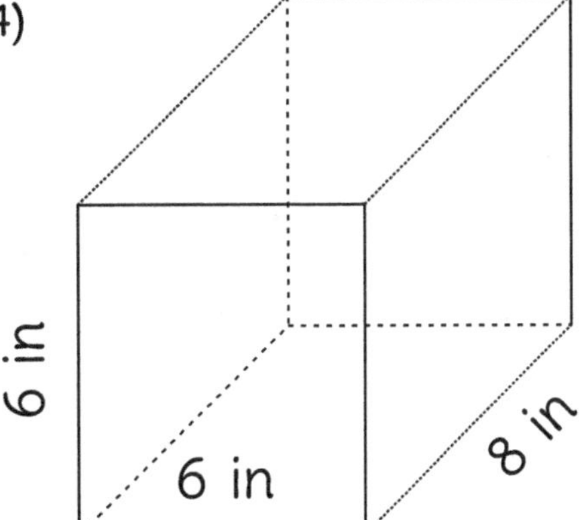

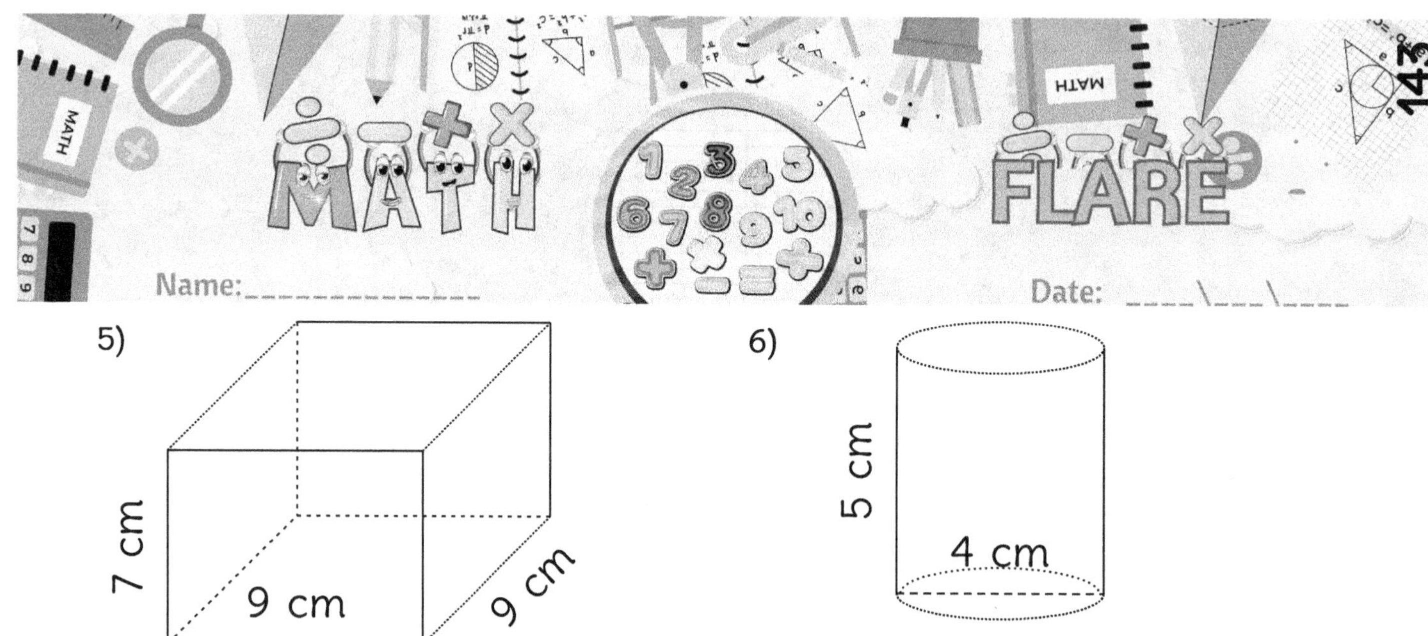

5)

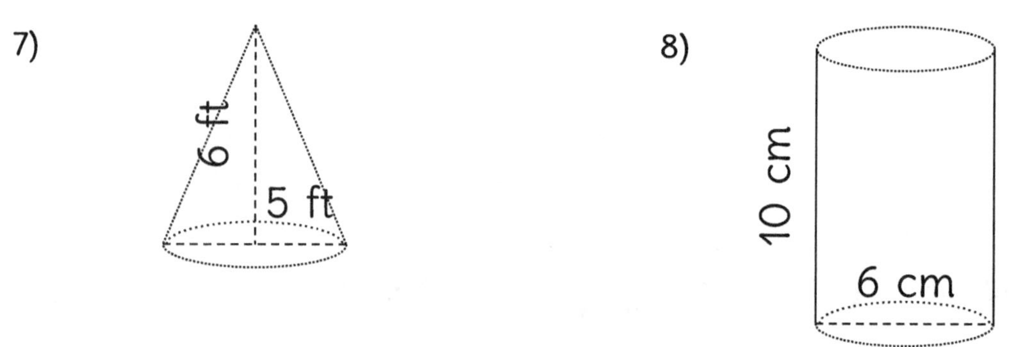

6)

7)

8)

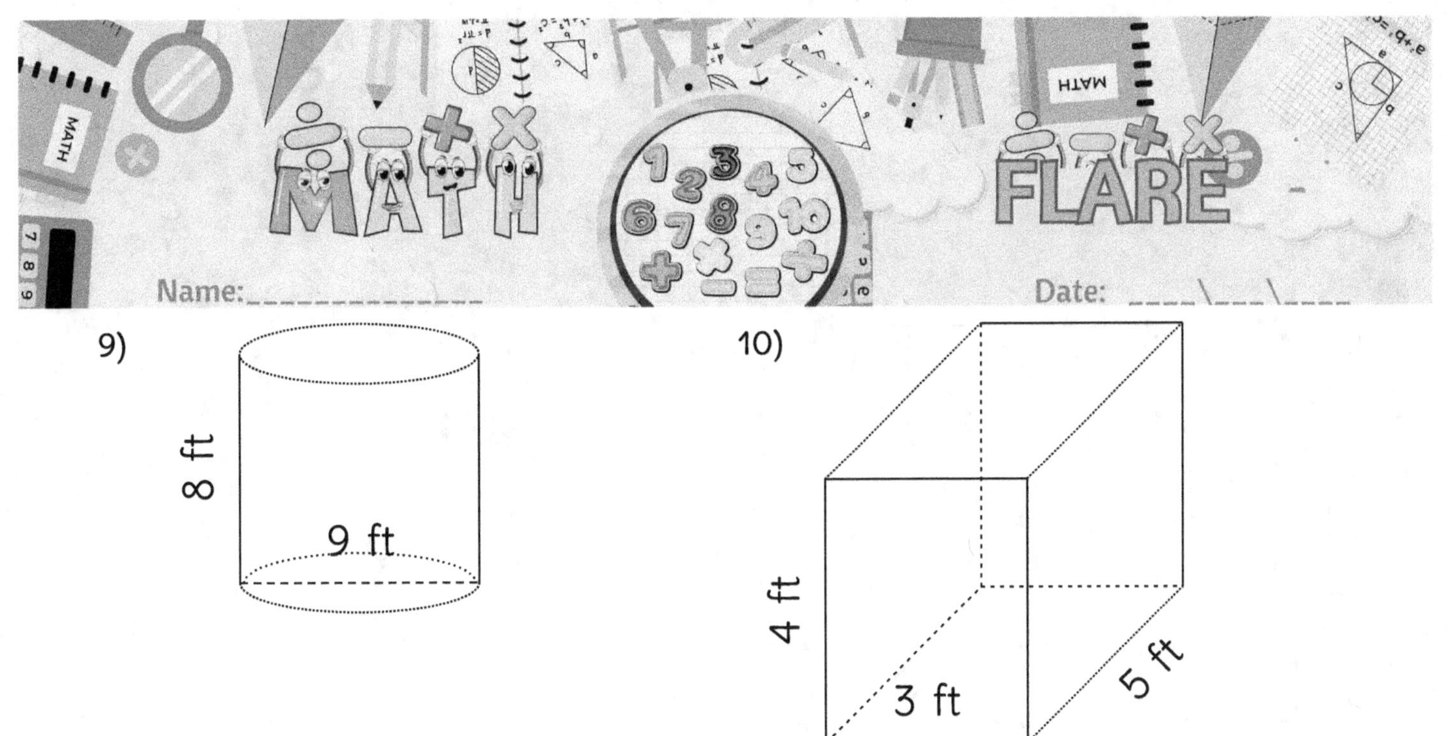

11) 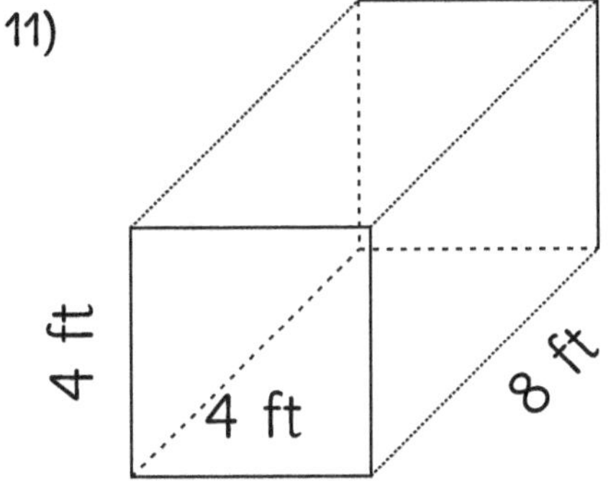

12) 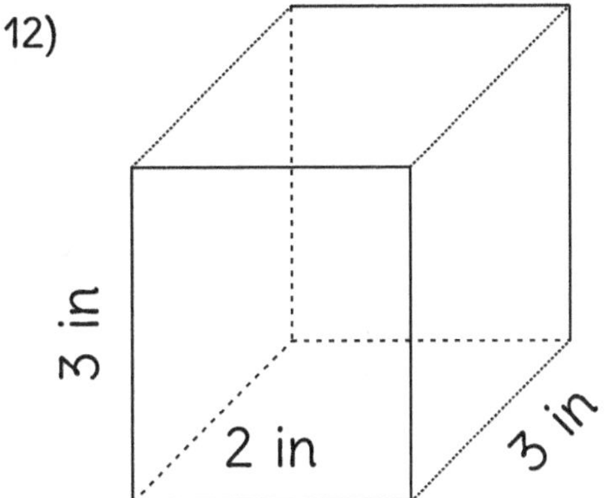

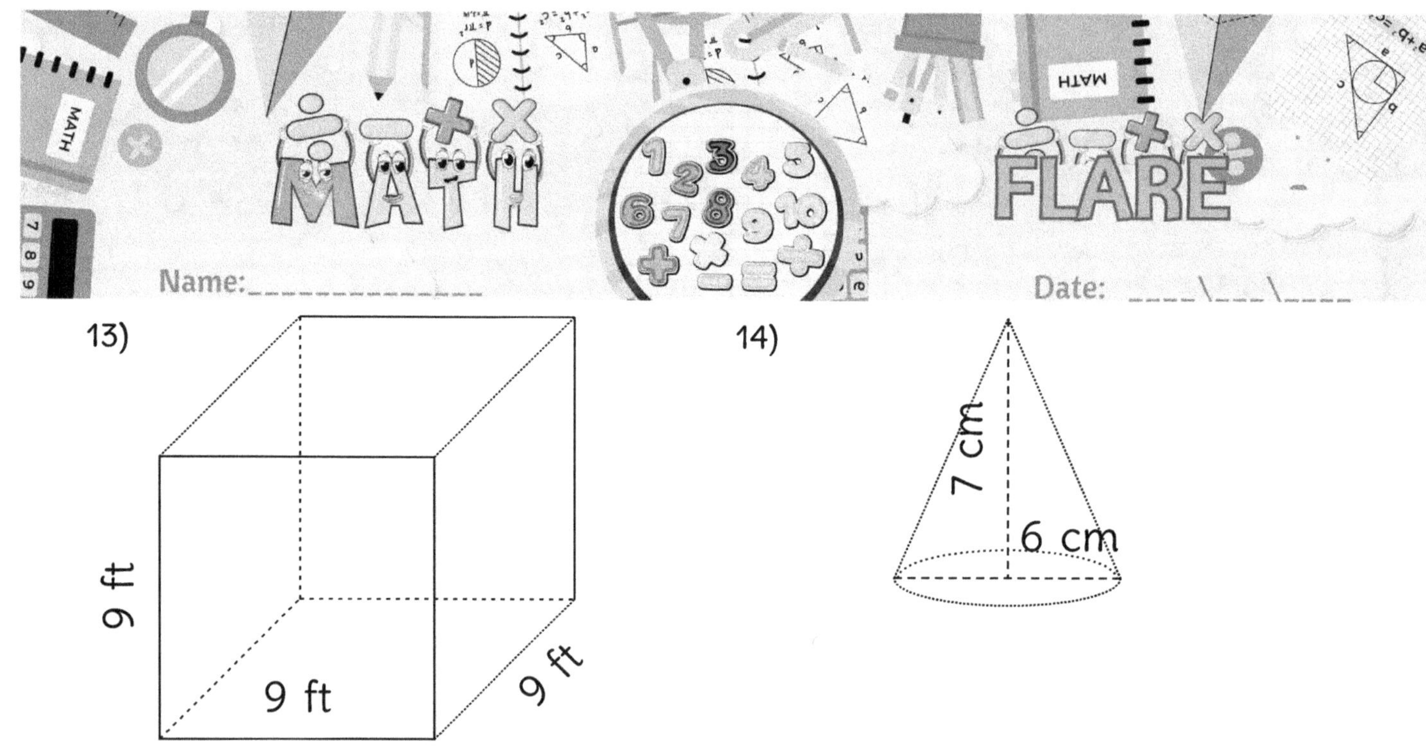

15)

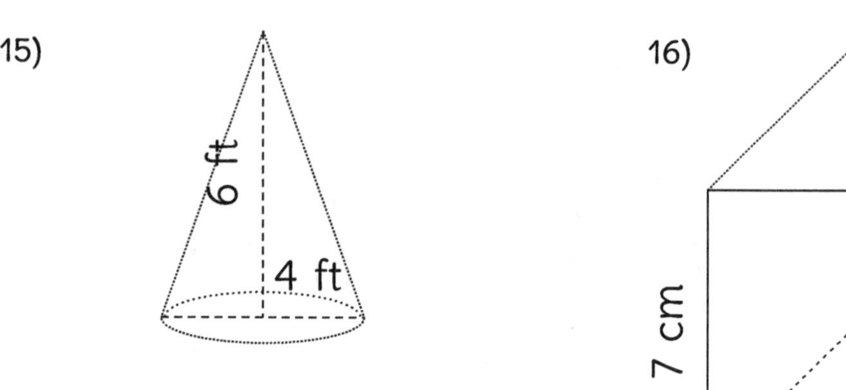

16)

17)

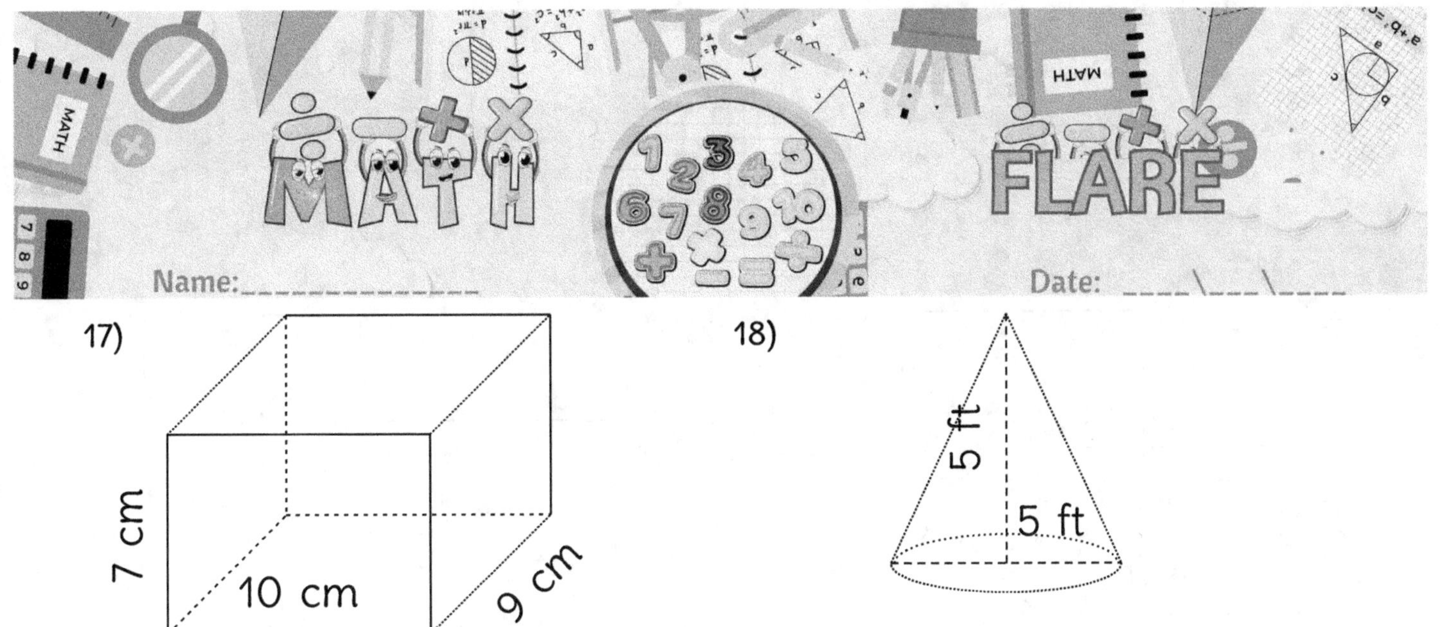

18)

19)

20)

MATH
FLARE
Name:______________
Date: ____________

21)

3 ft
4 ft
4 ft

22)

2 ft
3 ft
2 ft

23)

2 in
2 in
2 in

24)

8 ft
8 ft

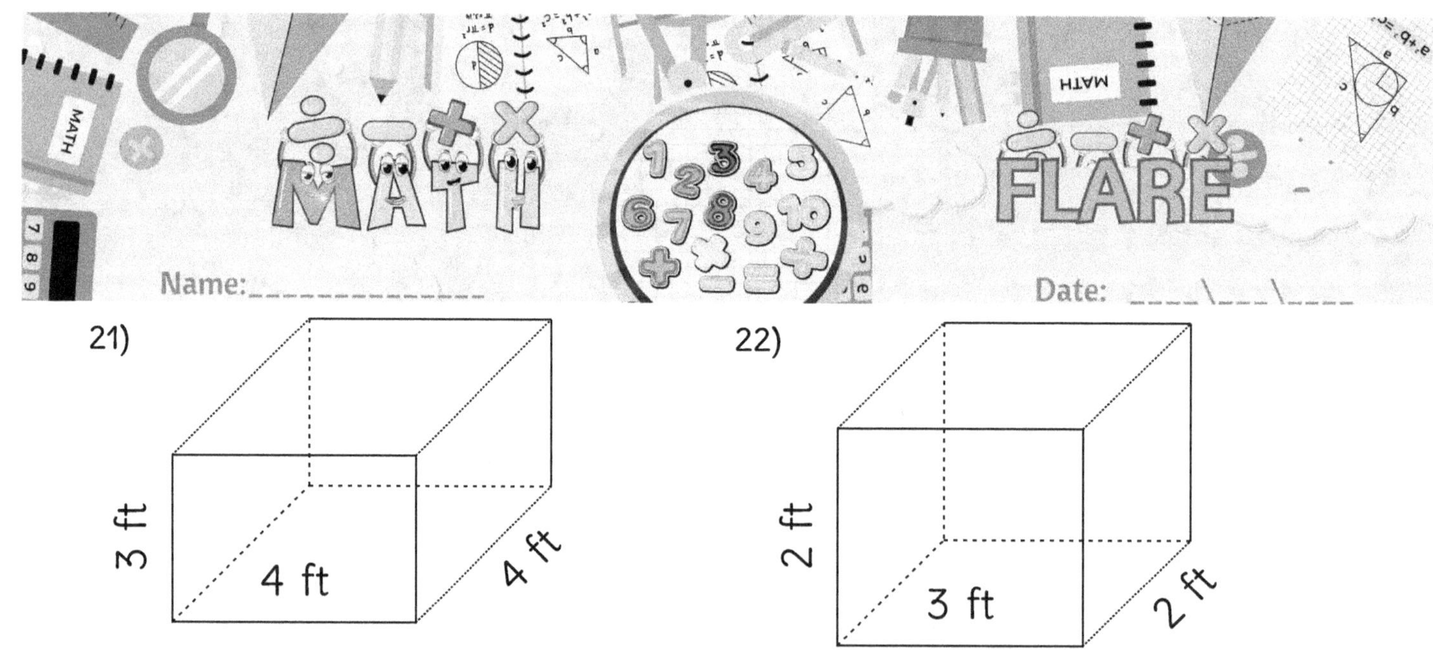

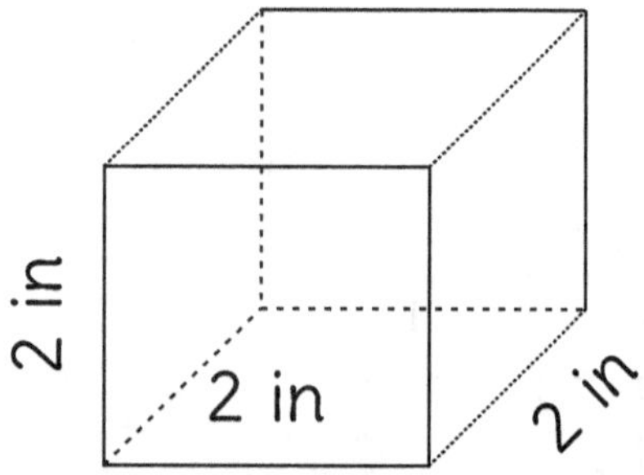

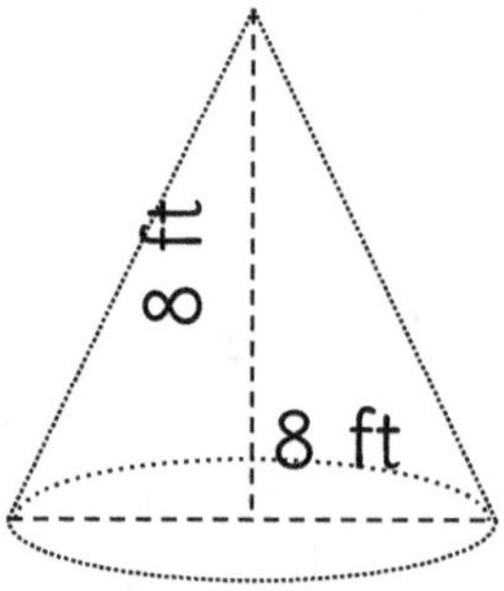

MATH
FLARE
Name:
Date:

25)

7 ft
9 ft
8 ft

26)

5 in
6 in

27)

10 in
10 in
7 in

28)

5 in
5 in
8 in

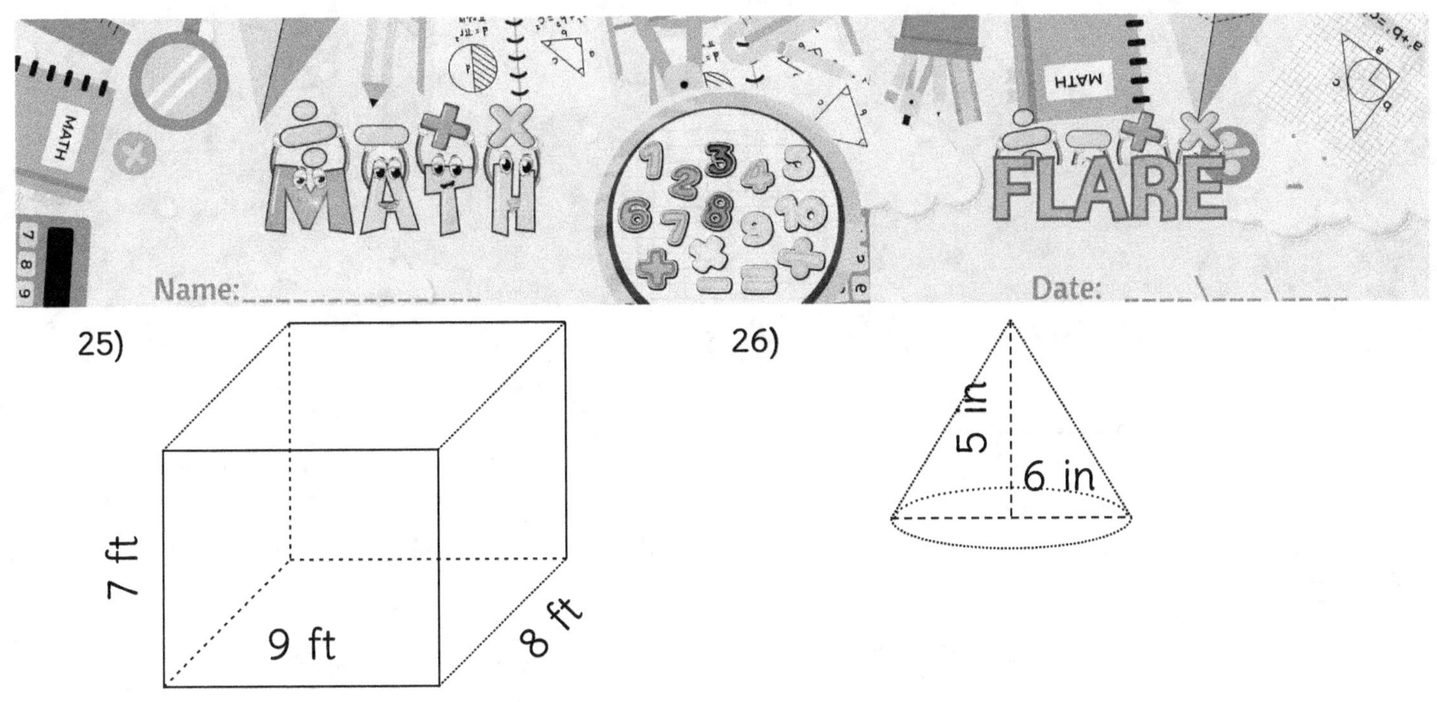

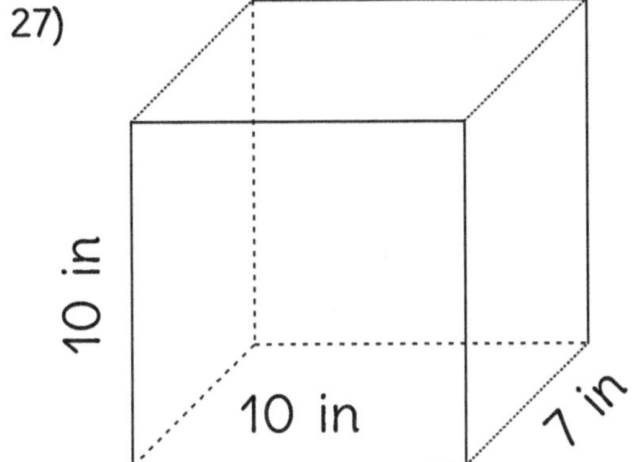

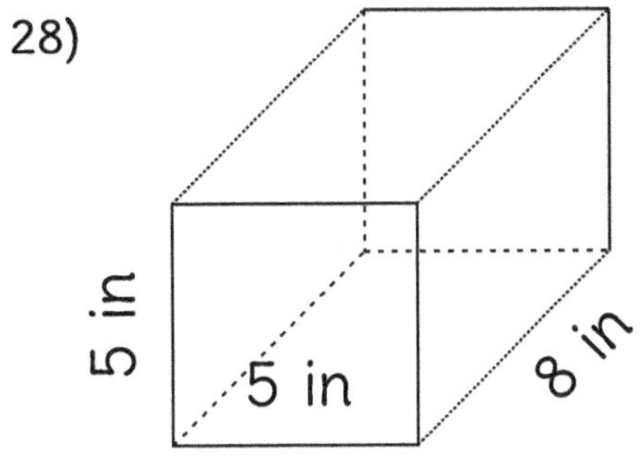

MATH
FLARE
Name:
Date:

29)

10 in
10 in
8 in

30)

4 in
3 in
3 in

31)

6 in
7 in
11 in

32)

8 cm
7 cm

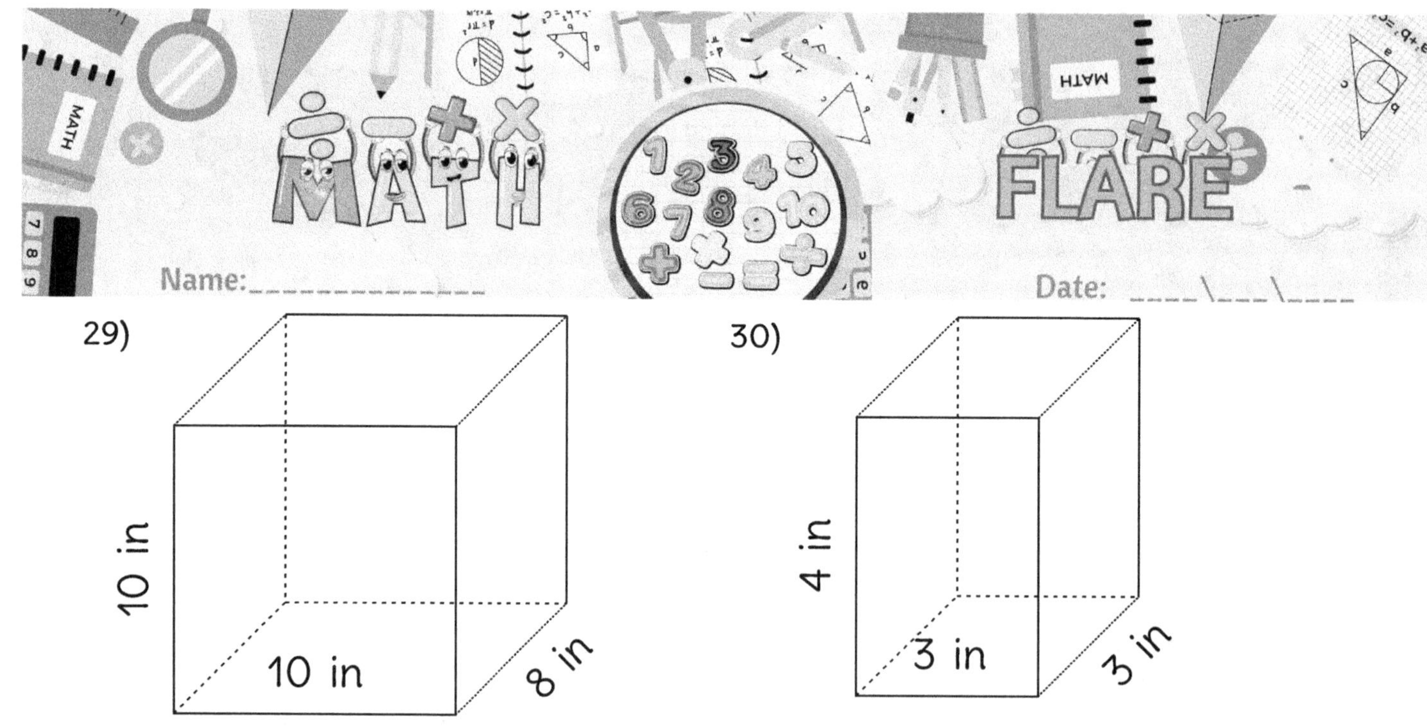

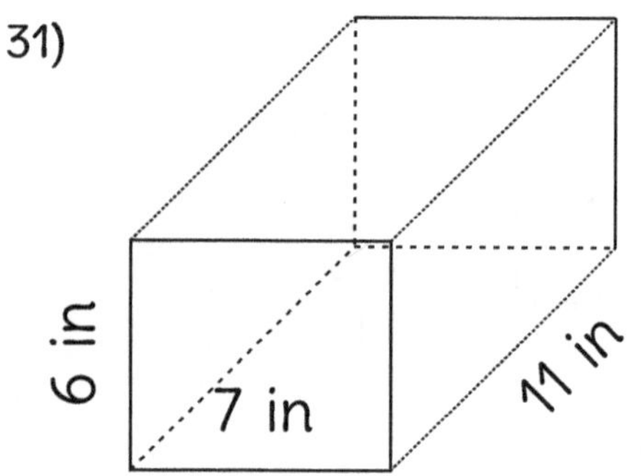

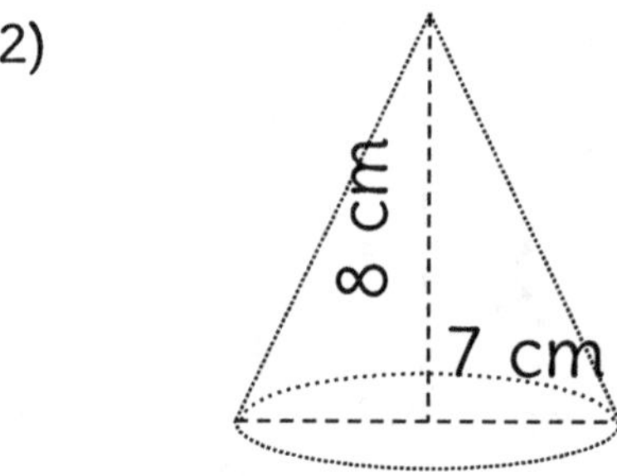

MATH
FLARE
Name: ______________
Date: _______________

33)

5 in
7 in
8 in

34)

7 in
6 in
8 in

35)

6 cm
6 cm
6 cm

36)

5 ft
6 ft
7 ft

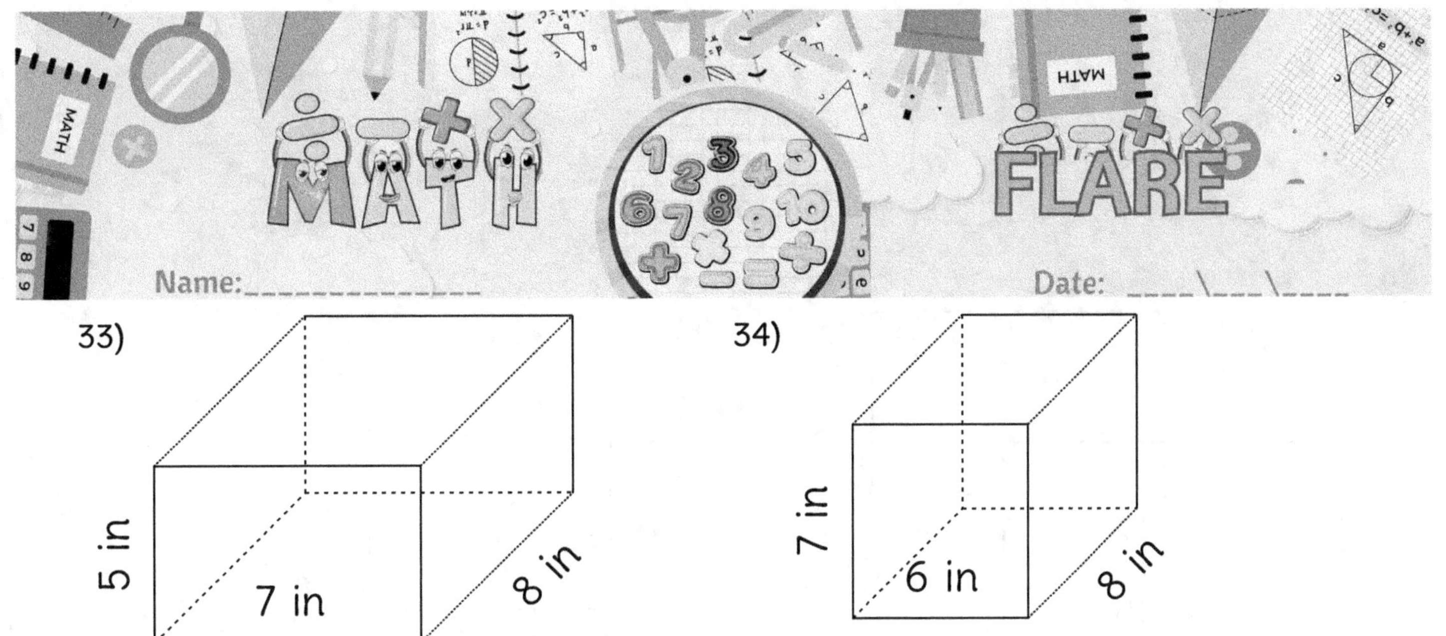

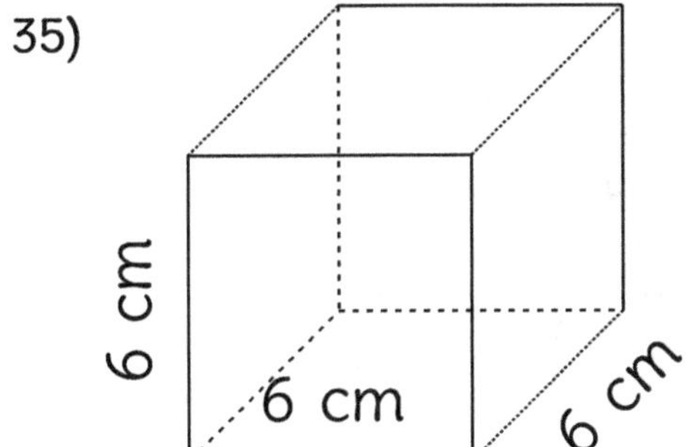

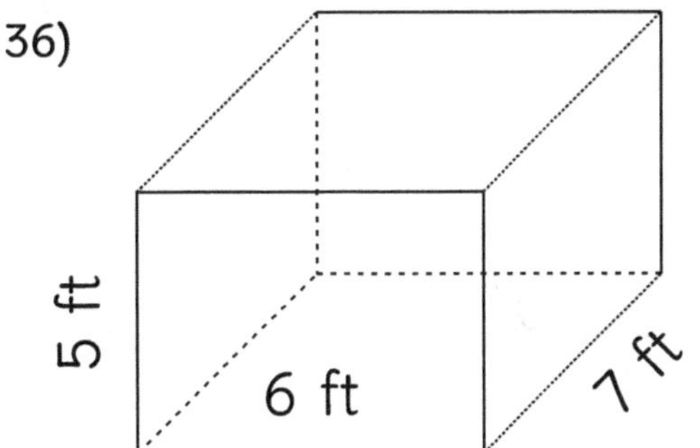

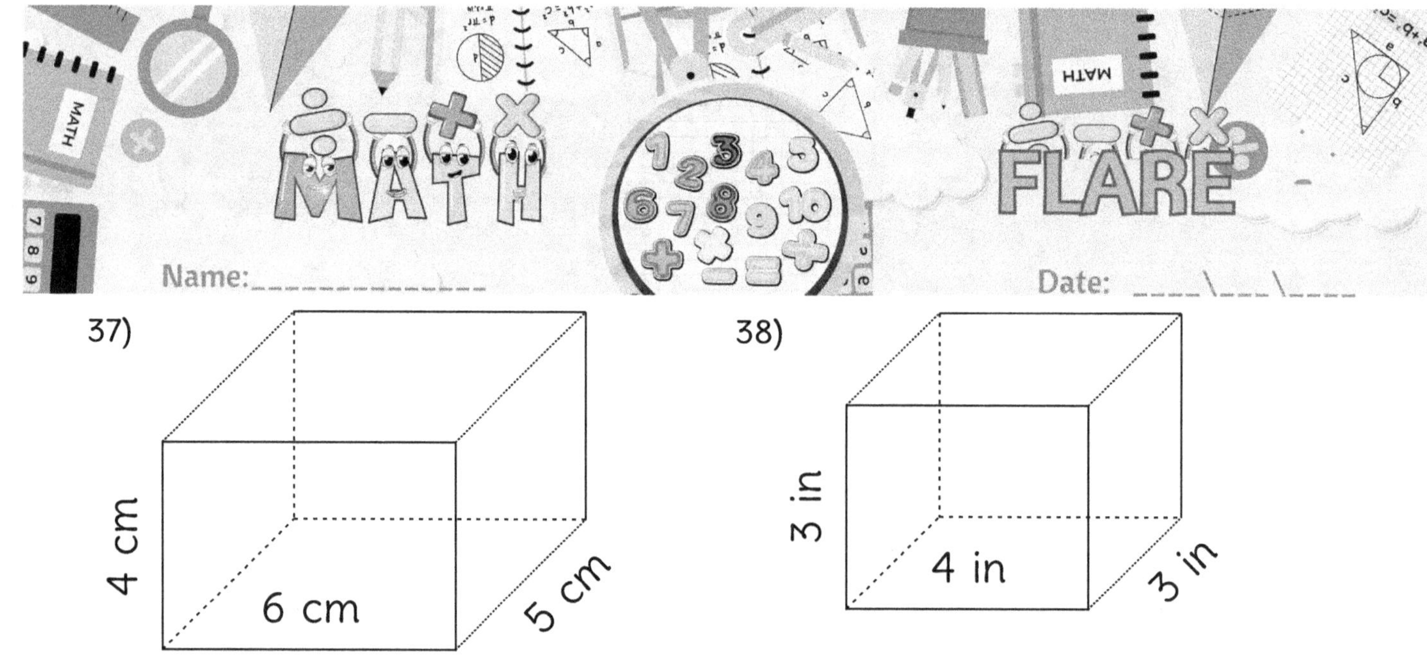

Name:
Date:
37)
4 cm
6 cm
5 cm
38)
3 in
4 in
3 in

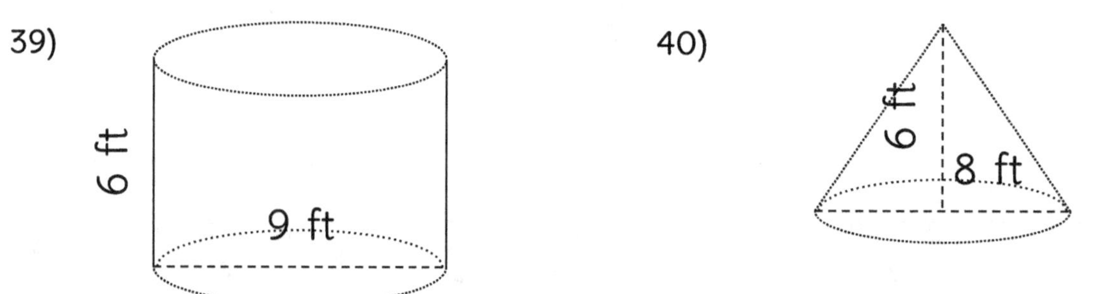

39)
6 ft
9 ft
40)
6 ft
8 ft

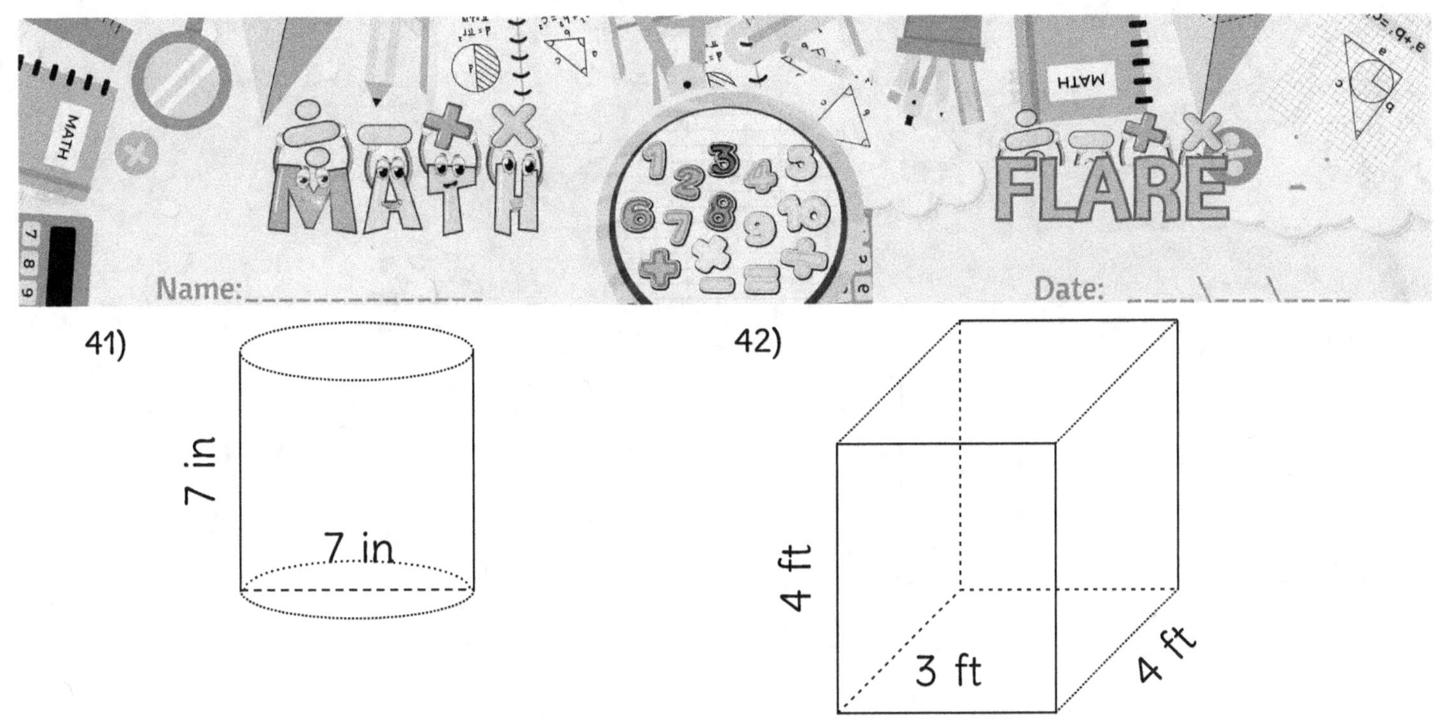

41)

7 in

7 in

42)

4 ft

3 ft

4 ft

43) 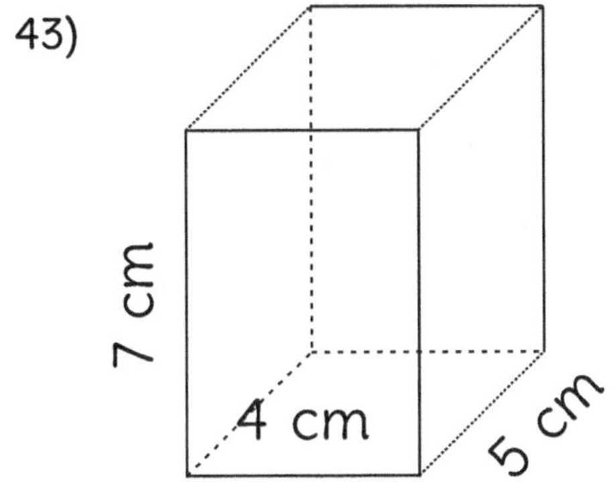

7 cm

4 cm

5 cm

44) 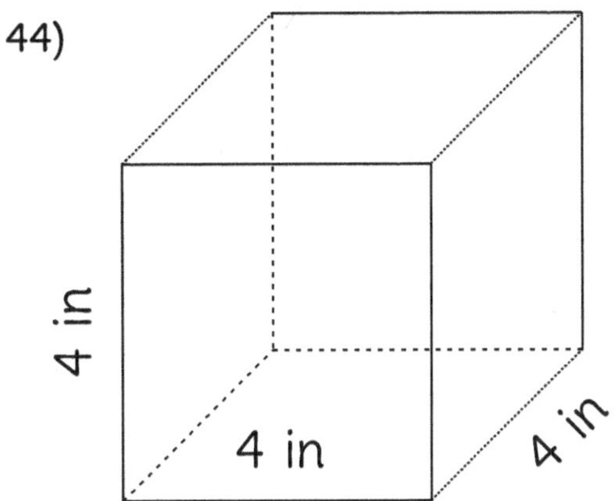

4 in

4 in

4 in

MATH FLARE
Name:
Date:

45)

5 in
6 in
7 in

46)

6 cm
9 cm
6 cm

47)

6 ft
4 ft
7 ft

48)

2 in
4 in

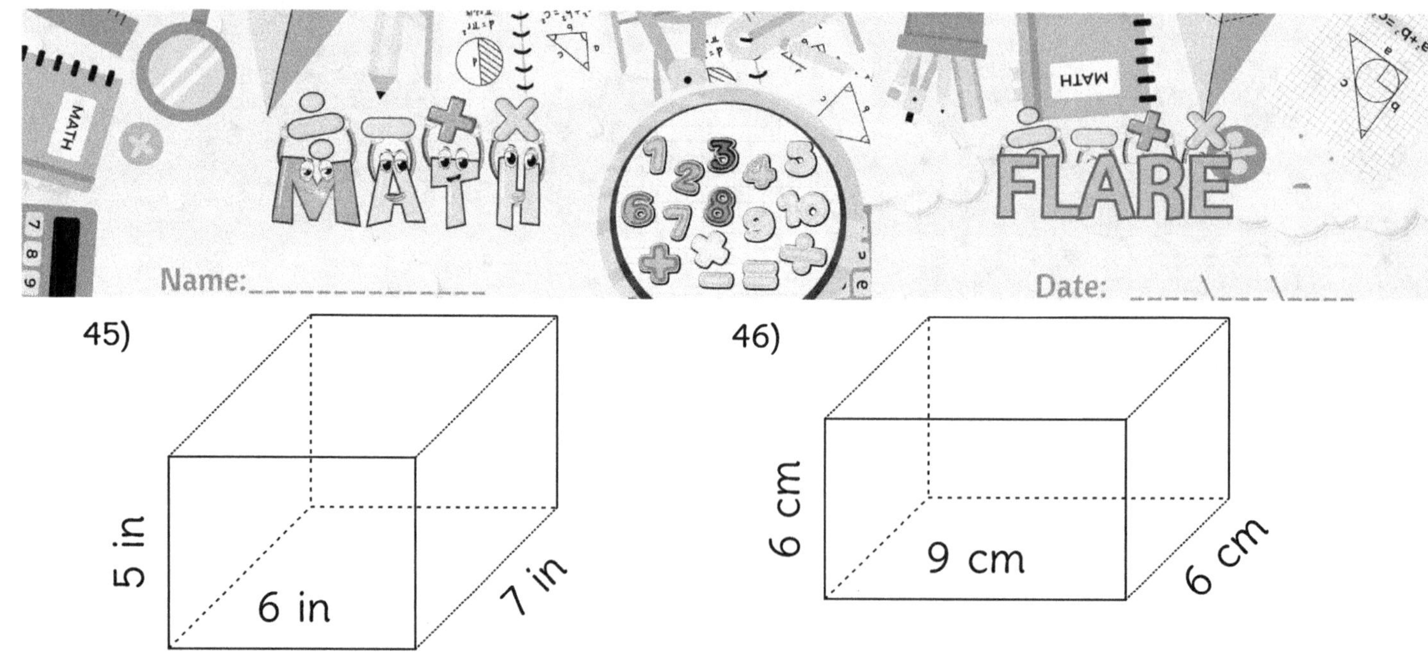

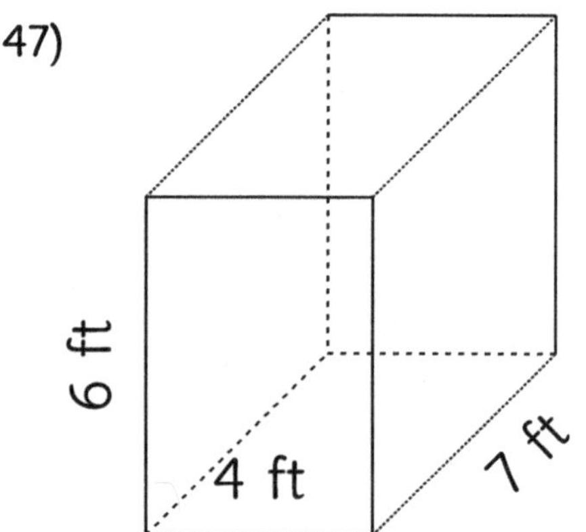

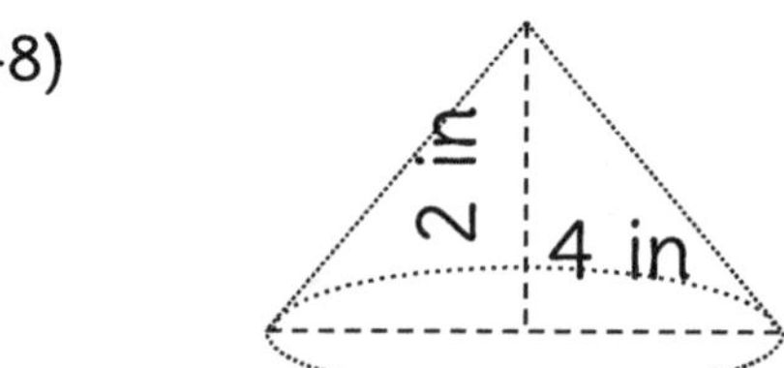

MATH
FLARE
Name:
Date:

49)

9 ft
7 ft
11 ft

50)

4 ft
3 ft
4 ft

51)

2 in
3 in
3 in

52)

4 cm
5 cm
6 cm

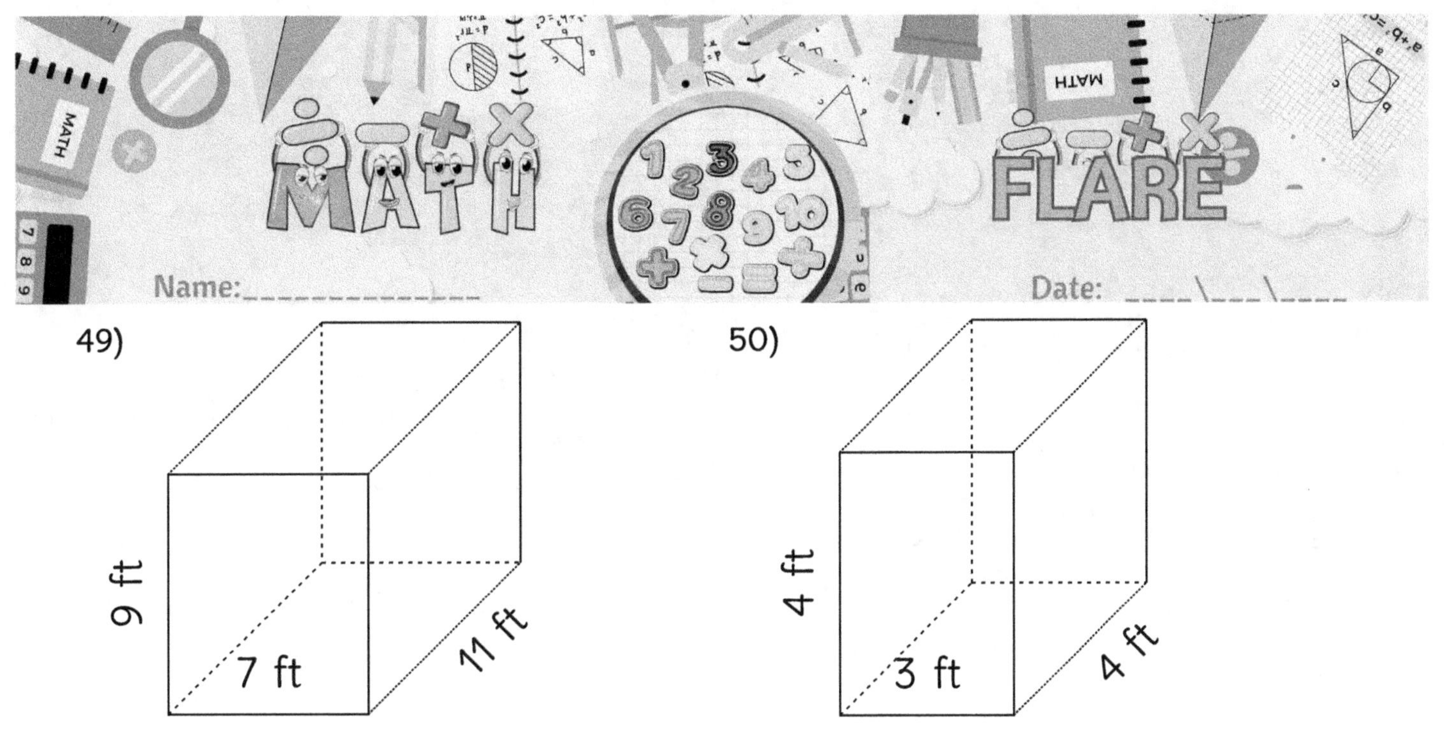

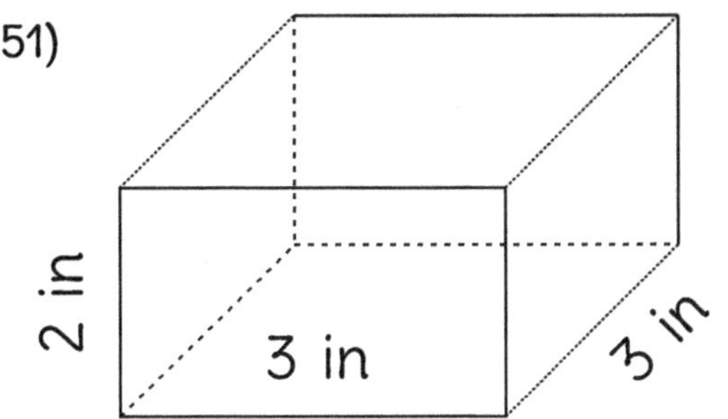

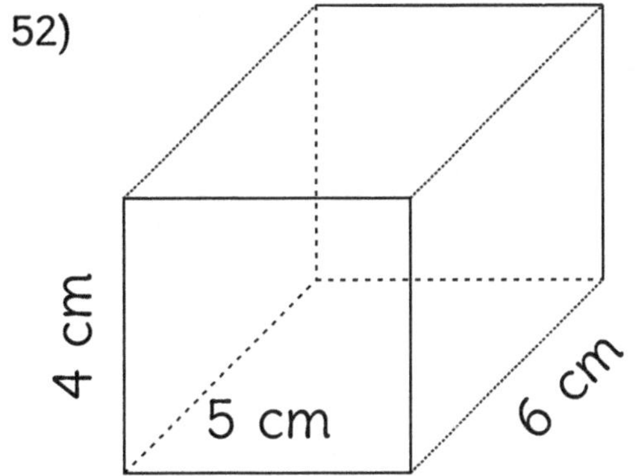

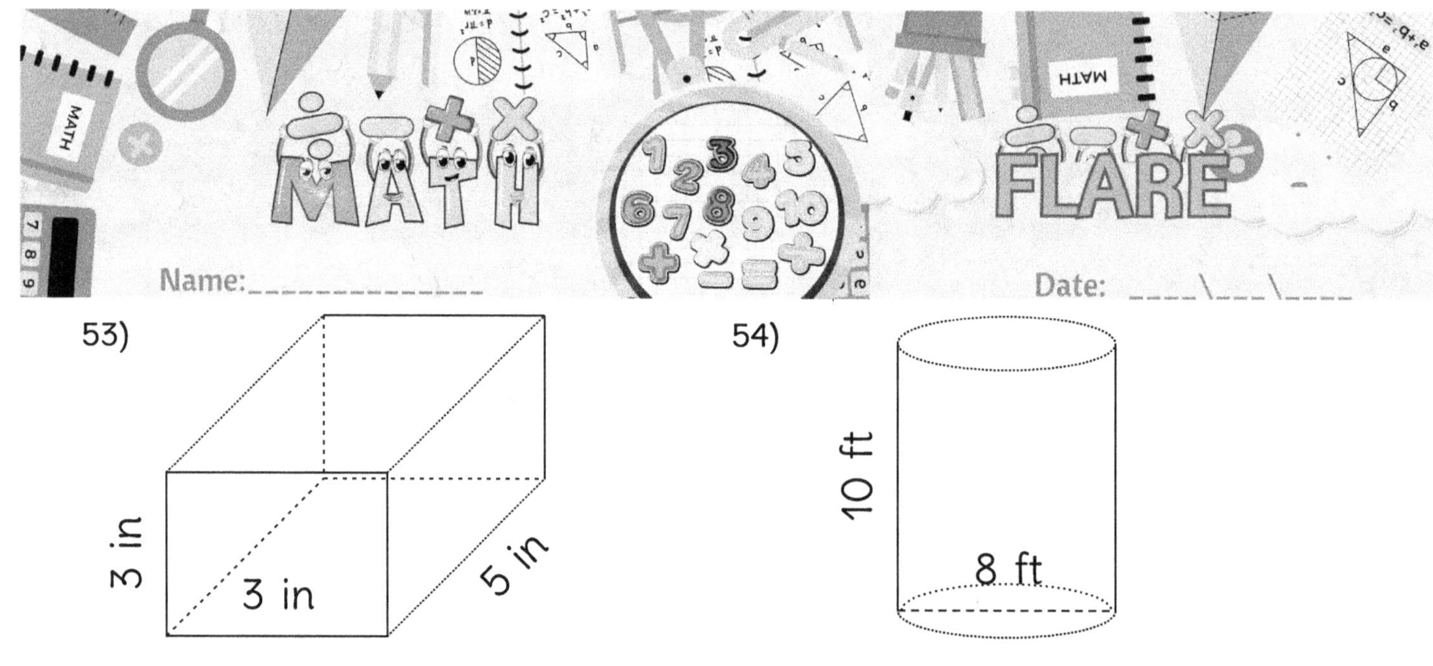

53)

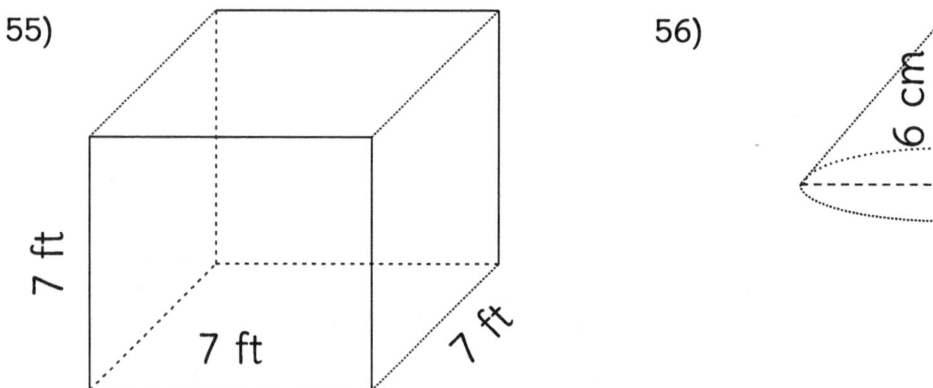

54)

55)

56)

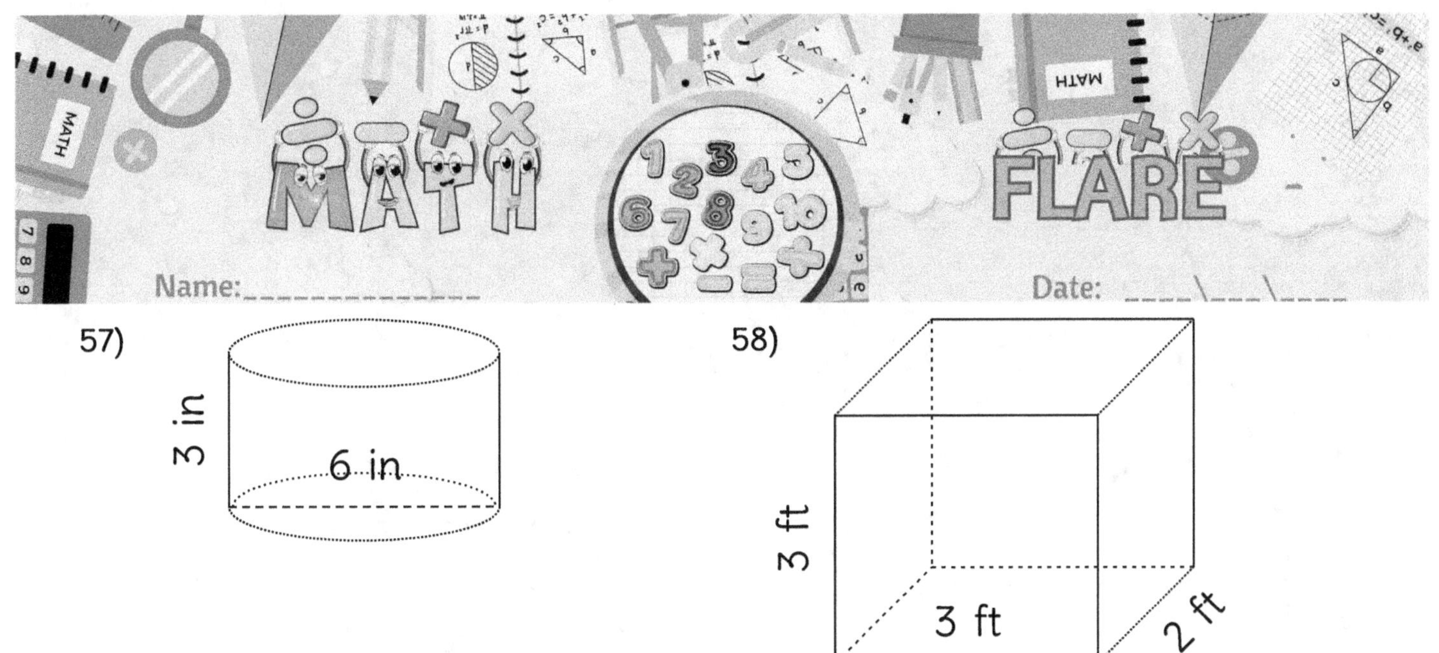

57)

58)

59) 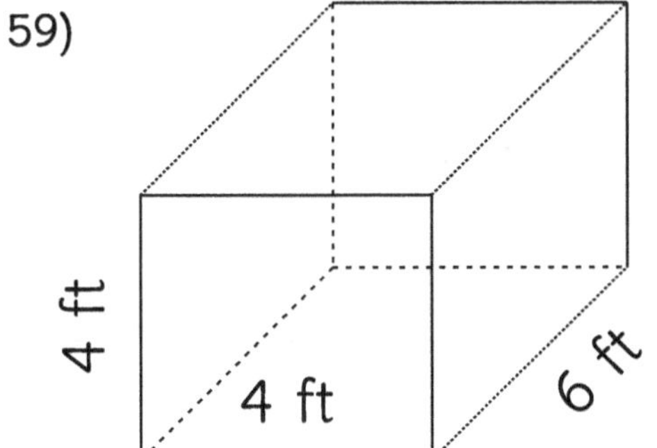

60) 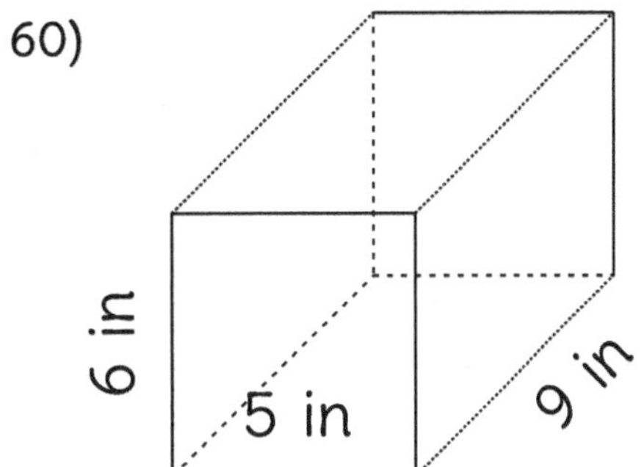

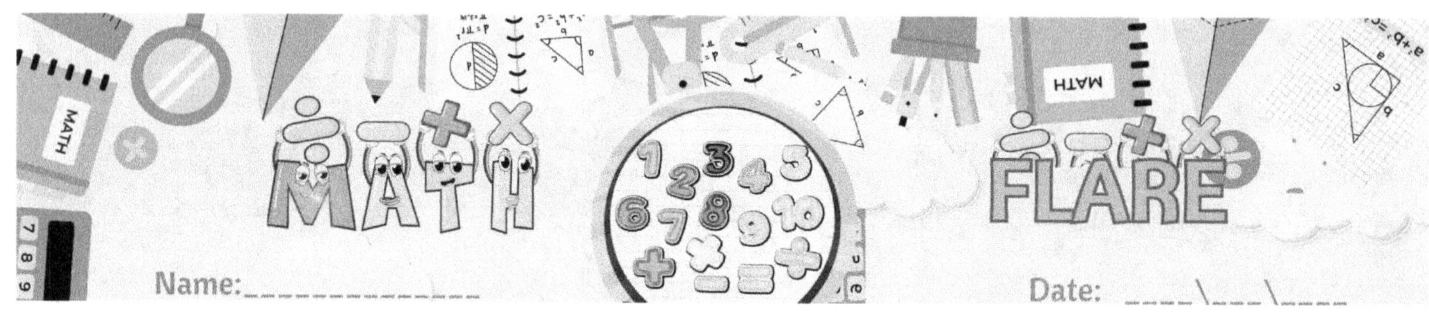

Identify and Describe Shapes

1)

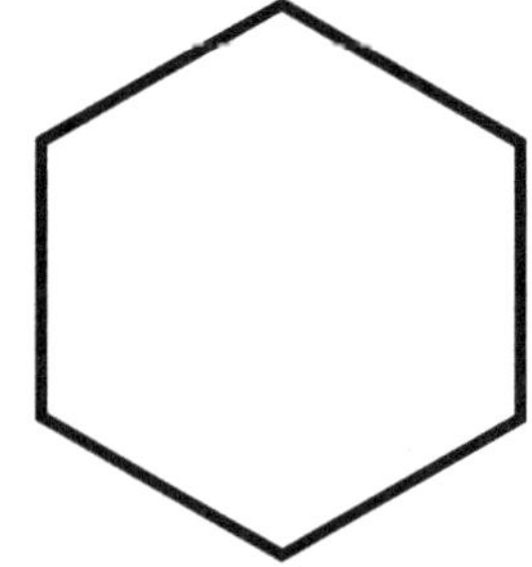

____

2)

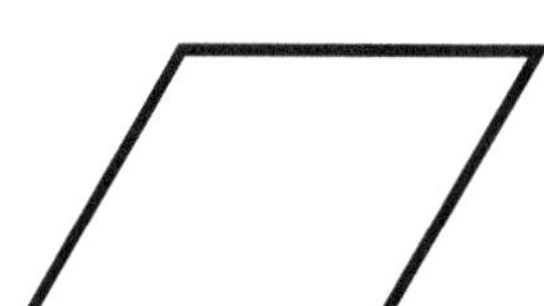

____

3)

____

4)

____

5)

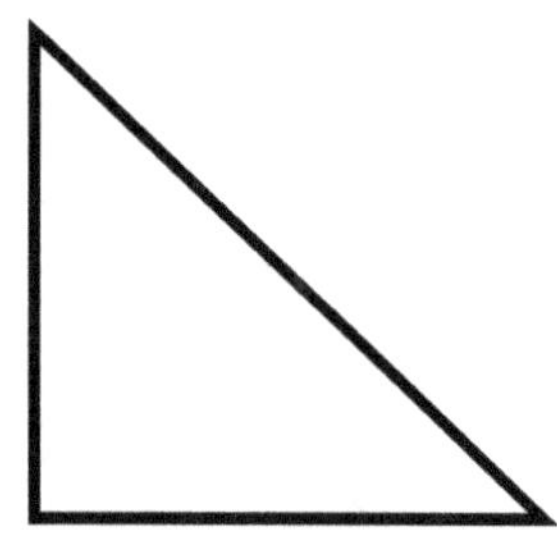

____

6)

____

Chapter. 05

Statistics

Mean

The mean, also known as the average, is a measure of central tendency.

To find the mean of a set of numbers:

- Add up all the numbers in the set.
- Divide the sum by the total count of numbers in the set.

For example: consider the set of numbers: 70, 72, 49, 69, 27, 76.

$$\text{Mean} = \frac{70 + 72 + 49 + 69 + 27 + 76}{6}$$

$$= \frac{363}{6} = 60.5$$

Median

The median is a measure of central tendency that represents the middle value of a dataset when the values are arranged in ascending or descending order.

To find the median of a set of numbers:

- Arrange the numbers in ascending or descending order.
- If the total count of numbers is odd, the median is the middle value.
- If the total count of numbers is even, the median is the average of the two middle values.

For example: consider the set of numbers: 70, 72, 49, 69, 27, 76.

$$27, 49, 69, 70, 72, 76$$

$$\frac{69 + 70}{2} = \frac{139}{2} = 69.5$$

Median =   2   2

Mode

The mode in statistics refers to the value that appears most frequently in a given set of data.

Let's consider the following set of numbers:

$$\{2, 4, 4, 5, 6, 6, 6, 7, 8, 8\}$$

In this set, the number 6 appears three times, more than any other number. Therefore, the mode of this dataset is 6.

It's possible for a dataset to have more than one mode if two or more numbers appear with the same highest frequency. In such cases, the dataset is considered multimodal. If no number repeats, the dataset is considered to have no mode.

For example:

$$\{2, 4, 4, 4, 5, 6, 6, 6, 7, 8, 8\}$$

In this date set, 4 and 6 appear three times. Therefore, this dataset is multimodal.

Range

In statistics, the range refers to the difference between the largest and smallest values in a dataset. It represents the spread or variability of the data.

For example, consider the dataset $\{68, 13, 30, 18, 45, 76, 11\}$:

To calculate the range:

1. Arrange the data points in ascending order.

$$11, 13, 18, 30, 45, 68, 76$$

2. Subtract the smallest value from the largest value.

- The smallest value is 11.

- The largest value is 76.

Range = Largest value - smallest value = 76 - 11 = 65.

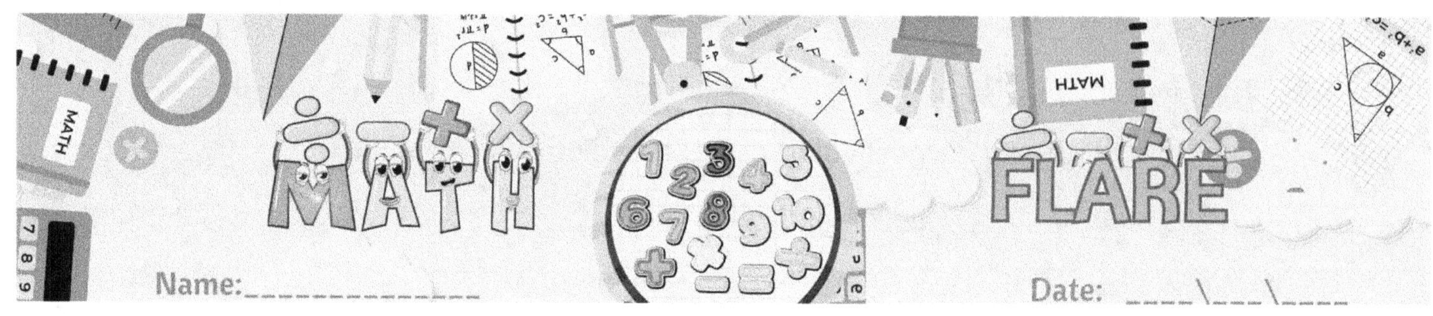

Mean, Median, Mode, and Range

Find the Mean, Median, Mode and Range of the following sets of data.

1) **7, 62, 5, 92, 16, 28**

   Mean = 35   **Median =** 22

   Mode = none **Range =** 87

2) 17, 92, 18, 1, 1, 26

   Mean = _____   Median = _____

   Mode = _____   Range = _____

3) 21, 10, 73, 95, 67, 12

   Mean = _____   Median = _____

   Mode = _____   Range = _____

4) 30, 48, 42, 93, 88, 10, 31

   Mean = _____   Median = _____

   Mode = _____   Range = _____

Name:_______________   Date: ____________

5) 6, 51, 26, 89, 38, 39, 30

   Mean = _______   Median = _____
   Mode = _______   Range = _____

6) 70, 13, 51, 15, 24, 80

   Mean = _______   Median = _____
   Mode = _______   Range = _____

7) 71, 34, 2, 22, 34, 80, 1

   Mean = _______   Median = _____
   Mode = _______   Range = _____

8) 91, 3, 33, 77, 88, 73, 57

   Mean = _______   Median = _____
   Mode = _______   Range = _____

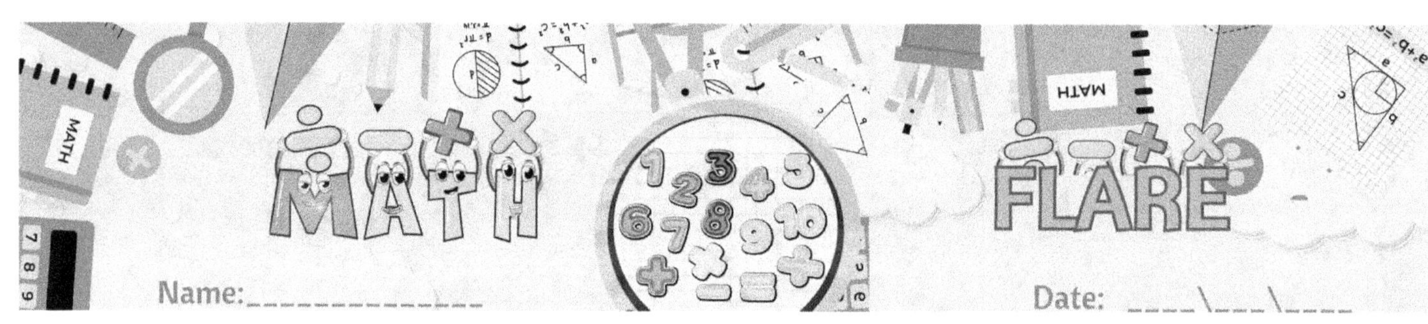

9) 63, 48, 78, 13, 73, 95, 61

Mean = _______   Median = _____

Mode = _______   Range = _____

10) 11, 76, 91, 4, 80, 62

Mean = _____   Median = _____

Mode = _____   Range = _____

11) 70, 56, 8, 58, 58, 72, 86

Mean = _______   Median = _____

Mode = _______   Range = _____

12) 40, 96, 47, 20, 59, 9, 10

Mean = _______   Median = _____

Mode = _______   Range = _____

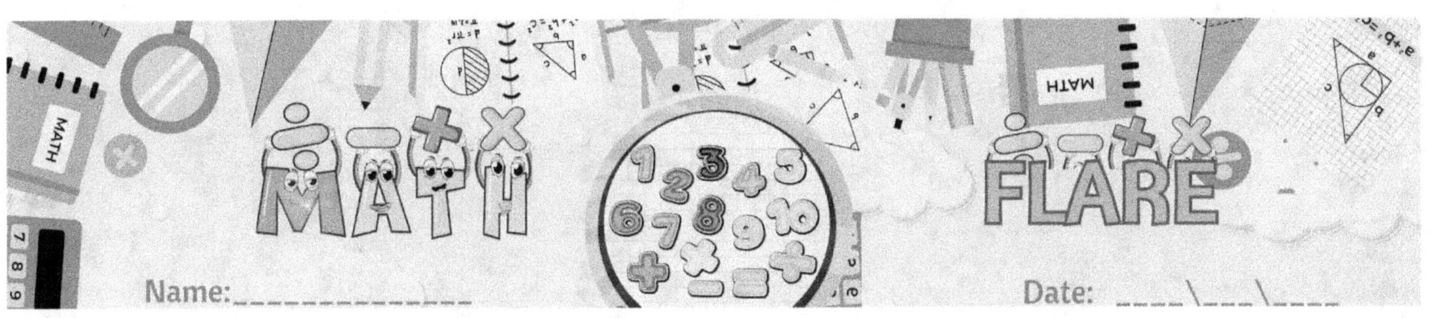

13) 39, 3, 19, 49, 1, 65

Mean = _______   Median = _____

Mode = _______   Range = _____

14) 82, 67, 22, 35, 39, 41, 29

Mean = _____   Median = _____

Mode = _____   Range = _____

15) 19, 61, 57, 11, 19, 54

Mean = _______   Median = _____

Mode = _______   Range = _____

16) 19, 30, 35, 95, 74, 19

Mean = _______   Median = _____

Mode = _______   Range = _____

17) 17, 86, 17, 66, 2, 58, 53

    Mean = ______   Median = ____

    Mode = ______   Range = ____

18) 64, 85, 23, 8, 58, 43, 3

    Mean = ______   Median = ____

    Mode = ______   Range = ____

19) 15, 79, 4, 34, 72, 20, 17

    Mean = ______   Median = ____

    Mode = ______   Range = ____

20) 43, 68, 79, 39, 37, 2

    Mean = ______   Median = ____

    Mode = ______   Range = ____

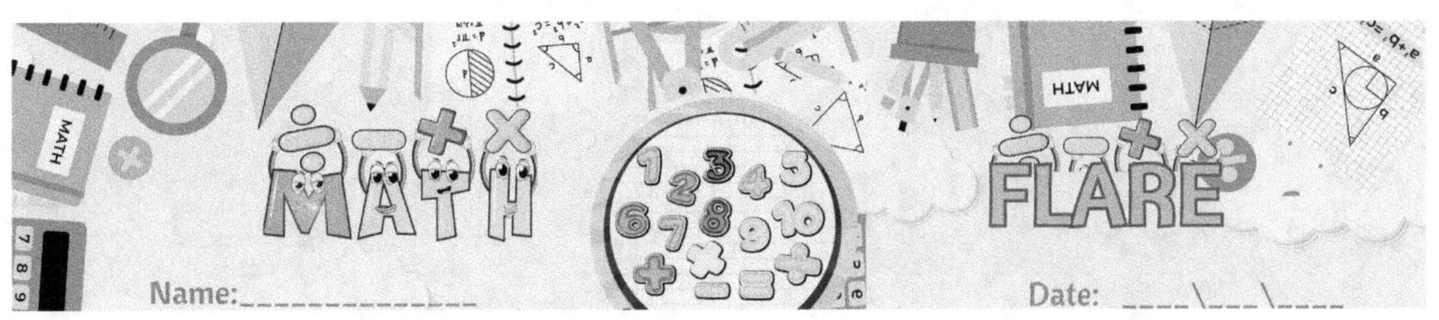

21) 6, 90, 80, 4, 8, 44

Mean = _______   Median = _____

Mode = _______   Range = _____

22) 30, 84, 78, 66, 1, 21, 76

Mean = _______   Median = _____

Mode = _______   Range = _____

23) 85, 77, 43, 96, 54, 99, 67

Mean = _______   Median = _____

Mode = _______   Range = _____

24) 17, 39, 39, 26, 1, 23

Mean = _______   Median = _____

Mode = _______   Range = _____

ANSWERS

Page 1:   Order of Operations (PEMDAS)

1. 88	2. 146	3. 323	4. 2,502	5. 107	6. 63
7. 204	8. 42	9. 36	10. 36	11. 0.3	12. 130
13. 91	14. 903	15. 1.8	16. 2.6	17. 3.8	18. 18
19. 19	20. 23	21. 11	22. 7	23. 560	24. 19
25. 225	26. 12	27. 4,910	28. 8	29. 14	30. 36
31. 325	32. 32	33. 14	34. 14	35. 83	36. 13
37. 2,406	38. 265	39. 244	40. 2,308	41. 22	42. 19
43. -0.8	44. 48	45. 132	46. 88	47. 12	48. -6
49. 35	50. 12	51. 56	52. 14	53. 230	54. 1,303
55. 12	56. 2				

Page 7:   Solving Equations: (One Step)

1. $y = 17$	2. $y = 6$	3. $x = 5$	4. $x = 2$	5. $y = 15$
6. $y = 11$	7. $x = 3$	8. $x = 5$	9. $y = 10$	10. $x = 5$
11. $y = 1$	12. $y = 12$	13. $y = 22$	14. $y = 2$	15. $y = 12$
16. $x = 2$	17. $x = 14$	18. $x = 5$	19. $y = 19$	20. $y = 16$
21. $y = 20$	22. $x = 4$	23. $y = 8$	24. $y = 20$	25. $y = 16$
26. $y = 19$	27. $y = 4$	28. $x = 2$	29. $y = 8$	30. $x = 2$
31. $x = 17$	32. $y = 11$	33. $y = 15$	34. $x = 19$	35. $x = 1$
36. $x = 7$	37. $y = 10$	38. $x = 6$	39. $y = 20$	40. $y = 19$

41. y = 7   42. x = 5   43. y = 12   44. y = 1   45. x = 1

46. x = 13   47. x = 20   48. y = 14   49. y = 11   50. x = 18

51. y = 3   52. y = 20   53. y = 12   54. x = 128   55. x = 17

56. x = 12   57. x = 9   58. y = 2   59. x = 2   60. x = 8

61. y = 133   62. y = 3   63. x = 8   64. x = 9   65. x = 4

66. x = 10   67. y = 200   68. x = 4   69. x = 16   70. x = 17

71. y = 7   72. x = 8   73. x = 16   74. x = 7   75. y = 16

76. y = 15   77. x = 10   78. y = 19   79. x = 17   80. y = 7

81. x = 1   82. x = 19   83. y = 17   84. y = 20   85. y = 9

86. x = 8   87. y = 10   88. y = 14

Page 16:   Equations (Two Steps)

1. x = 7   2. x = 7   3. y = 2   4. z = 7   5. y = 4   6. z = 6

7. z = 8   8. x = 4   9. x = 5   10. x = 1   11. y = 4   12. x = 8

13. y = 9   14. x = 4   15. y = 9   16. y = 9   17. z = 2   18. z = 1

19. z = 7   20. y = 7   21. x = 5   22. x = 4   23. x = 9   24. x = 2

25. x = 6   26. y = 7   27. z = 5   28. x = 8   29. z = 3   30. x = 2

31. x = 2   32. z = 9   33. z = 9   34. x = 2   35. z = 5   36. y = 9

37. y = 5   38. y = 2   39. x = 7   40. y = 6   41. x = 4   42. z = 2

43. x = 6   44. z = 1   45. y = 5   46. z = 8   47. y = 3   48. z = 6

49. y = 5   50. y = 4   51. y = 5   52. z = 6   53. x = 9   54. y = 4

55. z = 8   56. x = 1   57. x = 6   58. x = 3   59. y = 3   60. z = 1

61. x = 7   62. y = 7   63. y = 2   64. z = 6   65. x = 1   66. y = 4

67. y = 3   68. x = 8   69. x = 3   70. x = 1   71. x = 1   72. x = 8

73. z = 5   74. x = 8   75. x = 3   76. x = 3   77. x = 1   78. x = 6

79. y = 3   80. y = 9

Page 32: Evaluate Expressions

1. 19   2. 3   3. 5.5   4. 10   5. 4   6. 16   7. 7   8. 34

Page 33: Evaluate Expressions

1. 0   2. 3   3. 7   4. 10   5. 11   6. 5   7. 9   8. 4

Page 34: Evaluate Expressions

1. 5   2. 0.6   3. 19   4. 128   5. 9   6. 5   7. 3   8. 21

Page 35: Evaluate Expressions

1. 10   2. 268   3. 686   4. 21   5. 3.4   6. 6   7. 14   8. 0.8

Page 36: Evaluate Expressions

1. 784   2. -45   3. 12   4. 22   5. 15   6. 3   7. -1   8. 4

Page 37: Evaluate Expressions

1. 1.3   2. 3   3. 5   4. 56   5. 16   6. 576   7. 8.2   8. 1.5

Page 38: Evaluate Expressions

1. 1.8   2. 11   3. 1.2   4. 1   5. 3.4   6. 56   7. 2.4   8. 12

Page 39: Evaluate Expressions

1. 0   2. 24   3. 10   4. 9   5. 8   6. 17   7. 9   8. 2

Page 40: Evaluate Equations

1. 4   2. 9   3. 1   4. 4   5. 6

6. 9   7. 7   8. 9   9. 5   10. 2

11. 1	12. 7	13. 3	14. 8	15. 3
16. 8	17. 3	18. 2 or -2	19. 6	20. 1
21. 6	22. 2	23. 1	24. 6 or -2	25. 8
26. 1	27. 7	28. 7	29. 8	30. 4
31. 1	32. 6	33. 6 or -13	34. 6	35. 1
36. 8	37. 5	38. 4	39. 8	

Page 50: Find Numbers

1. 16	2. 5, 50	3. 26, 8	4. 4
5. 1, 3, 5	6. 6, 60	7. 8	8. 7
9. 5, 35	10. 6, 1	11. 5, 1	12. 2
13. 12	14. 8	15. 1	16. 9
17. 5, 7, 9, 11	18. 10, 8	19. 9, 7	20. 9
21. 14	22. 8	23. 3	24. 5, 7, 9
25. 1	26. 4	27. 9	28. 33, 5
29. 2	30. 6	31. 4, 2	32. 3, 5, 7
33. 1	34. 10	35. 0	36. 7
37. 12	38. 1, 9	39. 9, 2	40. 54
41. 4	42. 14	43. 9	44. 9
45. 12	46. 3	47. 6, 8, 10	48. 9, 36
49. 8, 72	50. 10, 12, 14	51. 4, 6, 8, 10	52. 3
53. 2	54. 4, 2	55. 5	56. 6, 12

57. 16, 9   58. 10, 4   59. 1, 7

Page 63: Solving Inequalities

1. $m \geq -2$ 2. $x \leq -5$ 3. $z < 3$ 4. $z \leq 5$ 5. $k \leq -3$

6. $m > -5/2$ 7. $y > 11$ 8. $x < -1$ 9. $y \leq -6/5$ 10. $y < 5$

11. $y < 5$ 12. $m < 2$ 13. $m \geq 9$ 14. $m < 0$ 15. $m \geq -17$

16. $k < 3/5$ 17. $z < -10$ 18. $x \leq -4/7$ 19. $m < 11$ 20. $m \geq -1$

21. $m \geq -24$ 22. $y > -3$ 23. $m \leq -3/2$ 24. $y > -5$ 25. $m < -5/4$

26. $m < -27$ 27. $m > -2$ 28. $k \leq 16$ 29. $k > -35$ 30. $x < -8$

31. $x \leq -6/7$ 32. $z < -10$ 33. $m < 17$ 34. $k \leq 5$ 35. $k \leq -5/6$

36. $k > 28$ 37. $k > -9$ 38. $m < -5/4$ 39. $m \leq 12$ 40. $k > 4$

41. $x \leq 16$ 42. $k > -6$ 43. $y < -8$ 44. $y > -3$ 45. $z \geq 5/3$

46. $m \leq 16$ 47. $z < -12$ 48. $x > -7$ 49. $y \geq 15$ 50. $z > 7$

51. $m < -2$ 52. $m > -5$ 53. $y \geq -4$ 54. $x > 1/2$ 55. $x \leq -1$

56. $y \leq 15$ 57. $m \leq -5$ 58. $k \geq 2$ 59. $y \geq -2$ 60. $y \leq 0$

61. $z > 3$ 62. $y < -18$ 63. $m \geq -3$ 64. $m > 14$ 65. $k < 24$

66. $z < 15$ 67. $z < -13$ 68. $k \geq 2$ 69. $m > -7$ 70. $k \leq 8$

71. $z \leq 16$ 72. $y < 1/2$ 73. $k > 12$ 74. $k \leq 11$ 75. $y \geq 3$

76. $k \geq 6$ 77. $k \leq -3$ 78. $x \leq -6$ 79. $z < 6/5$ 80. $z \geq -1$

Page 83: Proportion Relationship

1. 14   2. 8   3. 2   4. 33   5. 1   6. 8   7. 7   8. 8

9. 18   10. 3   11. 4   12. 4   13. 120   14. 4   15. 17   16. 12

17. 9   18. 14   19. 88   20. 24   21. 8   22. 10   23. 30   24. 5

25. 4   26. 7   27. 5   28. 70   29. 12   30. 11   31. 8   32. 2

33. 5   34. 17   35. 5   36. 54   37. 70   38. 75   39. 3   40. 9

41. 133   42. 30   43. 8   44. 52   45. 16   46. 96   47. 6   48. 18

49. 11   50. 56   51. 45   52. 7   53. 5   54. 20   55. 11   56. 24

57. 63   58. 14   59. 8   60. 42   61. 54   62. 12   63. 19   64. 110

65. 6   66. 4   67. 25   68. 14   69. 33   70. 4   71. 12   72. 6

73. 1   74. 48   75. 65   76. 27   77. 10   78. 3   79. 9   80. 4

Page 91:   Ratio and Proportion Word Problems

1. 3.4   2. 12   3. 14   4. 16.44   5. 1.83   6. 340.5

7. 765   8. 9.33   9. 27.33   10. 6.5   11. 39.67   12. 12

13. 8.77   14. 830   15. 3.3   16. 15.43   17. 2.74   18. 17.27

19. 641.33   20. 9.86   21. 25.19   22. 3.8   23. 88   24. 157.14

25. 2.67   26. 8.8   27. 2.25   28. 758.8   29. 13.5   30. 8.25

Page 101:   Percentage

1. 75%   2. 80%   3. 400   4. 300   5. 15%   6. 200

7. 5   8. 25%   9. 7%   10. 1%   11. 500   12. 0.2

13. 700   14. 200%   15. 36   16. 900   17. 75   18. 300%

19. 100   20. 100   21. 7   22. 60   23. 500   24. 300

25. 200   26. 300   27. 3%   28. 200   29. 100   30. 90

31. 4%   32. 42   33. 6   34. 350   35. 10   36. 40

37. 500   38. 90   39. 600   40. 9   41. 5%   42. 280

43. 15%   44. 1600   45. 800   46. 200   47. 6%   48. 210

49. 60%   50. 500   51. 9%   52. 500   53. 900   54. 270

55. 8   56. 800   57. 900   58. 300%   59. 800   60. 8

Page 106:

1. 0.094   2. 3   3. 8.8%   4. 1   5. 468

6. 18.06   7. 1.007   8. 0.1%   9. 0.18   10. 0.336

11. 0.774   12. 50   13. 0.036   14. 13.464   15. 904

16. 0.07   17. 5   18. 4   19. 7.3%   20. 710

21. 8.9%   22. 772   23. 712   24. 2   25. 949

26. 6   27. 152   28. 0.6%   29. 6.3%   30. 6.0%

31. 1   32. 7.1%   33. 6.882   34. 1.732   35. 2

36. 443   37. 3.649   38. 0.01   39. 8   40. 1.9%

41. 0.006   42. 82   43. 137   44. 123   45. 6

46. 0.783   47. 63.624   48. 69   49. 0.1%   50. 8.8%

51. 0.7%   52. 606   53. 0.266   54. 8.9%   55. 3.4%

56. 0.2%   57. 76.342   58. 1.383   59. 0.5%   60. 0.9%

61. 7   62. 697   63. 5.22   64. 4.332   65. 7.1%

66. 59   67. 252   68. 0.8%   69. 794   70. 8.9%

Page 112: Convert: Ratio, Fraction, Percent, and Decimals

1.

	Ratio	Fraction	Percent	Decimal
a.	3:4	3/4	75%	0.75
b.	16:17	16/17	94.1%	0.941
c.	9:14	9/14	64.3%	0.643
d.	2:2	2/2	100%	1
e.	8:17	8/17	47.1%	0.471
f.	11:14	11/14	78.6%	0.786
g.	2:6	2/6	33.3%	0.333
h.	4:16	4/16	25%	0.25
i.	1:8	1/8	12.5%	0.125
j.	12:13	12/13	92.3%	0.923
k.	9:17	9/17	52.9%	0.529
l.	8:16	8/16	50%	0.5
m.	8:14	8/14	57.1%	0.571
n.	1:6	1/6	16.7%	0.167
o.	5:10	5/10	50%	0.5

2.

	Ratio	Fraction	Percent	Decimal
a.	1:1	1/1	100%	1
b.	13:18	13/18	72.2%	0.722
c.	10:11	10/11	90.9%	0.909
d.	7:8	7/8	87.5%	0.875
e.	1:4	1/4	25%	0.25
f.	13:20	13/20	65%	0.65
g.	6:7	6/7	85.7%	0.857
h.	4:5	4/5	80%	0.8
i.	10:18	10/18	55.6%	0.556
j.	3:9	3/9	33.3%	0.333
k.	6:17	6/17	35.3%	0.353
l.	10:12	10/12	83.3%	0.833
m.	5:20	5/20	25%	0.25
n.	5:16	5/16	31.2%	0.312
o.	1:8	1/8	12.5%	0.125

3.

	Ratio	Fraction	Percent	Decimal
a.	11:15	11/15	73.3%	0.733
b.	7:11	7/11	63.6%	0.636
c.	11:18	11/18	61.1%	0.611
d.	4:19	4/19	21.1%	0.211
e.	1:4	1/4	25%	0.25
f.	1:6	1/6	16.7%	0.167
g.	3:8	3/8	37.5%	0.375
h.	1:1	1/1	100%	1
i.	6:12	6/12	50%	0.5
j.	7:12	7/12	58.3%	0.583
k.	4:18	4/18	22.2%	0.222
l.	3:14	3/14	21.4%	0.214
m.	12:18	12/18	66.7%	0.667
n.	3:10	3/10	30%	0.3
o.	2:13	2/13	15.4%	0.154

4.

	Ratio	Fraction	Percent	Decimal
a.	20:20	20/20	100%	1
b.	1:6	1/6	16.7%	0.167
c.	2:6	2/6	33.3%	0.333
d.	12:13	12/13	92.3%	0.923
e.	5:8	5/8	62.5%	0.625
f.	1:3	1/3	33.3%	0.333
g.	17:19	17/19	89.5%	0.895
h.	2:4	2/4	50%	0.5
i.	2:16	2/16	12.5%	0.125
j.	4:14	4/14	28.6%	0.286
k.	12:14	12/14	85.7%	0.857
l.	3:5	3/5	60%	0.6
m.	1:2	1/2	50%	0.5
n.	5:16	5/16	31.2%	0.312
o.	2:12	2/12	16.7%	0.167

5.

	Ratio	Fraction	Percent	Decimal
a.	1:2	1/2	50%	0.5
b.	6:16	6/16	37.5%	0.375
c.	1:1	1/1	100%	1
d.	5:17	5/17	29.4%	0.294
e.	13:18	13/18	72.2%	0.722
f.	2:5	2/5	40%	0.4
g.	1:6	1/6	16.7%	0.167
h.	2:9	2/9	22.2%	0.222
i.	5:10	5/10	50%	0.5
j.	6:8	6/8	75%	0.75
k.	3:6	3/6	50%	0.5
l.	14:17	14/17	82.4%	0.824
m.	4:5	4/5	80%	0.8
n.	4:11	4/11	36.4%	0.364
o.	12:17	12/17	70.6%	0.706

6.

	Ratio	Fraction	Percent	Decimal
a.	1:1	1/1	100%	1
b.	1:6	1/6	16.7%	0.167
c.	3:6	3/6	50%	0.5
d.	1:12	1/12	8.3%	0.083
e.	5:9	5/9	55.6%	0.556
f.	15:17	15/17	88.2%	0.882
g.	1:5	1/5	20%	0.2
h.	7:15	7/15	46.7%	0.467
i.	1:2	1/2	50%	0.5
j.	3:11	3/11	27.3%	0.273
k.	2:10	2/10	20%	0.2
l.	9:16	9/16	56.2%	0.562
m.	10:18	10/18	55.6%	0.556
n.	8:11	8/11	72.7%	0.727
o.	12:20	12/20	60%	0.6

7.

	Ratio	Fraction	Percent	Decimal
a.	8:19	8/19	42.1%	0.421
b.	5:5	5/5	100%	1
c.	2:7	2/7	28.6%	0.286
d.	15:18	15/18	83.3%	0.833
e.	6:7	6/7	85.7%	0.857
f.	11:13	11/13	84.6%	0.846
g.	5:7	5/7	71.4%	0.714
h.	9:11	9/11	81.8%	0.818
i.	2:12	2/12	16.7%	0.167
j.	12:13	12/13	92.3%	0.923
k.	1:2	1/2	50%	0.5
l.	7:17	7/17	41.2%	0.412
m.	8:20	8/20	40%	0.4
n.	4:16	4/16	25%	0.25
o.	16:19	16/19	84.2%	0.842

8.

	Ratio	Fraction	Percent	Decimal
a.	13:18	13/18	72.2%	0.722
b.	3:3	3/3	100%	1
c.	8:10	8/10	80%	0.8
d.	14:19	14/19	73.7%	0.737
e.	1:2	1/2	50%	0.5
f.	15:16	15/16	93.8%	0.938
g.	1:3	1/3	33.3%	0.333
h.	2:16	2/16	12.5%	0.125
i.	4:8	4/8	50%	0.5
j.	4:16	4/16	25%	0.25
k.	9:11	9/11	81.8%	0.818
l.	4:6	4/6	66.7%	0.667
m.	7:11	7/11	63.6%	0.636
n.	3:18	3/18	16.7%	0.167
o.	11:20	11/20	55%	0.55

9.

	Ratio	Fraction	Percent	Decimal
a.	1:13	1/13	7.7%	0.077
b.	4:6	4/6	66.7%	0.667
c.	20:20	20/20	100%	1
d.	5:7	5/7	71.4%	0.714
e.	8:12	8/12	66.7%	0.667
f.	8:20	8/20	40%	0.4
g.	15:20	15/20	75%	0.75
h.	9:19	9/19	47.4%	0.474
i.	1:4	1/4	25%	0.25
j.	4:8	4/8	50%	0.5
k.	12:19	12/19	63.2%	0.632
l.	17:18	17/18	94.4%	0.944
m.	10:12	10/12	83.3%	0.833
n.	1:12	1/12	8.3%	0.083
o.	8:16	8/16	50%	0.5

10.

	Ratio	Fraction	Percent	Decimal
a.	6:8	6/8	75%	0.75
b.	10:20	10/20	50%	0.5
c.	1:6	1/6	16.7%	0.167
d.	5:12	5/12	41.7%	0.417
e.	6:6	6/6	100%	1
f.	3:4	3/4	75%	0.75
g.	3:19	3/19	15.8%	0.158
h.	4:19	4/19	21.1%	0.211
i.	2:13	2/13	15.4%	0.154
j.	3:5	3/5	60%	0.6
k.	4:8	4/8	50%	0.5
l.	13:14	13/14	92.9%	0.929
m.	5:13	5/13	38.5%	0.385
n.	1:2	1/2	50%	0.5
o.	5:18	5/18	27.8%	0.278

Page 122: Area and Perimeter

1. P=25 A=29.02

2. P=62 A=136

3. P=44 A=99

4. P=30 A=41

5. P=26 A=28

6. P=37 A=45.63

7. P=30 A=43.3

8. P=40 A=66

9. P=34 A=72

10. P=52 A=169

11. P=50 A=126

12. P=21 A=21.22

13. P=46 A=126

14. P=24 A=24

15. P=44 A=93

16. P=44 A=65

17. P=41 A=72

18. P=17 A=13.62

19. P=27 A=32

20. P=52 A=168

21. P=30 A=41

22. P=60 A=186

23. P=38 A=72

24. P=49 A=104

25. P=42 A=84.87

26. P=36 A=54

27. P=25 A=28

28. P=29 A=40.18

29. P=30 A=43.3

30. P=32 A=53

31. P=52 A=108

32. P=46 A=78

33. P=42 A=75

34. P=27 A=32

35. P=24 A=27.71

36. P=24 A=23

37. P=31 A=40.5

38. P=48 A=110.85

39. P=48 A=140

40. P=42 A=73

41. P=26 A=26

42. P=38 A=62

43. P=36 A=47

44. P=35 A=42.66

45. P=36 A=60

46. P=52 A=112

47. P=48 A=96

48. P=34 A=37

49. P=78 A=110

50. P=16 A=9.66

51. P=41 A=72

52. P=31 A=31.32

53. P=29 A=29.6

54. P=58 A=144

55. P=43 A=75

56. P=60 A=181

57. P=55 A=128

58. P=40 A=80

59. P=72 A=323

60. P=22 A=30

61. P=36 A=62.35

62. P=50 A=132

63. P=64 A=120

64. P=23 A=21

65. P=24 A=27.71

66. P=32 A=64

67. P=36 A=62.35

68. P=82 A=192

69. P=42 A=61

70. P=40 A=71

71. P=32 A=51

72. P=60 A=171

73. P=39 A=73.18

74. P=39 A=60.48

75. P=26 A=40

76. P=37 A=60.5

77. P=44 A=60

78. P=38 A=60

79. P=50 A=91

80. P=51 A=112.5

Page 142: Volume and Surface Area

1. V=8 ft³ ft³ SA=24 ft² ft²

2. V=9 ft³ ft³ SA=27 ft² ft²

3. V=7 in³ in³ SA=23 in² in²

4. V=288 in³ in³ SA=264 in² in²

5. V=567 cm³ cm³ SA=414 cm² cm²

6. V=62.83 cm³ cm³ SA=88 cm² cm²

7. V=39 ft³ ft³ SA=71 ft² ft²

8. V=282.74 cm³ cm³ SA=245 cm² cm²

9. V=508.94 ft³ ft³ SA=353 ft² ft²

10. V=60 ft³ ft³ SA=94 ft² ft²

11. V=128 ft³ ft³ SA=160 ft² ft²

12. V=18 in³ in³ SA=42 in² in²

13. V=729 ft³ ft³ SA=486 ft² ft²

14. V=66 cm³ cm³ SA=100 cm² cm²

15. V=25 ft³ ft³ SA=52 ft² ft²

16. V=448 cm³ cm³ SA=352 cm² cm²

17. V=630 cm³ cm³ SA=446 cm² cm²

18. V=33 ft³ ft³ SA=64 ft² ft²

19. V=26 ft³ ft³ SA=57 ft² ft²

20. V=46 ft³ ft³ SA=78 ft² ft²

21. V=48 ft³ ft³ SA=80 ft² ft²

22. V=12 ft³ ft³ SA=32 ft² ft²

23. V=8 in³ in³ SA=24 in² in²

24. V=134 ft³ ft³ SA=163 ft² ft²

25. V=504 ft³ ft³ SA=382 ft² ft²

26. V=47 in³ in³ SA=83 in² in²

27. V=700 in³ in³ SA=480 in² in²

28. V=200 in³ in³ SA=210 in² in²

29. V=800 in³ in³ SA=520 in² in²

30. V=36 in³ in³ SA=66 in² in²

31. V=462 in³ in³ SA=370 in² in²

32. V=103 cm³ cm³ SA=134 cm² cm²

33. V=280 in³ in³ SA=262 in² in²

34. V=336 in³ in³ SA=292 in² in²

35. V=216 cm³ cm³ SA=216 cm² cm²

36. V=210 ft³ ft³ SA=214 ft² ft²

37. V=120 cm³ cm³ SA=148 cm² cm²

38. V=36 in³ in³ SA=66 in² in²

39. V=381.70 ft³ ft³ SA=297 ft² ft²

40. V=101 ft³ ft³ SA=141 ft² ft²

41. V=269.39 in³ in³ SA=231 in² in²

42. V=48 ft³ ft³ SA=80 ft² ft²

43. V=140 cm³ cm³ SA=166 cm² cm²

44. V=64 in³ in³ SA=96 in² in²

45. V=210 in³ in³ SA=214 in² in²

46. V=324 cm³ cm³ SA=288 cm² cm²

47. V=168 ft³ ft³ SA=188 ft² ft²

48. V=8 in³ in³ SA=30 in² in²

49. V=693 ft³ ft³ SA=478 ft² ft²

50. V=48 ft³ ft³ SA=80 ft² ft²

51. V=18 in³ in³ SA=42 in² in²

52. V=120 cm³ cm³ SA=148 cm² cm²

53. V=45 in³ in³ SA=78 in² in²

54. V=502.65 ft³ ft³ SA=352 ft² ft²

55. V=343 ft³ ft³ SA=294 ft² ft²

56. V=190 cm³ cm³ SA=236 cm² cm²

57. V=84.82 in³ in³ SA=113 in² in²

58. V=18 ft³ ft³ SA=42 ft² ft²

59. V=96 ft³ ft³ SA=128 ft² ft²

60. V=270 in³ in³ SA=258 in² in²

Page 157: Identify and Describe Shapes

1. Regular Hexagon S=6 V=6

2. Rhombus S=4 V=4

3. Parallelogram S=4 V=4

4. Square S=4 V=4

5. Right Triangle S=3 V=3

6. Rectangle S=4 V=4

1. Mean = 35, Median = 22, Mode = none, Range = 87

2. Mean = 25.833, Median = 17.5, Mode = 1, Range = 91

3. Mean = 46.333, Median = 44, Mode = none, Range = 85

4. Mean = 48.857, Median = 42, Mode = none, Range = 83

5. Mean = 39.857, Median = 38, Mode = none, Range = 83

6. Mean = 42.167, Median = 37.5, Mode = none, Range = 67

7. Mean = 34.857, Median = 34, Mode = 34, Range = 79

8. Mean = 60.286, Median = 73, Mode = none, Range = 88

9. Mean = 61.571, Median = 63, Mode = none, Range = 82

10. Mean = 54, Median = 69, Mode = none, Range = 87

11. Mean = 58.286, Median = 58, Mode = 58, Range = 78

12. Mean = 40.143, Median = 40, Mode = none, Range = 87

13. Mean = 29.333, Median = 29, Mode = none, Range = 64

14. Mean = 45, Median = 39, Mode = none, Range = 60

15. Mean = 36.833, Median = 36.5, Mode = 19, Range = 50

16. Mean = 45.333, Median = 32.5, Mode = 19, Range = 76

17. Mean = 42.714, Median = 53, Mode = 17, Range = 84

18. Mean = 40.571, Median = 43, Mode = none, Range = 82

19. Mean = 34.429, Median = 20, Mode = none, Range = 75

20. Mean = 44.667, Median = 41, Mode = none, Range = 77

21. Mean = 38.667, Median = 26, Mode = none, Range = 86

22. Mean = 50.857, Median = 66, Mode = none, Range = 83

23. Mean = 74.429, Median = 77, Mode = none, Range = 56

24. Mean = 24.167, Median = 24.5, Mode = 39, Range = 38

www.ingramcontent.com/pod-product-compliance
Lightning Source LLC
Chambersburg PA
CBHW081911120726
47996CB00010B/3288